GREYHOUND

Joanna Pocock is an Irish-Canadian writer living in London. Her writing has notably appeared in the *Los Angeles Times*, the *Nation* and *Guardian US*, and she is a contributing editor at the Dark Mountain project. She won the 2018 Fitzcarraldo Editions Essay Prize for *Surrender* and in 2021 she was awarded the Arts Foundation's Environmental Writing Fellowship. *Greyhound* is her second book.

Praise for *Surrender*

'Pocock's prose is understated and spare, and, like a cave painting, does perfect justice to her subject. It doesn't debase the living world by trying to overword it. It is just a sketch, and in its gentleness touches it perfectly ... This is nature writing that we need: standing in contrast to writing that forces the human into the picture as observer, or tries hard to pin the thing down exactly, with alienating expertise or florid description.... [Pocock's] is a perspective not of objectivity or voyeurism, but of participation in the web of life and in the land and communities as she writes them.'
— Abi Andrews, *Irish Times*

'This is a bewitching and deeply affecting book. Pocock's elegant interweaving of the intimate and the expansive, the personal and the universal, culminates in a work that forces us to consider our own place in, and impact upon, a world that could itself have more past than future.'
— Tom Smalley, *Spectator*

'Pocock is an environmentalist, yet she is also clearly a humanist. She is always willing to hear people out, no matter how extreme their points of view, and to accept the limits of her own knowledge.... Pocock's writing is a prism, refracting hidden nuance from her subjects and meaning from memory.... [W]hether it is climate crisis or midlife crisis, Pocock holds her themes lightly, allowing the "fluidity of life" to run its course.'
— Clare Saxby, *Times Literary Supplement*

'Land and water, flesh and blood. The planet and the body. Society and the person. *Surrender* maps these profound fractal relationships with a precision and sensitivity that stunned me. Here is a singular spiritual travelogue of the American West that is worthy of D.H. Lawrence.'
— Walter Kirn, author of *Up in the Air*

Fitzcarraldo Editions

GREYHOUND

JOANNA POCOCK

For Jason and Eve

'The Anglo-American... fells the forests and drains the marshes; lakes as large as seas and huge rivers resist its triumphant march in vain. The wilds become villages, and the villages towns. The American, the daily witness of such wonders, does not see anything astonishing in all this. This incredible destruction, this even more surprising growth, seems to him the usual progress of things in this world. He gets accustomed to it as to the unalterable order of nature.'
— Alexis de Tocqueville, *A Fortnight in the Wilderness* (1832), tr. Gerald Bevan

'O public road, I say back I am not afraid to leave you, yet I love you, you express me better than I can express myself.'
— Walt Whitman, 'Song of the Open Road' (1882)

'According to the Hedges Company, there were 286.9 million registered cars in the US in 2020. That's 0.84% more than 2019's 284.5 million units. The same study also suggests that by the end of 2021, 289.5 million vehicles would be roaming the roads of America. The US automotive industry has experienced its fair share of ups and downs. This is due to factors such as the oil and energy crisis, improvement of fuel economy, fluctuation of gas prices, innovative upgrades, and the COVID-19 pandemic. Some factors have a larger impact than others.'
— The Hedges Company at financesonline.com

¶ Travelling on a Greyhound bus, you can disappear.

The day hadn't yet begun as we pulled out of Detroit. We were heading to St. Louis through lashing rain under a black sky. The only sounds were the regular swish of windshield wipers and the rhythmic sucking of rubber tyres on wet tarmac. It was too early for conversation. The people around me seemed weary. Some looked like they hadn't slept in days. Others had come prepared with pillows, eye masks and blankets. The woman next to me appeared lost in her thoughts. No phone, no book, she was just sitting. I could sense she was working something out in her mind. The reading lights didn't work and I nodded off.

When I woke from a light sleep, I could just make out the skeletons of electricity pylons and the sprawling bodies of industrial buildings through the large foggy window. Every now and then the bright lights of gas stations and truck stops veered into view, signalling food, rest, a break from the grey monotony of the highway.

As I became more awake I noted fields, the outline of scrubby trees, ads for RV campgrounds, enormous parking lots, 18-wheelers, truck dealerships, farms, phone masts, a U-Haul storage centre with electric yellow windows lit from the inside, rusting CN boxcars, factories, the odd small opalescent body of water just about visible under the tungsten glow of the edgelands – a glow that dimmed with the brightening of the dawn. We passed a building whose chimney was on fire. No one seemed aware of it. The flames carried on burning in the muted landscape as we sped past.

It was March 2023 and I was on a Greyhound bus retracing a 2,300-mile journey from Detroit to Los Angeles – a trip I had taken in 2006. As a non-driver, my only options for crossing the continent solo consist of hitchhiking, train or bus. For several years, I'd felt a pull to remake this journey, to revisit the motels, diners, highways, parking lots, towns, cities, suburbs and truck stops. I was curious to see how the places I had travelled through in 2006 had changed, while simultaneously catching a glimpse of the person I had been then. A ragged person running away from loss.

Marc Augé, the late French anthropologist, sees these revisited 'places of memory' as opportunities to face 'the image of what we are no longer'. A place can offer a palimpsest of one's past and present: the superimposition of our current selves onto the memories we have of a place allow us to be, in Augé's words, 'tourists of the private'.

During the Covid-19 pandemic, I tried to satisfy my urge to strike out across the United States by immersing myself in the literature of the Great American Road Trip. My journeying would be a literary one, as I followed fictional characters and writers into temporal and spatial zones forbidden to me.

I travelled with Sal Paradise, Jack Kerouac's narrator in *On the Road*, in his search for the beating heart of the artist and visionary, for transcendence, for that sense of immensity and freedom that comes from racing across a continent chasing the unknown. And there was John Steinbeck, who in 1960, drove from Long Island to the Pacific coast and back again with his poodle and documented his 10,000-mile journey in *Travels with Charley*. In 1934, almost forty years before Steinbeck, the journalist and author James Rorty drove from Easton, Pennsylvania to Los Angeles, interviewing people along the way and describing their working conditions in fields and factories. *Where Life is Better: An Unsentimental*

American Journey is an extraordinary and angry work. 'I encountered nothing,' Rorty wrote,

> in 15,000 miles of travel that disgusted and appalled me so much as this American addiction to makebelieve. Apparently, not even empty bellies can cure it. Of all the facts I dug up, none seemed so significant or so dangerous as the overwhelming fact of our lazy, irresponsible, adolescent inability to face the truth or tell it.

The book that spoke to me the most was *Blue Highways: A Journey into America* by William Least Heat-Moon, a Missouri-born author of mixed Irish, English and Osage ancestry. In 1978, Least Heat-Moon lost his job teaching English. On the day that he was fired, his wife, from whom he'd been separated for nine months, announced that she was now seeing 'her "friend" Rick or Dick or Chick. Something like that.' Least Heat-Moon decided to head off in his van across the US the very next day. 'A man who couldn't make things go right could at least go,' he wrote. I knew this feeling well: a sense that fleeing was the best way to face change and loss.

Once the pandemic began to lift and my thoughts returned to the Greyhound, I wondered how I would feel sitting in the enclosed space of a bus. Would I be imagining the vectors of aerosols from my fellow passengers as they talked? Would I be envisioning traces of the virus on my armrest tracked in from a motel reception area? The innocent and unquestioned sharing of air with other people had become infected with fear. But my desire to revisit these places and a younger version of myself became too insistent to ignore.

I needed to know what it would be like as an older woman, a less vital and sexually adventurous one, a more circumspect one, to revisit my 2006 journey and re-engage with the world in our post-pandemic landscape. I wanted to see how I would respond to the sleeping head of a passenger as it tilted towards me on the bus, how I would react to the offer of sharing a pair of headphones or a bag of crisps. Would it be met with the Covid-infected knee-jerk 'No, thanks' of self-preservation and paranoia? Or the grace, humour and gratitude from the *before times*?

I would not only be revisiting the motels, cities, highways, parking lots, edgelands and upholstered seats of the Greyhound (that is, if they still existed) – I would also be revisiting my younger self. I would be trying to recapture Marc Augé's 'fugitive feelings ... where all there is to do is "see what happens."' I put away my books and my fear and bought an airline ticket so I could make the journey that seventeen years earlier had emerged from a sense of profound grief.

¶ It was a cold January morning in 2006, when my husband Jason and I got to the Royal London hospital. I knew it was dead. I had been mourning my sister Mary for eighteen months and now there was another death, but this one was inside me. The familiar jelly was rubbed onto my stomach and the nurse standing at the ultrasound machine gave me the news I was expecting: there was no heartbeat. It was my third miscarriage. I had become adept at recognizing the exact moment life ceased inside me: my morning sickness lifted, the metallic taste in my mouth disappeared, fatigue drained from my limbs and my appetite returned. I no longer retched when I smelled coffee, alcohol or frying garlic.

My husband Jason's face wore a sombre expression. We said nothing to each other for some time. There really was nothing to say. It took several weeks for us to return to those normal conversations about what we might cook for dinner, what film we might watch, which friends we might invite over, how work was going. I worried that the double punch of another miscarriage with the death of my sister could damage me for life, that I might never again experience any sort of levity or joy, that I had to accept life without children, life as a trail of disappointments and deaths.

I held these losses close and while turning them around in my mind, I decided that I needed to do something that I would not have been able to do if I were cradling an infant in my arms. I decided that what I needed was to travel, to move, to remind myself how good it felt to be unencumbered. I wanted to escape my desire for a child, and my grief, and revel in being unburdened by domesticity. I could achieve this, I thought, by crossing the United States from east to west on a Greyhound bus.

Jason gave me £1,000 to help with my trip; in 2006 that

19

covered most of it. Then, I got out the maps. I spent weeks staring at them, reading out the names of places while working out my route. So many of the names were stories, erasures, fabrications and myths. The place names in Kentucky seemed the most visceral and evocative: Decoy, Subtle, Mud Lick, Mummie, Neon, Minnie, Mousie, Hazard, Viper and Defiance. But my route wouldn't be taking in Kentucky: I would start in my home province of Ontario and finish in Los Angeles.

While my sister in Toronto was dying, a fictional character called Karl Jones appeared in my imagination. A no-bullshit, androgynous eighteen-year-old from Napanee, Ontario, she became my companion as well as the central character in a novel I had started writing which opens with Karl nursing her terminally ill father. After his death, Karl (like me) is grief-stricken. During her father's final weeks, Karl's estranged mother, Jean, has begun calling and leaving desperate messages. Karl hasn't spoken to Jean in thirteen years. The phone calls are like guerrilla attacks: her mother is broke and wants the house in Napanee. Freed of her caring duties, angry and uncertain about her future Karl gets on a Greyhound bus and heads to Las Vegas where Jean is working as a waitress at the El Cortez. I would travel in Karl's footsteps and stake out her friends, see where she grew up and look out the Greyhound bus partly through the eyes of a smart, funny teenager. That way I could grieve and keep moving and I had something to write, a character and a plot to develop. Having a project and a plan filled the gaps left in the absence of joy and the sense of a future worth heading towards.

When I landed in Toronto on 10 March 2023 to begin my most recent cross-country journey, I walked under a glowering sky from the airport concourse to a bus stop where I was to board a Megabus to Napanee. Snow was coming down in large clumps and I had that awful post-long-haul flight taste in my mouth: of bad food, cheap wine, no sleep and recirculated air. And I was about to face a five-hour bus trip.

I stood next to pillar C8 in the departures area, where the Megabus app told me I would find my stop. A blizzard was whirling and I worried that my bus might not show up. Inside the airport, I found an information desk and asked the woman behind the counter whether buses would be running in this weather. She leaned forward to look out a window where wind was smearing dirty white gobs of snow across the glass. She looked at me, puzzled. 'Oh, this is nothing. Nothing at all! Your bus will be fine.' I had been out of Canada for too long. I had forgotten what winter was like here.

I waited in the warmth of the airport, with one eye on pillar C8. Nearby, a young woman with three kids sat on the floor Facetiming someone on her phone. She was crying. Her kids were playing with a luggage trolley, blocking out her tears by inhabiting their own alternate reality. The woman was begging for something, but I was too far away to hear what she was saying. A security guard showed up and squatted next to her. I could tell from his body language and the tone of his voice that he had come to offer help rather than to move her on. She was sobbing now and her phone was on the floor next to her, her face in her hands, her children ignoring what was going on. I headed out into the blizzard to stand by pillar C8, feeling haunted by this woman. She wasn't wearing a winter coat, nor were her kids.

The bus shelter was on a paved section of the airport departures area where people were being dropped off

21

by taxis, friends, family. It was dark now and very cold. A young guy showed up and stood next to me in the little bus shelter. He was holding one long-stemmed white rose.

'Do you know if this is the bus stop for Kingston?' he asked.

'Yes, I'm going to Napanee and I think it's the same bus'.

'Where are you from?'

'London,' pause, 'England.' You have to say 'England' in Canada or people will think you mean London, Ontario.

'Cool. What are you doing going to Napanee?'

I told him I was working on a book, a travel book. I hadn't decided what I would tell people yet when they asked, which I knew they would. I am superstitious about talking about my writing. The white rose guy wanted to know more. I said I was writing about crossing the US on a Greyhound bus.

'Sweet,' he said. And then I got his story: he was twenty-one, had studied firefighting – structural, rather than wildfires – and he was going to visit his girlfriend in Kingston, hence the rose.

'But *you're* having a real adventure,' he said.

Looking down at my phone for the live Megabus route, I noticed that the little bus icon had passed the airport and was on the way to Napanee. White Rose Guy checked his phone and it said the same thing. We both panicked and questioned whether the bus could have shown up while we were chatting. Did we miss it? How could we? It was dark and blizzarding, but we could see the road right next to us. By this time, it was 7 p.m. in Toronto, which made it 2 a.m. for me. I was cold and tired and worried that I'd have to conjure somewhere to sleep. Just as White Rose Guy and I were discussing what we might do, the bus appeared, a ghostly apparition in the snow. It hadn't passed us at all; the Megabus app was wrong.

The ride to Napanee was treacherous. Snow turned to freezing rain. High winds made the bus feel unstable on the road. The highway was littered with accidents and vehicles were stuck in snow drifts. Snowplows and large trucks outnumbered cars. Our bus skidded. I could feel ice under the wheels. There were no overhead lights so I couldn't read, but I was too anxious to sleep. All I could do was stare out at the occasional flashing lights of emergency vehicles emerging from the whiteout.

We got to Belleville at ten o'clock. An older passenger got off the bus and was greeted by a young man. Both of them in parkas. They hugged like bears.

I got dropped off just after eleven at a giant Petro-Canada station on Highway 41 bordering the outskirts of Napanee. Eighteen-wheelers were parked in rows next to a 24-hour Denny's. I found myself in a brilliantly lit oasis in the snow, like a frozen stage set constructed to showcase a diner, a gas station, semi-trailer trucks and giant cars. Across the highway from this bright petroleum-fuelled tableau and through the flying snow I could just make out the backlit Royal Napanee Inn sign. I ran across the empty road and rang the bell. Despite the late hour, someone magically appeared to hand me my room key. There was no one around, just gigantic snow drifts, sleeping trucks and neon signs designed to be seen by drivers in their cars from miles away. I flopped into bed.

I was woken at 7.30 in the morning with a noise that took me straight back to childhood: the scrape of a metal shovel on icy concrete. I opened the door of my motel room onto

blinding sunlight, reflecting off dazzling, fresh snow. The person shovelling – or scraping – the hardened snow from the motel steps was Betty, a sweet woman in a knitted tuque embroidered with 'I ♥ CANADA'. She lived rent-free in the motel in return for doing jobs around the place.

I showered, dressed and headed across the highway through a maze of parked fuel trucks in the forecourt of the Petro-Canada station. All these machines looked strangely beautiful covered in glittering snow under a pure, clear blue sky. In Denny's, I was greeted by a small sea of baseball caps and chequered shirts, and made my way to a table by a window where dust motes danced in the rays of sunshine. The talk among customers was last night's blizzard. I looked out onto the parking lot at the polished, silver tanker trucks.

'So nice to see the sun, eh, after last night's storm,' the waitress said as she poured my coffee.

After breakfast I checked out of the Royal Napanee Inn. I had stayed there for logistical reasons: it was the only motel within walking distance of the bus stop. My actual destination had always been the Fox Motor Inn, where I had stayed in 2006. I asked Roger, the owner of the Royal Napanee Inn, if he could call me a taxi. He needed to know where I was going and I had to come clean.

'It's a shame,' he said. 'I could have offered you a deal on two nights.'

What I didn't tell him was that the Fox Motor Inn was where my previous trip had begun, when I had gone looking for the house of the fictional Karl Jones who, at the beginning of my novel, is working as a catering assistant. Instead, we wished each other well and I thanked him.

As I waited for my taxi in the parking lot, a guy pulled

up in a Dodge RAM 1500. 'You need sunglasses,' he shouted. His English was accented. Russian, maybe. He got out of his truck waving his arms frantically. 'Your brain can't compute all these rays going into your retinas.' He went on about the percentage of the sun's rays going into our bodies and how they are processed by our minds and the damage I was doing to myself standing in this parking lot. I squinted at him as he stood against the rising sun. I was unable to comprehend what he was telling me and I needed coffee.

I was grateful when my taxi arrived. It dropped me in front of the Fox Motor Inn, an anonymous chalet-style motel sprawled along Highway 2, a road which began its life as a stagecoach trail and was now a paved highway stretching across southern Ontario. My diary entry from 2006 also mentions a taxi journey to the Fox Motor Inn. The date was 3 April 2006, a date which was to take on huge significance the following year, though I did not know this then. There were no Ubers, so I had shared a cab to the motel with a guy a few years younger than me, in his mid- to late-thirties, handsome in a clean-cut sort of way. He asked where I was from, and I told him I was from Canada but that I now lived in England. He was from Buckinghamshire but lived in Napanee. Our driver piped up. He had come from Dorset as a child to work in Canada. I was the only Canadian-born person in the cab, but I didn't live in Canada, which felt somehow very *Canadian*.

There were no shared taxis on this recent trip. Jim, the owner, greeted me and asked how I'd liked the Royal Napanee Inn.

'How did you know I stayed there?' I asked, confused.

'When you called me earlier to ask about an early check-in, I recognized the phone number.'

'Oh,' I replied.

'But, it's fine. We're friends, Roger and I. We're both from India.'

The Hotel Wars in Napanee seemed convivial enough.

March can be an ugly time of year in Ontario. The snow is often just beginning to melt, and scruffy yellow patches of grass appear like small, hairy scabs. In 2006, I had arrived terribly underdressed, having forgotten that spring could be so cold. This time, I bought a puffy down coat especially for the trip. I looked like the smallest figure in one of those nesting Russian dolls, tiny and rounded. Fresh snow was piled high on every surface, from spindly tree branches to gabled rooves like towers of marshmallow fluff. A big blue sky hovered above everything.

After checking into the Fox, I walked along the main road into town. The outskirts hadn't changed much, but as I approached the centre, I noticed many of the cafés and restaurants I remembered were no longer there, although a couple of new ones had sprung up. The frozen banks of the Napanee River looked the same: like jagged teeth around the liquid mercury tongue of the water.

I was sad to see the Superior Restaurant & Tavern on Dundas Street had closed. The place had been decorated with larger-than-life photomurals of autumn woodlands, waterfalls and undulating farmland. Moose antlers, taxidermy, dusty Christmas decorations and knickknacks had made their way into every corner. Back in 2006 the owner had greeted me with the Greek welcome, *tikanis*. There had been only one other customer that night: a man eating alone. I remember ordering the vegetarian moussaka.

The other diner, who was at a nearby table, shouted,

'Good choice! Not like that Kraft stuff, that *white* stuff,' he mysteriously added.

After we'd both eaten our meals in silence, he approached and told me how he used to be into photography but now that he was blind, he had to see what everyone else sees in his own head. He asked how I'd liked my moussaka and whether I was a tourist. Before I could answer, he said that there were better months to be a tourist in Napanee.

'My timing is always terrible,' I said.

He replied, 'Your timing is beautiful because I got to talk to you,' and then turned and walked out.

As I left the Superior that night, snow began to fall, great huge flakes of it.

The Superior Restaurant has now become the Touch of Class Fashion Boutique, 'a "one stop shop" for women of all ages filled with smart casual wear, resort, formal wear, shoes, jewelry, handbags and accessories'. There was no one there to tell me my timing was beautiful.

I wandered around Napanee in the cold, taking photographs until my fingers froze. At Conservation Park, the 'Greater Napanee' sign read 'Greater for Many Reasons'. I marvelled that someone had presumably been paid to provide branding of such extreme vagueness. Two joggers in shorts and sneakers were heading in my direction. I was wearing boots and could easily navigate the snowbank, so I scrambled aside to give them space. They both effusively huffed a very Canadian 'thank you'. I walked along County Road 2, the first paved road in Canada, which joins Kingston and Toronto. It turns into the town's main street, Dundas Street, where it crosses the Napanee River. There were fewer restaurants and bars, fewer places where people could gather. This would turn out to be a

portent of what was to come.

As the sun dipped and the sky turned a cold, hard black,
I headed to the Loaf N' Ale, one of the few downtown
restaurants still going. I sat at the bar nursing a glass of
wine from the vineyard of the much-loved Canadian
hockey player Wayne Gretzky. The place still flew its
union flags, but it had been refurbished and updated. I
remembered the conversation I'd had here back in 2006.
The man next to me at the bar had been talking to the
barmaid about Gerard, who had smoked like a chimney,
worked hard and played hard; he'd died of a heart attack
a few days before my visit. The wake was to be that very
night. The guy next to me kept saying, in his British accent, 'It is just too damn bad about Gerard.' The barmaid
replied, 'He tried to smoke his troubles away,' shaking her
blonde head.

Another man at the bar, this one in a tweed jacket and
a flat cap, noticed me writing in my journal and came
over to tell me that his wife had just written a novel. He
asked where I lived and when I told him, he said he hated
London because there were too many 'different colours
and people from all over' – words that tumbled straight
into my journal. The owner of the Loaf N' Ale heard I
was from out of town. He sat on the stool next to mine
and told me he had emigrated from Kent. He was another London-hater. 'No-one bloody speaks English there!'
They all laughed.

I had always known Karl would leave Napanee. It was
becoming clearer to me why.

As I got my wallet out to pay, the Englishman said, 'It's
already been taken care of.' I felt ashamed that despite my
protests about London being not at all as they described
it, these men still saw me as *one of them*.

After my glasses of Wayne Gretzky wine, I walked along the icy, deserted streets back to the Fox Motor Inn. It was a Saturday night, but no one was out. I slipped into bed and wondered how different this trip would be to the one I had done all those years ago. How many of the changes I was noticing were inside me – as fugitive feelings – and how many were in the landscape, on the pavement, in other people and in the ether?

Downtown Napanee on a Sunday morning offered very little by way of cafés or diners. Some shopfronts were boarded up – possible casualties of a lethal combination of Covid-19, the exodus to online shopping and big-box stores out of town. Thankfully Tammy's, a diner serving bottomless cups of coffee, was still going. I rocked up at four minutes to eight on the morning of my departure. An elderly couple was waiting in their truck for the place to open. As soon as a waitress appeared, they stepped out of their vehicle. The elderly gentleman held the diner door open for his wife and then for me. They took their seats at a window table. A man in Day-Glo orange gloves, hunting cap, jeans, a red and black chequered shirt walked in gingerly using a cane.

'Hello Den,' the elderly couple said in unison.

The waitress asked, 'Do you need a menu, Dennis?'

'Nope', Den said as he took a seat.

The talk this morning was about daylight savings. The elderly gentleman noted that the restaurant was quieter than usual.

'I guess everyone is sleeping in 'cuz the clocks changed,' the gentleman said, although it was still only twelve minutes past eight on a Sunday morning. As people parked up outside the large plate glass window and entered, they wiped their feet, greeted each other with a

tip of the hat, a handshake or a pat on the back. They all knew each other by name.

I am wary of romanticizing the excruciating claustrophobia and conservatism that can exist in small communities where everyone knows who's getting divorced, whose kids are buying weed, whose teenager has just had an abortion, and so on. But this wariness exists in tandem with my knowledge that our state and public institutions are often failing when it comes to looking after our welfare. Communities are left to do the work that larger public bodies have been tasked with, but can often no longer provide. What I sensed here in Tammy's was the cohesiveness of a close-knit community. I could imagine the casseroles left on back porches for bereaved families, the sandwiches tucked into a kid's backpack by someone who knows his parents are struggling financially, the offers of a drive to that difficult hospital appointment, the quiet, unremarkable kindnesses that make up the social fabric of small towns. It was palpable in this restaurant at 8.15 on a Sunday morning.

The waitress refilled the coffees of the elderly couple. 'How is everything tasting,' she asked.

'Excellent,' the gentleman replied, 'as always. It never changes, which is how I like it.'

I knew what he meant.

I finished eating and wandered with my suitcase into town towards the VIA Rail station where I would be getting a train to Toronto and then onto Windsor, where I'd catch a shuttle bus to Detroit. That was where my *real* trip would begin. I bought a sandwich for the journey from the one place open, the unfortunately named 'Butter My Buns'. Armed with a giant Havarti roll, I bumped into the guy who had lectured me outside my motel about UV rays

and the damage they were doing to my retinas. He didn't recognize me. Again, he came a bit too close: 'You know the terrible thing is that the only people who *actually* care are the Karens! Everyone gets them wrong. They are the *only* people who care.'

He wandered off.

A woman caught my eye and leaned in, 'I see you've met the Crazy Mathematician,' she whispered. 'He was in Tim Horton's and I had to leave. I just couldn't take it anymore. I couldn't take all of them. One guy was literally talking to the wall.' She looked a bit sad herself. 'But the thing is, they've got nowhere else to go.'

I got to the train station early. It was empty. By 'empty', I mean derelict. It was boarded up and graffitied and looked to be out of commission. I wasn't expecting a human to be there, but I thought maybe there would be a sign with some information, or a timetable on a wall somewhere. Perhaps a bench. I wondered whether the station's permanent closure meant that trains no longer stopped here. I had a ticket, but maybe there was another station I didn't know about. I looked online and it seemed Napanee had only one train station and that I was standing at it. What I could see in front of me – a deserted and boarded up station – did not correspond to what I was seeing on the screen of my phone. I was forced to trust the algorithm and was feeling unmoored by this disassociation between reality and its online version.

I stood outside in the cold wondering where I could find a warm place to wait when the Crazy Mathematician re-appeared. He lived in Montreal, he told me, and he had been planning to buy a house in Belleville where the 'jobs were plentiful and the girls were pretty', but he'd missed that boat. Belleville was booming so he was going to buy in Napanee instead. As he talked, he scoured the ground picking up cigarette butts. He claimed to be looking for his cell phone. He asked me where I was going. 'Toronto, Windsor, then Detroit,' I told him.

He told me he was from the Czech Republic and then added, 'You know women make more incorrect statements than men. It's a fact.'

I tried projecting disinterest. My reading glasses were on, my finger still firmly holding the place in my book.

He added cryptically, 'When a man forces himself on a woman, it's a boy. When he is forced to pull out early, it's a waste.'

A car pulled up. A guy with long grey hair sat in the driver's seat smoking a joint, listening to Bob Marley. Canada geese flew in formation overhead. Finally, my train arrived.

¶ From Napanee I had to get myself back to Toronto, where I spent a night with family, in order to get the 6 a.m. train to Windsor, Ontario – which is just across the American–Canadian border from Detroit. It was dark when I set out for Union Station and the Toronto streets were covered in slush. Greyhound Canada went out of business in 2021, so I would have to make this journey by train. In my carriage, people either hunkered down over laptops or slept. As we approached Windsor, a flat disc of sun emerged from behind thin metallic clouds. Snow fell faintly. The ground turned the colour of zinc. The scene was oddly romantic in a grim way, like the background to an early Gus Van Sant film where the protagonist's yearning doesn't extend much beyond the need to 'get out'. I wandered around Windsor's train station looking for a coffee shop. Everything was shut. It was freezing. I gave up and walked back to the train station to get a taxi to the Windsor–Detroit terminal. My taxi driver said he wasn't sure the buses to Detroit were running.

'Why not?' I asked.

'They stopped running during Covid. I'm not sure they're back up yet.' I felt that familiar fear creep up inside me. Whenever I cross a border, I am hit with neurotic guilt as if I've committed a crime unknown even to myself. There is also the fear of simply getting everything wrong, of reading the instructions incorrectly.

'Most people take a taxi across to Detroit,' he said.

'How much does that cost?'

'Sixty dollars.'

'Well, the bus is $7.50, so I'm going with that.'

'*If* it's running,' he said, fixing me with a stare in his mirror.

'Right. *If* it's running,' I repeated.

As we drove along the river towards the Tunnel Bus,

the snow got heavier. Big, proper flakes. The kind that as a child I would run outside for, to feel them melt on my tongue. Even in this fluffy white blanket, the border town of Windsor looked bleak. It's sometimes referred to as the smog capital of Canada, partly because of its own car industry and also because it is at the end of a peninsula which juts south and west into Lake Erie and almost hits Detroit, a town with its own pollution problems.

The Detroit River, which separates Canada from the US, was named by the French: *détroit* meaning the 'strait' or the 'narrow' of a waterway. In 1701, the French explorer Antoine de la Mothe, sieur de Cadillac, gave the waterway the full name of 'le détroit du Lac Érie', as it joined the smallest of the Great Lakes with Lake St Clair. In 1908, *Detroit News* called the river 'the Greatest Commercial Artery on Earth'. By then it was carrying almost 60 million metric tonnes of cargo from Detroit to ports around the world. To put this in perspective, in that same year, the port of London shipped fewer than 17 million tonnes and New York 18 million tonnes.

This beast of a waterway has carried birchbark canoes, freighters loaded with lumber, ships filled with furs, minerals and liquid chemicals. And there it was in a fog of frozen mist as we whizzed past. My cab driver dropped me at the station, where a bus was leaving for Detroit in thirty minutes. So much for the taxi driver's *if it's running*. I looked for somewhere to get coffee and found nothing nearby. I had been up since 5 a.m. and it was now 11, and I had been running on adrenaline. I sat next to my bag on the floor, leaned my back against the wall and closed my eyes.

On this grey, drizzly morning only six of us were heading from Windsor, Ontario to Detroit, Michigan. The last time I had crossed this same border, I had been grilled by the customs officer. Canada still had Greyhounds running in 2006, so I had taken the bus from Napanee to Windsor, which then connected to the Tunnel Bus. At the border, we filed out of the bus into a small immigration office where a guard interrogated me. I explained that I was taking a Greyhound bus trip because I needed a break, I needed to get away, I'd lost another baby, I was sad. None of this went down very well. Where was my husband, she asked. In London, I replied. She wasn't happy with this either. When she asked why I was *really* going to the US, I mumbled something about my dead sister and travelling as a way of getting over my grief. Her stare got more penetrating and she crossed her arms. It was one of those situations where the truth seemed to get me nowhere. I tried one more thing: I told her that I was writing a novel and my character was making this trip to find her estranged mother. At this her face lit up. I got to hear about the college course she was taking in novel writing. She was top of the class, working on her first book. She stuffed my things back into my bag and wished me a pleasant stay.

When I emerged from the tunnel in Detroit on that trip, it was all smoking manhole covers, burnt-out buildings and overly large cars from the 1970s and 1980s spewing exhaust. People pushed shopping trolleys loaded with broken computers, keyboards, cans of food, stuffed toys and clothing. An indescribable sadness seeped straight up into me from the pavement. Beautifully ornamented Art Deco buildings sat empty. Back then, only the property developers seemed hopeful. Façades were hung with large plastic banners advertising 'LOFTS FOR SALE'. I could hear the real estate jargon about up-and-coming neighbourhoods, revitalization, creative

community hubs and curated retail spaces.

Off Detroit's main drag were side streets lined with turreted late Victorian red brick houses like structures brought to life from an Edward Hopper painting, except none of Hopper's yellow lights burned inside. Much of downtown was populated by pigeons and people who had either shot up or smoked something or were looking to. Karl, I thought, would want to stay in Detroit, at least for a night, to explore this foreign place. It was so close to Canada and yet it felt so completely alien.

While planning my 2023 bus trip, I tried to find small, independent motels close to the Greyhound stations I'd be stopping in. Detroit had none. The first thing that came up when I Googled 'Motel in Detroit' was:

> Fugitives | Kara | Detroit Become Human
> Walkthrough – To sleep in the motel, Kara needs to steal money from the grocery store and the clothes inside the laundromat. Kara doesn't need the gun from Todd's house to steal the money. Once both items were stolen, simply go towards the motel and use the money there.

This was followed by several questions:

> How do you get into the abandoned house in Detroit: Become Human?
> Can you escape the camp in Detroit: Become Human?
> How do I cut a human fence in Detroit?

I couldn't make sense of it. After several readings, I realized that the motel in Detroit that Google wanted me to walk through was virtual and part of an elaborate game. So, I added an 's' to my search: 'Motels Detroit' and I got several in Windsor, which is not even in the same country. This trip would need patience.

The only cheap room I could find in the centre of Detroit was in a small building owned by a company called Sonder. I had tried to resist staying anywhere that required an app or that boasted of a 'digital concierge' and a 'self check-in' but here I was forced to give into the appification of travel. The Tunnel Bus from Windsor dropped me right around the corner from the Sonder. My check-in time was three in the afternoon. I still had several hours to wait until I would hear my phone ping with the code for the building.

It was freezing. Snow was falling. The sky was grey and low. Downtown Detroit was not how I remembered it. Where burnt-out buildings with gaping windows lined the empty streets in 2006, there was now a Gucci, a Lululemon, vegan restaurants, cocktail bars and cash-free cafés selling $7 croissants. I was stunned by the change.

Smartly dressed Detroiters walked down the street clutching creamy pink coffee cups emblazoned with the word 'Cannelle' in a pretty, old-fashioned script. I headed in the direction they were coming from. This small café on Griswold Street was one block up from State Street, where Seymour Finney, an abolitionist tailor from New York, ran a livery stable in 1850 that served as a crucial hideaway for freedom-seeking enslaved African Americans, en route to Canada on the Underground Railroad.

When I went to pay for my coffee in Cannelle, my Canadian debit card wouldn't work, nor my British one. (I also had a Montana bank card which was equally useless.)

Unlike many of the cafés and restaurants I was to visit, this one still accepted cash. I excavated the 'emergency' $100 bill from my wallet and handed it to the server. 'Oh, an old one,' she said holding the bill up to the light. 'Did you make it this morning?'

'I brought it with me from the UK via Toronto,' as if telling her my itinerary would go some way to explaining the 'old' money.

'Oh, so you made it yesterday,' she quipped.

A familiar nervousness rose in me.

Our steady march towards a cashless society has created a growing sense of unease within me. When you have to rely on the digital realm for the privilege of buying food or other essentials, you are being asked to trust in something other than a belief in the value of money. You are being asked to trust in technology – the very same system that monitors us, harvests and sells our data and nudges into our social media with misinformation and advertising. This move towards a cash-free world fuels an existential anxiety that I will be denied service, be shut out of the smooth running of society by having my physical money rejected. During the height of the Covid pandemic, many businesses had become 'cash-free', ostensibly for safety and hygiene reasons. And many have remained that way. This is yet another form of exclusion. It leaves out those who work in a cash economy while simultaneously keeping the rest of us plugged into the giant database tracking our consumption, our movements, our 'spending power'. It increases the divide between the haves and the have-nots, the tracked and those who aren't 'in the system'.

I tuned into the French chansons, Francois Hardy, Jacques Brel, Edith Piaf playing in Cannelle. I felt incredibly tired but logged onto my laptop to see if any of the urban farms I had contacted had replied. In 2006, these places were only just springing up. I had heard that there were now over 200 acres of urban farms in and around Detroit. Not one had replied to my requests to visit. This was partly because everything was still frozen – it was minus 10 degrees Celsius, and nothing would be growing outside of a greenhouse. The volunteering that urban farms rely on for planting seeds, transplanting seedlings and harvesting had not yet begun. I had arrived in Detroit just a bit too early in the season.

My phone beeped with the code for my room at the Sonder. I was surprised that it was the same as the code for the front door on the street. Shouldn't they be different? In a frenzy of panic partly fuelled by sleeplessness, I wrote the number on my hand, in my journal, in the 'notes' on my phone and emailed it to myself. I had covered every potential code loss. Then I received a text saying that one of the texts from the Sonder wasn't secure and could be spam. How could I know what was spam and what was genuine? How can any of us know? I ignored the text, hoping that when I got to the building, the code would work. It did.

It is odd staying in a building that is not a hotel, nor an apartment building. One feels untethered in these spaces. There was a security person at the front desk and elevators to take you to your floor, but the place had a strange in-between feeling to it, akin to watching a cleverly made advertorial – you sense something is off but it's hard to put it into words. All communication with the Sonder is done via the app or via email. There are no humans involved. I know this is the way everything is moving, but it's destabilizing.

The apartment was spacious. The bedding was well

made. It was clean. I Googled 'who owns the Sonder' just to give myself a sense that there might be a person behind it, to make me feel that it wasn't a completely disembodied space. The co-founder and CEO, Francis Davidson, had studied at McGill University – like my mother and two of my nephews (a link!). A deeper dive took me to an article Davidson had written. He talked of the 'culture' he was creating with his business – the culture that is 'lived day-to-day' by his employees. Davidson went on to define culture:

> Culture isn't perks, or fun events organized by the company. It's a much broader, more meaningful idea which defines the behavioral code of every person in the organization. A well communicated culture should clearly spell out what behaviors are expected, and which are deemed unacceptable. This is accomplished by filtering who joins, who's asked to leave, who rises up, and how everyone adapts their way of working and communicating to fit the management system.

This business-speak, with its focus on efficiency and behaviour management, is chilling. 'New recruits', Davidson wrote, 'are filtered through a systematic hiring process. Onboarding feels close to a culture shock – much needs to be unlearned as new habits are formed.' Onboarding? The forming of new habits? Isn't this the language of cults? There was more: 'The goal isn't to get everyone to recite all values on day 1. The goal is to drive behavior. It's OK if it takes months, or even years, to master all principles.' Here I was sleeping in a bed built by corporate ideology and zealotry. There was a dishwasher, a washing machine, a tumble dryer, a shower and ample, good-quality toiletries. I was safe. I was warm. And yet it

52

all felt so wrong.

The contrast between my night in the Sonder and my first night in Detroit, seventeen years ago, was stark. In 2006, I had planned to stay at the Temple Hotel, where it was rumoured Harry Houdini had visited in the 1920s – a detail Karl would have enjoyed. I called in advance but the woman who answered the phone told me that the owner wouldn't let her give out the rates over the phone. When I got there, I realised it was a flop house. It was falling apart. People were lying on the front steps in various states of intoxication and the rooms were rentable by the hour. Number 72 Temple Street is now a vacant lot. After wandering off from the Temple Hotel, I had found myself in Greektown, where I came upon the Golden Fleece Restaurant, which back then had those classic blue and white chequered tablecloths and a simple, cheap menu.

Before taking my order, the owner, Vassilis, asked for ID before giving me a beer.

'I'm forty years old,' I retorted.

'It's the law.'

Vassilis joined me for a drink while the young and very pretty waitress showed customers to their tables. He asked me the same question as the woman at the border, 'Where's your husband?'

This was to become a refrain I would hear over and over during the next couple of weeks on that 2006 trip. I had never been asked this anywhere else in the world.

There are only three accounts of women undertaking the Great American Road Trip that I know of: Simone de Beauvoir's 1948 *America Day by Day* (beautifully translated by Carol Cosman), British writer Ethel Mannin's travelogue, *An American Journey*, written twenty years later and *The Great American Bus Ride* by Irma Kurtz which was published in 1993. Unlike accounts by male writers, all three of these involve travel by Greyhound bus.

Born in New Jersey in 1935, Kurtz travelled to Europe in the late 1960s. In Paris, she was excited to see Simone de Beauvoir and Jean Paul Sartre in a Left Bank café. 'I was expected to marry a lawyer, live in Connecticut and have two cars,' she told an interviewer in 2016. Instead, she ended up in London in the early 1970s, where she wrote books and worked as a journalist as well as *Cosmopolitan* magazine's agony aunt from 1975 until her retirement in 2015.

Kurtz set off on her epic Greyhound trip because, in her words, she was 'a hussy of low appetites who always yearn[ed] shamelessly for rough travel'. Her desire to revisit her home country was one I, as a Canadian living in London, could understand: 'Life is a circular journey; as soon as my son turned nineteen and I could plan on open-ended travel for the first time since his birth, it had to be ... to the most baffling of all places, my unknown homeland.' Kurtz's focus in *The Great American Bus Ride* is on the people she meets, the conversations, the over-heard snatches of dialogue, as if she wants to get to know where she came from through the people who live there still. Her journey is not a straightforward one from east to west, but rather loops around in an idiosyncratic way. Because of this unusual trajectory, the book doesn't focus on a particular destination. She doesn't need to be any-where at any specific time, and the reader quickly realizes that the wayward conversations are her destination.

In male accounts of the Great American Road Trip, there are fewer conversations with strangers, the individual is paramount and the car is a symbol of intoxicating, virile freedom. When John Steinbeck set off across the United

States with his French poodle Charley, he was forty-eight years old, wealthy and famous. By this point he'd written half a dozen novels and won a Pulitzer Prize for *The Grapes of Wrath*. Steinbeck saw the 'ten or twelve thousand miles driving a truck, alone and unattended, over every kind of road' as 'the antidote for the poison of the professional sick man'. He equated his trip with manliness, pointing an accusing finger at those middle-aged men who slowed down, worried about their cholesterol levels and entered a semi-invalid stage of life. 'I see too many men delay their exits with a sickly, slow reluctance to leave the stage. It's bad theatre as well as bad living.'

I was curious to see what it would look like today to cross the United States without the machismo, the individualism and the car. The communal aspect of travelling by Greyhound is crucial to seeing a side of 'America' that very few people want to acknowledge and even fewer actually inhabit, even fleetingly. Passengers travel by bus because it is the cheapest way to move from one place to another. There are more stuffed garbage bags on a bus than suitcases on wheels. The Greyhound is where you meet those who, despite wanting and deserving a better life than the one they have, are stuck for various reasons: luck, fate, bad choices, unfair circumstances or illness. 'Traveling by Greyhound is no pleasure trip,' Kurtz writes, 'Bus journeys in America are purposeful expeditions, no frills or affectations.'

Then there are the criminals or patients who've been released from institutions far from where they have friends, family or a parked car. Many of those I met on both of my trips had had their driving license revoked because of a DUI (Driving Under the Influence) or some other infraction. Often people were physically unable to sit behind the wheel of a car because of a broken bone, eyesight problems or chronic conditions like epilepsy. Or, rarely, like me, because they never learned to drive.

In 1930, two years after the very first Greyhound Bus pulled out of Los Angeles heading in the direction of New York City, bus travellers, according to Carlton Jackson in his book *Hounds of the Road*, 'reflected a cross section of American society. They included salesmen (but not the expense account executive), workmen, housewives, tourists, sportsmen, school teachers, old people and youngsters.' Like many of today's passengers, 'Bus people generally wore sports clothes, were very friendly, and were easy to get acquainted with.'

Simone de Beauvoir had been sent on her trip by her publisher to document a lecture tour. Although she does see the US in part from a Greyhound bus, *America Day by Day* often reads like a who's who of artists, authors and intellectuals of the post-war period: she shares a taxi with Marcel Duchamp and ends up in a home where his piece *The Bride Stripped Bare by her Bachelors, Even* is on display (it had been damaged en route). She meets the Hollywood director William Wyler at a party in Los Angeles, where she also drinks with Man Ray, who tells her of his 'disgust' for Hollywood. In New York she meets Joan Miró and Carlo Levi at a party full of architects and painters and later goes to a gathering where Le Corbusier and Kurt Weill show up. This is also where she meets Charlie Chaplin, of whom she writes, 'From the moment he arrives, there's no question of anyone talking with anyone else. A circle forms around him, and he talks for three hours nonstop.... His hair is completely white, and in his aging face, only the eyes and the smile remain young.' But de Beauvoir is more interested in observing his wife, 'who is seated dejectedly in a corner' and who is 'pregnant as usual.... His wife is very much a brunette and is very beautiful in a violet dress with large gold earrings. The daughter of the playwright Eugene O'Neill, she had a brilliant youth; now she seems crushed by the weight of their conjugal glory... [I]t can't be very easy being Charlie Chaplin's wife.' Conjugal glory: the couple had eight children together.

De Beauvoir goes to 'Billie Holiday's place' on 52nd Street, where she describes Holiday as 'very beautiful in a long, white dress, her black hair straightened by a clever permanent and falling straight and shiny around her clear brown face. Her bangs look like they've been sculpted in dark metal. She smiles, she is beautiful, but she doesn't sing. They say she's on drugs and sings only rarely now.' But the person whose spirit and intellect suffuses *America Day by Day* is Richard Wright, whom de Beauvoir had already met in Paris. His autobiographical novel *Black Boy* had only just been published in 1945 and, four years previously, his novel *Native Son* had had a complicated reception. James Baldwin called it a 'pamphlet in literary disguise'. Wright takes de Beauvoir to dance halls and clubs and they see Sidney Bechet play live.

It is on this trip that she meets Nelson Algren, with whom she had a long and complex affair. They visit seedy bars in Chicago where the morphine addicts, alcoholics, petty thieves, prostitutes and gamblers congregate. In one dive bar, addicts bunk down and shoot up in rooms upstairs. De Beauvoir is shocked when the female bartender there asks, 'How is Malraux doing on his latest novel?' and then enquires after Sartre. She writes, 'This woman spends all her nights supervising this bar, which is also an overnight shelter; her favourite amusements are reading and drugs.' De Beauvoir's discerning eye looks at America through the lens of an outsider, an America always on the move.

De Beauvoir notices that in 1947 she didn't often see women travelling alone. 'American women', she wrote, 'drive in the cities, but they rarely take a trip without a masculine escort – this is about the extent of their independence.' Throughout *America Day by Day*, we encounter de Beauvoir's views on freedom and feminism – she was after all about to write *The Second Sex*. 'I'd imagined that women here would surprise me with their independence,' she writes, adding:

> "American woman", "free woman" – the words seemed synonymous.... In the women's magazines here, more than in the French variety, I've read long articles on the art of husband hunting and catching a man. I've seen that college girls have little concern for anything but men and that the unmarried woman is much less respected here than in Europe.

She describes a dinner she had been to at a woman's apartment. Another young woman had also been invited. Both of them were single. 'For the first time in my life,' de Beauvoir writes, 'a meal with women seems to be a meal "without men". Despite the martinis, despite the good cheer, we were surrounded by a conspicuous absence.'

Almost sixty years later, my travelling as a woman 'without a man' was still somehow shocking. The people I met seemed to see a 'conspicuous absence' around me. Vassilis, the owner of the Golden Fleece, simply couldn't understand why my husband would let me travel on my own, and I couldn't understand how he could think I might need either permission or a chaperone. We laughed about it because there was no way we were ever going to agree. The very pretty waitress added that if she didn't have kids, she'd love to travel on her own across the

58

country. Vassilis said he was happy she had kids because it meant he got to have a pretty waitress. De Beauvoir would have had the perfect barb for this. I simply kept quiet and drank my beer.

Thankfully, in 2023, no one asked me where my husband was or whether he trusted me. Maybe this is partly a function of being an older woman. My value had waned over the past seventeen years. Perhaps older women are expected to be single once their sexual attraction and procreative capacities are behind them. Being alone could perhaps be seen to be the *only* acceptable state for an older woman past her prime.

A guy in his late fifties entered the Golden Fleece with two women – one on each arm – who looked half his age. He asked Vassilis for a table for three. 'If there's a spare woman in the place, I'll take a table for four,' he shouted. Vassilis pointed at me and asked him if I was too old. 'Yes,' came the reply. At forty, I was too old. The pretty waitress showed them to a table and I paid for my spanakopita. Vassilis hadn't charged me for the two bottles of beer.

I sauntered in the direction of the Milner Hotel, recommended by the waitress in the Golden Fleece. The sunny day had turned grey and damp and I was cold. I found the handsome nine-story building on a short, tree-lined street. It dated from 1917, when the city was bursting with money and industry and optimism. The Milner's slogan then was, 'A bed and a bath for a buck and a half'. The street was perfectly situated near the Fox Theatre with its glitz and gilt, where tourists would have parked their new Ford motor cars, built at the plant twelve miles down the road. There would have been fur coats and sleek leather shoes with thin straps and mother-of-pearl buttons.

In 2006, the Milner was shabby and in disrepair, but the rooms were cheap. Karl would be able to afford it. It would be her first night sleeping outside of Canada: a milestone for her. It was just within walking distance of the bus station and it was dawning on me back then that not being able to drive would force me to stay in the often dodgy downtown areas of cities, many of which were still being hollowed out by the exodus of the middle classes to the suburbs. Not being mobile was, and still is, a problem in the US. In Irma Kurtz's words, 'America is a road country. To be without wheels in America is to be lame.'

The elevator rattled as it took me up eight floors to my room. Water dripped from the ceiling next to where the electric light fizzed and blinked. My room was filthy and the dresser was missing a leg, which meant that if you opened a drawer, the entire piece of furniture toppled over. There were cigarette butts on the floor. The sink and bathtub were dotted with small, singed-brown crescent moons. It was enormous, though – the size of a suite. After staring out the window through the foggy night at the old Tigers baseball stadium, now called Comerica Park, after the Comerica Bank, I slid into bed in this room that hovered above Detroit. There was contentment in the fact that no one knew where I was. For the first time in a long time, I was really alone, a mountaineer on top of a solitary peak. I almost didn't exist. This sensation of being uncontactable, out of digital reach, is so rare now. I was not to know in 2006 that this was possibly the last time I would ever have the luxury of not being able to be found or tracked.

'And so the earth revolves in the quiet of the night with this shining wound in its side,' wrote de Beauvoir of Los Angeles. Any great industrial city could be described as a shining wound, yet despite these wounds the Earth

revolves and we with it. And now with our web of online connections, we carry the tools that carve these industrial wounds in our hands and pockets.

While planning my most recent trip in spring 2023, I had looked into staying at the Milner again. I found out that in 2012, it had been sold and turned into condos in what *Deadline Detroit* called a downtown 'boomlet'. I also found an online review written two years after I had stayed there: 'Upon opening the door at one point, the WINDOW FELL OUT OF THE WALL. It literally just...freaking flopped right out. Big gaping hole in the wall. .... THE WINDOW FELL OUT OF THE WALL?!?!?!?! Need I say any more?'

On a cold, sunny day, I walked to 1538 Centre Street to see the physical evidence of this boomlet. Indeed the old Milner Hotel had morphed into an expensively appointed apartment block with an awning edged in hunter green announcing *The Ashley* in fancy script. A small one-bedroom apartment would set me back over $1,500 a month. It doesn't make sense to me that cities can transform themselves so rapidly. I guess this is called progress. But who is doing the progressing and who's being left behind? The disappeared motels and hotels I had stayed in back in 2006 had not closed solely because of the Covid-19 pandemic; they had been torn down in the pursuit of gentrification, urban renewal, upscaling, restoration, development and the digital colonization of the analogue. In other words: progress. 'Plastic scrimshaw, carnival rides, condos,' wrote William Least Heat-Moon, 'That was what history had come to.' He goes on, 'To melt warships into Ferris wheels, that had to be progress.'

Greektown in Detroit was polished and expensive now. The Golden Fleece Restaurant had been revamped and was out of my budget. For food, I headed to the City Market downtown, near the Sonder, where I bought a tin of lentil soup, some bread and fruit. The shop reminded me of the small supermarkets in New York's Lower East Side in the 1980s. Everything from diapers to guacamole crammed into wonky shelves. I ate supper in my room watching the snow fall. I was happy to get an early night. I would have liked to see what film was on Turner Classic Movies, but the TV didn't have normal stations. All I could get were reruns of *Antiques Road Show* (the flipped hair and Laura Ashley clothing made it obvious these were from the 1980s); *The Price is Right*, with its hysterical canned laughter; Bob Ross episodes showing how to paint trees; *Ice Road Truckers* (at least dating from this millennium); Hallmark films about dead mothers and God; and clips from out-of-date FOX newscasts. It wasn't a television – it was a digital streaming device called ROKU. It was the size of a small cinema screen and I had no idea how it worked. I turned it off.

That night as I lay in bed, it hit me that, being in my fifties, I had become more aware of my fragility. All through my twenties, thirties and forties, I was fearless and didn't think twice about wandering around alone at night. But here in Detroit, I imagined violent scenarios. It wasn't helped by one of the online reviews for the Sonder, left by someone called Michael: 'The 2nd night two men entered my apartment, held me down, sexually assaulted me and then robbed me of all my belongings. After the assault I frantically ran downstairs for help. The guard on duty looked at me like I was insane.' Since it is an online review it may, of course, not be real. Perhaps there is a grudge behind it or some kind of fantasy at play. Whether it was real or not, it planted in me a seed of anxiety, made worse by the fact that this reviewer stated that the back door to the building was never locked. I hadn't checked because I didn't want to know. Perhaps part of my fear and sense of fragility could be put down to this feeling that reality itself is now fragile. We don't live embodied lives anymore. Our reality has moved into the digital realm – a realm with no end or beginning, just an endless stream of data, algorithms, reruns, cash-free exchanges and customer reviews.

On this trip to Detroit, I didn't go to the Motown Museum. Nor did I sit, as I had in 2006, smoking and drinking bad coffee in the Cass Café, next to a guy wearing a T-shirt that said, 'Thanks for not breeding'. He sat on his own reading *The Magic Mountain*. I went to French cafés where women wore yoga pants and where men were expensively groomed. And as with all expensive urban centres, there were dogs. Small ones on laps and in handbags. Detroit was slick now, real estate had value.

Unfortunately, most of the photos I took in 2006 have since been lost. Faced with the derelict buildings, I was at once stunned and excited, and had wanted to record what I was seeing. This was before I had seen any of those glossy coffee table books of Detroit Dereliction Porn. This kind of urban landscape was new to me then. It looked like a war had been fought and lost there. In fact, Daniel, a cab driver I met in 2006, who took me on a tour of the city, had told me Detroit sometimes reminded him of images of war zones he saw on the news. I had wandered around, peering into buildings where chandeliers just about clung onto crumbling plaster ceilings. Chunks of ornate Victorian moulding lay on the ground around abandoned sleeping bags. Fragments of gilt picture frames sat in pieces on marble floors. It didn't titillate me; it made me incredibly sad. Why had I wanted to document this? What good would it do? Who would benefit from it?

¶ Dearborn, Michigan is a city ten miles west of down-town Detroit. It is home to the Ford Factory. The Uber driver who took me there was an Iraqi poet. He told me about his favourite poets, Badr Shakir al-Sayyab and Nazik Al-Malaika, whom I had never heard of. I learned on this ride that Urdu poetry translated into Farsi keeps its rhythm. I also learned that the prose poem first appeared in Iraq. My Arabic poetry lesson came to an abrupt end as we approached the Ford Museum and Factory.

Like many corporations, Ford would like to be seen to be addressing human-made climate disruption. To show their commitment, the company installed a 'living' roof. If you take a tour of the Ford plant, as I did recently, you can hear all about their Ballardian-sounding 'Xero Flor Green Roof System'. In their literature about the 600-acre, 2-billion-dollar Ford Rouge Complex, they write proudly of the plant's 'people-friendly features such as overhead safety walkways, day lighting, team rooms, cooler air in the summer months and relaxing places to congregate' which, if you strip away the adjectives, sound like pretty basic requirements for any building where people might work.

In 2004, Ford's 10.4-acre 'greenroof' was recognized in the *Guinness Book of World Records* as the world's largest living roof. But in a Ford Motor press release from 2000, Henry Ford's great-grandson, Bill Ford, makes clear that his effort to balance 'the needs of auto manufactur-ing with ecological and social concerns' does not stem from 'environmental philanthropy': it is simply 'sound business'.

Outside the Ford Factory building, I stopped to take photos of the flocks of Canada geese. The word 'frunk', which had been used on the factory tour, was running around in my head. It consisted of a trunk ('boot', in the

UK) at the front of the vehicle and was, according to a tour guide, one of the most useful innovations since the truck bed.

I heard footsteps behind me as someone from the Ford factory approached. He asked, 'So, where are you visiting from?'

'England.'

'Well, here's a sticker as a souvenir.'

'Oh, thank you.'

'Did you get all the information you wanted?'

'Yes, I did, thanks.'

'I saw you writing stuff down.'

'Yes, I was taking notes.'

'Are you just curious, or...' he trailed off.

'I always carry a notebook.'

'Well, I've seen a lot of changes.'

'I bet you have.'

'It's gotten really environmental over the years.'

'Yes, I can see that.'

'We've got a green roof.'

'Yes, I saw that. And beehives.'

'You got it! Your bus to the next part of the tour is leaving in three minutes.' He pointed to the shuttle bus, sitting with its door open.

I got on knowing that it wasn't leaving for another ten minutes.

The narrative Ford is putting forward now is the one we all want to believe: the reformed sinner making amends. And yet, many of us who grew up near Detroit and the Great Lakes remember seeing apocalyptic photos well into the 1970s of plumes of black smoke jetting hundreds of feet into the air above the River Rouge. Up until the 1940s, the industries around Detroit were dumping six million gallons of waste oil into the Detroit and River Rouge every year. This oil not only sat on the surface, but it soaked into anything and everything else lying around, from bird eggs to scrap wood. All that was needed to set a giant bonfire was a dropped acetylene torch, which is exactly what happened in 1969. The fire could not be extinguished; it was merely contained until it eventually burnt itself out along with every living thing in and around the river. The federal government approved the National Environmental Policy Act the following year, which was the start of pollution regulation for companies who were responsible for such environmental catastrophes. Some of us can also remember the 1980s, when the River Rouge was still 'one of the worst pollution "hot spots" in the Great Lakes area'. Nor can we forget how oil-dependent corporations like Ford were part of the industrialization that led to the ecological devastation of this watershed in the first place.

Volunteer and government organizations rallied together in a 900-million-dollar clean-up of the River Rouge area and, in 2005, the year before I first wandered the streets of Detroit with Karl, it had been deemed a 'Green Corridor'. How to square this then with the fact that according to the American Environmental Protection Agency (EPA), the River Rouge (which they confusingly call the Rouge River in their report) is still contaminated with 'heavy metals, polychlorinated biphenyls (PCBs), polycyclic aromatic hydrocarbons (PAH), mercury, oil and grease' which 'affect fish and wildlife habitat and populations as well as recreational opportunities'? In its literature, the government agency still lists problems with the River Rouge, such as:

Eutrophication or Undesirable Algae

Degradation of Fish and Wildlife Populations
Beach Closings
Fish Tumors or Other Deformities
Degradation of Aesthetics
Degradation of Benthos (the flora, fauna and sediments found on the bottom of a sea or lake)
Loss of Fish and Wildlife Habitat

Faced with the environmental legacies of companies like Shell, Mobile Oil, Amoco, Ford and General Motors, a one-inch Xero Flor 'pre-vegetated', 'pre-cultivated' mat stuck onto the roof of Ford's truck assembly plant feels not only inadequate but borderline schizophrenic.

There is a tension in Detroit that I couldn't help but tune into: a sense that the good jobs and the company benefits earned during the city's heyday were never going to last, because, like the Xero Flor roofing, they were short-termist and only a thumb's width deep. The very products being made here were seeding the town's demise.

Back in 1934, James Rorty in *Where Life is Better* described the factory tours of Ford's River Rouge plant, which were like 'a mechanically gifted child's dream of heaven'. Every day, he writes,

thousands of wide-eyed American children of assorted ages, from seven to seventy, walked through the gates of this heaven for to admire and to see. These tourists saunter along the platform beside the assembly line, just as a week before, perhaps, they had sauntered along the boardwalk above Niagara Falls.... The tourists didn't know each other, or speak to each other – they were the heterogeneous, atomic middle-class drift of a continent. The workmen who struggled frantically to keep up with the implacable crawl

of the belt conveyors – they too barely knew each other.
They were the labor drift of a continent, here today, gone
tomorrow.... They were merely the minimum ingredient
of man-power necessary to the manufacture of mobility....
They were a part of the nightmare and those who watched
it were a part of the nightmare. We are all part of the
nightmare.

So, what about those Pontiacs parked around my childhood neighbourhood in Ottawa in the 1970s? They
were named after the Odawa Chief Pontiac who lost to
the British in 1763. Was that model named specifically to
rub it in? We never thought to question such things then.
When you think back to being a child riding in your dad's
battered second-hand Cadillac you marvel that no one
ever told you it was named after Antoine Cadillac, who is
credited with 'founding' Detroit in 1701, erasing the place
names belonging to that land and its people with French
nomenclature, like his re-naming of the Rivière Rouge,
which as 'River Rouge' has retained the French syntax. I
have asked one of my Anishinaabe First Nations relatives
in Canada for what this river would have been called in
Anishinaabeg, and so far he hasn't been able to find anyone who knows.

The American writer and academic Lauret Savoy gets
to the heart of the naming of places in her book *Trace*.
'The project of illuminating terra incognita's darkness
made certain ways of inhabiting and relating to this place
called "America" natural,' she writes. 'In their placemak-
ing these newcomers not only set out to possess territory
on the ground. They also lay claim to territory of the mind
and memory, to the future and past.' When you erase the
words for a place, what else are you erasing? The names
given to towns, mountains, bodies of water and geological

74

formations – these all possess within their original names the collective memory of those who first saw them and lived by them; in time places come to reflect the political ambitions of those who bring new names to them. There was a time when none of the continent was named; it simply existed as land, water, snow and ice.

At 125 miles long, the River Rouge is a relatively small ribbon of fresh water, but it is this fresh water that brought people to fish and hunt in the region in the first place. Even before the First Nations people settled around the fertile Great Lakes, the area was home to the Mound Builders – a culture known for their embankments and sacred man-made hills. There was a ceremonial site at the mouth of the River Rouge where it meets the Detroit River but, over a hundred years ago, it was destroyed. Bela Hubbard, the nineteenth-century naturalist and writer who also made his name in lumber and real estate, noted in 1887 that 'for nearly half a century', this mound 'has been dug away and removed, by wagon load and boat load, and little notice of its contents, until now it is but a miniature of its former self'. He goes on, 'Much as has been lost by the wanton destruction of this instructive monument, enough is disclosed to show that this huge mound has been the memorial of many.' In other words, these were possibly ancient graves.

The Mound Builder culture collapsed around 1200AD, giving way to a succession of Native American tribes who enjoyed an abundance of food, fish and ample fresh water until French trappers arrived. 'The fur trade reduced the available game, set one Native American tribe against another, and made them dependent on traders for weapons, needles, blankets, traps, and metal tools,' writes the historian David Nye. Then came the British, whose victory in the French Indian Wars allowed the colonial project to take off with even more velocity. Steamboats arrived in 1818 and, along with them, industry. Lumber was needed for the expansion and building of cities and towns in the treeless Great Plains to the west of Michigan, and timber was also needed for railway ties. In the 1850s, Detroit was finally joined to other centres of commerce by rail. An industrial park came along soon after, enticed by the copious amounts of fresh water and the existing infrastructure.

Henry Ford must have been thrilled when, in 1915, he sent a team to scout out the Detroit area for his car factory. So much of the groundwork had already been laid for him. It was here that Ford developed his famous assembly line, an idea that seems so obvious now, but was a breakthrough in terms of labour exploitation. Until Ford came along, it was the workers who moved to different parts of the factory to fix or build commodities, but with his new set-up, it was the parts that were delivered to stationary labourers. This created what the geographer David Harvey has termed the 'compression of space and time', which has since become one of the backbones of an economic system that rewards efficiency and productivity over human welfare. James Rorty again:

> In Detroit, more clearly than anywhere else in America, one sees the bare bones of the cultural nightmare we Americans have dreamed for ourselves, believing, in our greedy haste, our barbaric innocence, that it was a thing we could live by and with; that human life could flourish as a kind of parasitic attachment to an inhuman, blind, valueless process, in which money begets machines, machines beget money, machines beget machines, money begets money.

In *Where Life is Better*, Rorty includes segments of

documents written by workers at the Ford factory. In the early 1930s, one worker told a journalist that 'production used to be 1,300 motors for the day and afternoon shifts'. When a general strike of the auto industry seemed imminent, 'production was cut down to 900, without reducing the working force', and for the first time in years, this Ford factory worker said, 'we were able to work almost like normal human beings'. The strike was called off, but production in this worker's department 'was stepped up to 1,450 for the two shifts and three workers out of 37 were laid off.' The workers were punished for their attempts to work like 'normal human beings'.

Rorty coined a term for the absolute power held by Henry Ford: Fordismus, which has come down to us more commonly as 'Fordism'. 'Where else in the world, and at what other period of history could a lean, pale, fixed-eyed pioneer mechanic have imposed his rule of thumb economics, his small-town morality, upon a whole society?... Mr Ford has had Fordismus all his life. He will die of it, and I think society will die of the same thing.'

When you look at a map, it is clear that the last two miles or so of the River Rouge, as it approaches the Detroit River, suddenly fall into an almost straight line. This is the canal that was built to allow larger ships to dock at Detroit. Grids were imposed on this land with no thought of their effect on the soil, the plants, people and animals living there.

Many of the grand buildings lining Detroit's avenues today are from the heyday of the Ford empire, when his was the largest factory in the world, employing over a hundred thousand workers. A middle class grew until the Crash of 1929, when half of Ford's employees were laid off. Over 3,000 workers, many of them from Ford, marched in protest to the River Rouge plant. When they

wouldn't turn back, the police opened fire, wounding hundreds and killing four men in what became known as the 'The Ford Hunger March' or the 'Ford Massacre'.

During the Second World War, Ford turned his plant into a military production facility, making tanks and weapons. It wasn't until the 1970s, when the oil crisis hit, that the post-war uplift in car production began to slacken. When the Japanese market emerged, Ford had to scrap the idea of being a self-sufficient factory and began buying in the components for its cars. As Nye explains, 'Many buildings fell into disuse or closed, and parts suppliers went bankrupt.... This "internationalization" eliminated well-paid jobs in Detroit.' And this is the background story to so many of the boarded-up mansions with their cracked crystal chandeliers, the windowless houses and the rooms in crumbling apartment blocks littered with needles, single shoes, soiled mattresses and crumpled Kleenex tissues.

Just outside my Sonder apartment was a city block that had been taken over by the not-for-profit Greening of Detroit. This downtown patch of land known as Lafayette Greens was filled with raised beds for growing plants, metal sculptures, trellises and gardening implements. It looked surreal surrounded by towering buildings, a giant Westin Hotel and the flashy red, white and blue lettering of Coney Island Hotdogs. Snow-covered, the raised beds were dormant and there were no volunteers about, but this particular organization has been running since 1989. Since their inception, they have planted over 100,000 trees and they estimate that as far back as 2013 there were already between 1,500 and 2,000 urban gardens being tended by residents, which seems high for a city that had a population of 692,000 at the time. It was in relation to

Detroit's urban farming scene that I had first heard the terms 'gangster gardening' and 'guerrilla gardening', named thus because in some parts of the city, planting seeds and growing food is either illegal or so tightly controlled as to make it impossible.

Despite the cold, the snow and the season, I wanted to see a bigger urban farm, so I boarded the number 6 bus along Jefferson Avenue to visit Earthworks on the east side of Detroit. I got off at Mount Elliott and walked up a snowy lane that looked more rural than urban. Rabbit and squirrel tracks criss-crossed my path and birds of prey circled. Solitary wooden houses, some with turrets, gingerbread detailing and large wrap-around porches were in various states of decay. One of the industrial buildings was still in use and there were workmen hauling lumber. I walked up and asked a guy lifting a 2-by-4 if he knew where the urban farm was. 'Honestly, I have no idea,' he replied. 'But I hear they're everywhere.'

'Until you start looking for them,' I replied.

He laughed.

There was no-one else around.

'All cities need to be walked in to get the "feel" of them,' Ethel Mannin said of her time in the US. Yet so few people see American cities from the sidewalk. Most experience them from the seat of a car. I kept walking and came to more abandoned houses. Then a few dwellings appeared with signs of life. Cars parked outside with fresh tracks in the snow. Plants in windows. 'Beware of Dog' signs. Porch lights on. Eventually I saw the Capuchin Soup Kitchen, which is run by an order of Franciscan monks. It was founded to help those affected by the stock market crash of 1929 'in the spirit of St. Francis of Assisi'. They grow food, prepare and serve it, and also provide showers, household items, clothing for adults and art therapy

for children.

The Earthworks urban farm produces tens of thousands of kilos of fruit and vegetables from their compact 1.25-acre organic farm. Their On the Rise Bakery employs people who need help rebuilding their lives after bouts of incarceration or periods of substance abuse. There is a small residential treatment facility for men recovering from addiction.

On the day I visited, the soup kitchen was packed and their hoop houses looked poised to get going for the season. In line with St Francis's respect for all living beings, one of the driving missions of the Capuchin Soup Kitchen is to restore our connection to the environment and community. As it was off-season and the workers serving lunch were busy, I spoke to a neighbour who lived next to one of the hoop houses in a row of small clapboard homes. He was a handsome Black man, maybe in his sixties or early seventies. He was scraping ice from the top of a large wooden box surrounded by half a dozen tabby and ginger kittens. I asked if he knew anything about the food being grown just on the other side of his picket fence.

'Oh, that's the Catholic Church doing that. You can go there and get some food, though.'

'Thank you.' I paused.

'Hey, you from Canada?' he asked.

'Yes, you got it,' I replied, amazed.

'Well, I remember meeting you right over there,' he said pointing to a spot in the lane behind his house next to where I was standing. 'I remember you saying you were from Canada.'

'I'm not sure we've met before. I was last in Detroit in 2006 and I live in England now.'

'Oh, well. My daughter says we have some history in Wales. Our name "Price" was spelled "Pryce". That was our slave name. I'm Tommy Price.'

I remained silent to let him continue.

'I've been watching PBS and all those programmes about slavery, but the thing is, it was all God's will. God's plan.'

I wasn't sure where he was going. He carried on, talking about the twelve tribes of Israel. I couldn't keep up with his narrative. He spoke too quickly and in non-sequiturs.

I asked if he belonged to any church.

He pointed to his chest, 'My church is in here.' He paused. 'I've had visions of people in white robes. My wife said I was dreaming but over there where there used to be a green gate, there were fluffy white clouds, which is what you'd expect in the afterlife, isn't it.' He laughed. 'My wife told me to go lie down.'

I was beginning to feel a chill seep through my puffy winter coat. Tommy was wearing a chequered shirt, a thin jacket, jeans, no hat or gloves or boots – just a pair of running shoes. He didn't seem in the least bit cold.

'This Covid vaccine is killing people,' he said. 'They're experimenting on people, on *babies*!' He looked at me hard. 'You haven't been vaccinated, have you?'

'Yes, I have.'

His eyes widened. 'Oh, dear. Everything is about money. Every shot they give, they make money. Basically the plan is to reduce the population.' He stopped and looked out onto his lane, where he thought we had once met. 'I have five more kittens inside if you'd like to take them?'

'I can't unfortunately. I already have three cats.'

'Oh, wow!'

He smiled and waved, and we said our goodbyes.

I went back to the soup kitchen. Just as I got to the door, three men were leaving. They held the door for me and I noticed the 'no guns or knives' sign just inside. The large room was still heaving with men sitting at long tables. The people working there looked intensely busy and some were chatting with men who looked in need of help, so I turned and crunched through the thick snow back to the bus stop. It was beginning to get dark and I felt a strange mixture of sadness and hope.

The burgeoning urban farm phenomenon in Detroit is partly down to the fact that land in the city is cheap. It is also the result of groups of people coming together to plant seeds, pass on skills and create communities around the common goal of building food sovereignty. This is particularly crucial for those who are marginalized and living in food deserts – places where fresh food is either unavailable or so overpriced as to be inaccessible.

I was invited to meet with someone I had heard was an enemy of the grassroots movement of urban farming in Detroit: Mike Score, president of Hantz Farms. The mission of Hantz Farms is to create the world's largest urban farm on underutilized land in Detroit. 'The simple focus of our investment,' Mike Score wrote to me in an email, 'is truly liveable neighborhoods where long-term residents are the first rewarded by our investment, and our work is guided by grace, gratitude, generosity and fidelity.' The number 9 bus again took me out along Jefferson Avenue. I walked up McClellan Avenue to number 2140 at the corner of Amity Street (with the Elliot Smith song running around in my head, 'Amity, Amity, Amity, good to go...'). It was a bright sunny day, but the emptiness of the streets was daunting. More burnt-out houses and industrial buildings, more empty lots, piles of cut timber from clearing land. The wind whistled through the telephone wires overhead.

There was no sign or number on the Hantz Farms building. I just had to guess from the fact it looked well cared for that this was Mr Score's office. He greeted me with polite friendliness. Tall, casually dressed in a chequered Carhartt shirt and beige slacks, he had a warmth about him that immediately made me drop my guard. He had what I call a 'non-coastal' look, like someone you'd meet in a diner in Montana or Idaho or any of the Intermountain West states. I wasn't expecting this. I was expecting someone slick and a bit shifty. I had made a list of questions for him about pesticide use, social justice, how he planned to feed people, how he might ensure biodiversity and soil health, how he would combat the food deserts. Did he call what he does 'rewilding'?

As soon as he led me to the table where he had laid out a pitcher of water and offered me a coffee, I knew that our conversation would take a turn I hadn't counted on. Because of what I'd read about him, I had been prepared to be on the offensive. But the problem was that I immediately liked him. He told me how his family had emigrated to the US from Poland after the First World War. His great-great grandfather had owned a block of houses in Detroit in the early 1900s. His mother and father grew up together in the city and he felt a piece of him was rooted here. His background was in farming, he had worked in sustainable agriculture at Michigan State University and had also done agricultural work in Kentucky and in Zaire with the Mennonite Church, but he always felt a pull back to Detroit.

'In Detroit you could squat land and grow stuff from free or cheap seeds,' he said, referring to a mission he had started to help recovering addicts grow food. He got frustrated, however, when some of the addicts sold the food for money to get their next fix. At this point he prayed to God and what came to him was the image of a large farm that would 'replace the blight with beauty'. It was such a powerful idea that he convened any friends who were bankers, architects and lawyers, and put together a business plan. He tried getting this project off the ground and in 2008 a phone call came through from his boss at Michigan State University saying that there was a businessman in Detroit who wanted to 'replace blight with beauty'. The synchronicity in this was remarkable. This businessman was John Hantz – a wealthy, cigar-smoking entrepreneur. They met serendipitously and John offered Mike a job as president of Hantz Farms, which he accepted.

The fact that these white, wealthy men have bought up land and are creating competition for smaller, grassroots and more marginalized urban farmers has stoked tension in Detroit's urban farming communities. Mike Score, however, feels that buying up just over 200 acres of land dotted with abandoned and condemned buildings will be transformational. The original idea was to grow food, but this proved difficult on such a large scale. The men altered their plans and focused on growing a mixture of hardwood trees, mostly sugar maples, oaks – burl, white and swamp – tulip poplars and black cherry. On one day, with the help of 1,500 volunteers, Hantz Farms planted 15,000 trees.

Mike and John put their own money into the venture. It was this commitment that led the City Council to approve Hantz Farms' proposal. The council members saw Mike – and indeed the whole venture – as authentic and trustworthy. His vision, in the end, is a neighbourhood creation scheme with trees and well-built homes – what might at one time have been seen as a 'typical American neighbourhood' – rather than a community farm.

The existence of Hantz Farms, with its backing of privilege and wealth in a city reeling from racial inequality, ongoing issues of poverty and a painstaking recovery from its bankruptcy in 2013, still rankles many in Detroit, like Malik Yakini, the executive director at the Detroit Black Community Food Security Network (DBCFSN). Yakini said in a 2019 interview that 'a dangerous precedent for the city' had been set through the sale of such a 'huge amount of land to an individual basically just because the guy had the money to buy it'.

I contacted DBCFSN, but their volunteering sessions hadn't begun and there was no one around when I was in Detroit to meet with me. Their farm, known as D-town, is the largest in the city and has been running since 2008. On seven acres, they grow over thirty kinds of fruits and vegetables using only sustainable, regenerative methods. Their focus is on community building, education and, according to their website, 'Black food sovereignty for people of African descent to access healthy and culturally appropriate food produced through ecologically sound and sustainable methods, and their right to define their own food and agriculture systems'.

The only urban farm open to volunteering was Keep Growing Detroit. Its hoop houses are near the famous Eastern Market, which sells produce from local growers. Keep Growing Detroit's mission, much like that of DBCFSN, is to create food sovereignty and to provide healthy, affordable food to Detroiters that is grown within the city limits.

I decided to walk there from downtown, which was a little optimistic. I got lost several times among abandoned buildings on streets without signs, which made Google

maps useless. It took well over an hour and saw me running across roads with several lanes of speeding traffic and no pedestrian crossings. I had left myself plenty of time and arrived early at the farm. As I wandered around the site, with the recognizable pallets, buckets, outdoor taps and chalk boards of urban farms, I spotted another volunteer who looked as lost as I did. We went into the main hoop house together where we met Rosebud, who would show us and half a dozen others how to separate the fine filigree roots of cauliflower seedlings. We potted the seedlings into large trays with popsicle sticks stuck into the soil to identify them. It was a cold, grey afternoon and we tended these tiny plants in silence. Eventually we introduced ourselves and then the chat opened up onto books and plants and ecology. It reminded me of the volunteer work I do in London at a small medicine garden. There is something universal and timeless about groups of people tending to plants, working with their hands. Conversation is gentle, tentative. There is often laughter.

It may seem to some that transplanting cauliflower seedlings in a hoop house in Detroit to sell in a farmer's market is fiddling while Rome burns. But for some of us, being with like-minded people – those who see the connections between unsustainable farming practices and the distribution of food requiring thousands of air miles with the proliferation of plastics and the burning of fossil fuels – is a form of active hope, a reminder that we are not alone and that we are not the crazy ones.

Planting seeds is in fact one of the most rebellious acts of resistance out there, which is why giant corporations like Monsanto are in the business of patenting seeds. By doing so, they are effectively making it illegal for farmers and Indigenous people around the world to grow the

91

(313)
567 7788
THE WORKING MAN'S STORE
MATS
POTS, PANS & UTENSILS
SHOPPING CARTS
PIGGY BANKS
DOLLAR ITEMS

food they have been relying on for millennia. In 2013, a 75-year-old Indiana farmer, Vernon Hugh Bowman, lost a case against Monsanto. Bowman had bought soybeans from a grain elevator near his farm in Indiana. He used these to plant a late-season second crop. From these plants, he kept seeds for planting future crops. He didn't think this would be a problem as he had bought the seeds from a third party who had put no restrictions on their use. But, Monsanto's patent, according to the ruling, covers all future seeds from plants grown from the original seeds. Despite being backed by the Center for Food Safety (CFS) and the Save Our Seeds campaigning groups, Bowman lost, and his case has now set a precedent. In their research into Bowman's case, the CFS said 'it had tracked numerous lawsuits that Monsanto had brought against farmers and found some 142 patent infringement suits against 410 farmers and 56 small businesses in more than 27 states. In total the firm has won more than $23m (£14.8m) from its targets.' More than 53 per cent of the world's commercial seed market is controlled by just three firms – Monsanto, DuPont and Syngenta. Seeds will become even more politically charged and will gain in value as food scarcity increases and climate disruption makes it more difficult to grow food. Those who own the patent on seeds will be able to control what can be planted and who is able to harvest the results.

Planting seeds and growing food is a political act. Not only do these activities keep one connected to the seasons and the cycles of life, but they are a means of creating a sustainable food source should the links in the global food system collapse. When looked at from this wider perspective, transplanting cauliflowers in a hoop house in Detroit looks very sane indeed. Urban farms are accessible to people without cars, without money, without photo ID. You don't need an app or an iPhone. They are places of community and learning. They are the places I feel most at home.

On my last night in Detroit, I went to the Greenwich Time Pub downtown. It had become my favourite hangout over these past few nights. The beer was cheap, the lighting just bright enough to write in my diary but still low enough to allow one to disappear into the shadows. At one end of the room, stained glass in tones of yellow and orange cast a warm glow. A tall, thin Black man named Tony took a seat next to me at the bar.

'I want to buy you a drink to spread the love.'

Tony had a wad of hundreds and was spreading love among many of the customers. When his lively conversation with the young, blonde bartender ended, he turned to me and we had the usual polite chit-chat one has in drinking establishments in foreign cities. Then he told me a story about a bar around the corner that wouldn't serve him. When he approached the manager to ask why he was being ignored, she said 'What can I get you?', not 'How can I help you?'

'Can you see the difference?' he asked.

The manager felt that a free drink or a bar snack would make him happy and keep him quiet, when really what he wanted was for her to listen. The distinction was subtle, but it was there.

I was getting ready to leave when he said he'd like to show me the bar he was talking about so I could avoid it. We left together. It had started snowing again and Detroit looked beautiful. Whenever I step out into a dark night in a big American city I hear Stevie Wonder say 'Wow, New York, just like I pictured it. Skyscrapers and everything.' We walked along for a minute or two towards the bar

where he had been treated rudely. Then he asked, 'So, where you staying?'

'Downtown.'

'Where Downtown?'

I laughed. 'Do you really think I am going to tell a guy I've just met in a bar where I am staying?'

As I walked to the Sonder, I remembered my final night in Detroit in 2006. I had walked to the university area where I passed a shop selling Verizon cards and put some money onto my phone, which I barely used. In 2006, calls were expensive, and I wasn't in the habit of using a cell phone. No one was. Karl didn't even have one. She always used payphones.

I found a café playing British music from the 1980s, where I could sit and write in my journal about Karl. The blue-haired clientele with visible (and no doubt invisible) piercings were her people. And just beyond Karl there was always my sister Mary – my two invisible travelling companions on the road back then.

I left the café in the evening and as I walked to the Milner Hotel, I clocked that I was being followed. The man caught up, walked alongside me for a while, and then shouted in my ear, 'Hey, can I ask you a question?' Although it was dark, I could make out several bloody cuts on his face. His arm was in a cast. I walked faster but he kept up his pace. His girlfriend had recently dumped him. He had paid all the bills, worked a double shift, but still that wasn't enough for his lady. 'How can I keep her?' he yelled at me.

I don't remember what I answered, if anything, but whatever it was, he must have taken it to mean I was making fun of him. He started shaking his fists in front of his face and I walked faster. I knew I was going in the general direction of my hotel, but I didn't know the route very well, nor the name of the street I needed to turn down. I couldn't pull out my map, so I just carried on walking. Eventually he stopped and I continued. He shouted after me: 'What do I need to do to keep her?'

On that night in 2006 after being followed, I had turned on the TV to find George Cukor's *Edward, My Son* with Spencer Tracy and Deborah Kerr. The eponymous son, Edward, was a study in entitled monstrosity. He reminded me of the character of Cliffie in Patricia Highsmith's *Edith's Diary* – another son showered with unconditional motherly love who ends up a narcissistic, alcoholic delinquent.

Back then I spent a lot of time thinking about fictional characters with overly devoted mothers. The character of Karl was a child whose mother had abandoned her. And then, of course, there was the child I couldn't seem to conceive and who, although he or she did not exist, was someone I thought about constantly. And then there was Mary, the sister I loved dearly who part raised me. Stories about mothers – particularly weak mothers and their psychologically damaged children – I couldn't get enough of them.

The following morning I had to cross Greektown to get to the Greyhound bus station. Back in 2006, that area was much less polished. I stumbled upon the Acropolis Bakery, which looked more like a wholesale outlet than a shop. Freshly baked goods were stored on tall metal shelves waiting to be bagged up and delivered. I popped my head in and asked where I could buy some bread and the guy in a white floury apron said, 'Right here. How many loaves do you want?'

'I just want one of those small rolls,' I said, pointing to a soft white bun.

'One roll?'

'Yes.'

'You can't buy just one roll,' he said laughing. 'You can *have* it.'

Next door was a small supermarket and I ran in to buy some hummus. The guy wouldn't sell me any hummus unless I took some Turkish bread to go with it. 'But I have this,' I said holding up my Greek roll. He waved it away. It was the wrong thing to have with his hummus, he told me as he slid a long slab of fresh Turkish bread into my bag at no extra cost. In 2006, I received biblical amounts of bread and beer from total strangers in Detroit.

In the Greyhound terminal, with my bag of Turkish bread, Greek roll and tub of hummus, I stood in the queue for St. Louis behind to two large Hispanic men. As I took my place, we smiled at each other in that polite Greyhound way I would become familiar with – one I didn't see as much of on my most recent trip. It was a kind of, 'We're all in this together' look – weary, accepting, but with some levity and knowledge of the potential absurdity of our fellow humans, with an awareness that 'anything could happen'.

On the wall next to where we were standing a pay-phone started to ring. We glanced at each other and laughed. After it rang again, I picked it up. The Amish people in the queue shot displeased looks in my direction. But what if someone needed help or had left something on a bus? I couldn't *not* answer it. The guy on the other end of the phone asked, 'Espanish?' in a thick accent. I tried to coax English from him, but my lack of Spanish meant we didn't get very far. I handed the phone to one of the men standing next to me. He took it and spoke in Spanish for some time. The guy on the other end had recounted a long story about looking for a woman he'd

98

met and how the last number she had given him was this one. He would never find her now. She probably didn't want to be found, I thought. The man shrugged. It could have been Karl who had given this man the phone number for the Greyhound bus platform. She had a sense of mischief. She was the type to memorize a payphone number for just such an occasion. Handing it out to a guy she wasn't interested in would have given Karl pleasure, but this detail would date the novel. As I travelled, on my recent trip, I came to see that every payphone in every Greyhound station has now been ripped from the walls.

¶ At Toledo, Ohio, only an hour from Detroit, I got off and stretched my legs. A message popped up from the Sonder asking me to rate my stay. I ignored it and reboarded the bus. A guy with a southern accent also embarked and told the driver that he had been trying to get to Atlanta, but his bus had broken down and dropped him at Toledo. He got there too late to get the connecting bus to Atlanta. He'd spent the night on a bench outside the station. Our driver told him to go back inside and wait out of the rain. True to his word he called the Greyhound dispatch and pleaded this guy's case: a broken-down bus, a missed connection, not his fault, no money to buy another ticket. Then he asked if he could take him to another connecting bus even though the man's ticket was for the previous day.

I was sitting close enough to the front to hear the dispatcher's response:

'His ticket was for yesterday?'

'Yes,'

'Then it's not valid.'

'So I can't take him?' The driver paused. You could hear the mounting frustration in his voice. 'I'm trying to do a good thing here.'

'No, you can't take him.'

The driver hung up and then said, under his breath, 'Well, God bless America.' He got off and went into the station to break the news to the guy stranded in Toledo with no money.

We had a stopover in Lima, Ohio (pronounced Lye-Mah), so I wandered around taking photographs. Shops were shut or having 'Closing Down' sales and the streets were empty. Every now and again a train whistled in the background, lending a feeling of longing to the atmosphere. I

103

eventually found a café with Wi-Fi. A *Guardian* headline popped up in my email inbox: 'Ohio train derailment: levels of carcinogenic chemical near site far above safe limit'. The Wi-Fi wasn't strong enough for me to read the article, but the headline came as no surprise. Before I had left on my trip, I had seen photos of the fiery plume of smoke shooting hundreds of feet into the sky.

Six weeks previously, on 3 February 2023, a Norfolk Southern train with 38 carriages derailed in East Palestine, a mere two hundred miles from where I was sitting in this café in Lima, Ohio. Safety concerns at Norfolk Southern had been raised for months and had been registered about this particular train, which was almost two miles long, had been weighted in a dangerous manner and was full of hazardous chemicals – notably vinyl chloride. Those concerns were disregarded, as were other safety issues raised by employees and union members. Over the past decade, derailments have increased. In 2022, 818 trains in the US were derailed or damaged. Over half of them were carrying hazardous materials.

Some reports on the East Palestine accident stated that the number of cars carrying hazardous material was five, whereas others said it was greater. Even one car of vinyl chloride is capable of poisoning land, water and humans for miles around. The photos of the East Palestine disaster were horrific: blackened boxcars, their bellies full of a lethal cocktail, lying scattered like toys, some on fire, others charred – all of them close to houses and businesses.

Experts who had been studying the crash site for several days decided that the safest way forward was to ignite the chemicals in a controlled burn. Some scientists believed that this would prevent a chemical reaction that could create a catastrophic explosion. On 6 February, 'vent and burn' was actioned. Locals watched a giant toxic fireball of black smoke erupt over their homes and businesses. The black cloud could be seen for miles. The debris from the fireball fell around the township, poisoning farmland, animals, humans and rivers. Thousands of fish died. Food grown in this agricultural part of Ohio and in neighbouring Pennsylvania would have to be destroyed. We've known for a long time that burning chlorinated chemicals like vinyl chloride creates dioxins. This group of chemicals is notoriously persistent – often being dubbed 'forever chemicals'. Not only do they never go away, they can be lethal.

The most toxic form of dioxin, 2,3,7,8-tetrachlorodibenzo-p-dioxin, shortened to TCDD, is found in Agent Orange and has been responsible for some of the most tragic environmental catastrophes in the United States, such as the disaster at Love Canal – a name that lingered in the history of that area and gave me nightmares as a child.

Love Canal was a neighbourhood of Niagara Falls, just on the border with Canada. The abandoned canal attracted Hooker Chemicals and Plastics Corporation who, throughout the 1940s and 50s, used it to dump almost 22,000 tons of chemical waste and dioxins, including polychlorinated biphenyls and pesticides. These were by-products from the manufacturing of rubber and synthetic resins. In the early 1950s, Hooker Chemicals filled in the site, and in 1953 they deeded it for a dollar to the Niagara Falls School Board. The contract's liability limitation clause included a caveat purporting to release the company from all legal obligations should lawsuits occur in the future. Despite this subtle warning, the site was ringfenced for the construction of a school. The architect hired for the project noticed upon inspection that the kindergarten playground was directly above a chemical dump. The playground was moved a few feet away. He cautioned that there were other problems to do with chemical waste, but the building went ahead. It was completed in 1955, with 400 students attending. In its first year, a twenty-five-foot area of ground near the school collapsed, exposing rusting chemical-filled metal drums. When it rained, this giant hole became a toxic pond where children played. Another school opened the same year, just six blocks away.

Heavy rainfall in 1975 and 1976 raised the groundwater table in Niagara Falls. Around this time, residents began complaining about bad smells in their backyards and in playgrounds. Black sludge was appearing in basements. I remember seeing photos of small children the same age as me jumping in polluted puddles. Residents of Love Canal were experiencing higher-than-average rates of miscarriage, birth defects and premature deliveries. The city finally hired a company to undertake an environmental study of the area and in 1978 it was discovered that toxic vapours and liquids from over eighty chemical compounds, including benzene, chloroform, toluene, dioxin and various kinds of PCB – many of them known carcinogens – were present in the basement of homes directly adjacent to Love Canal. The US government declared a National Emergency.

The state of New York then purchased the land. After a string of lawsuits, 1,300 past residents of Love Canal won a 20-million-dollar settlement against the city of Niagara Falls and the Occidental Chemical Corporation, who had taken over Hooker. But as with all stories of chemical leaks, there is no ending.

No amount of money can compensate for the high incidences of chromosomal damage, the cases of leukaemia and other serious health problems that plagued the people of Love Canal, which was eventually evacuated. The Environmental Protection Agency (EPA) admitted that residents exhibited a 'disturbingly high rate of miscarriages ... [and] toxic materials in the milk of nursing mothers'. The report states that 'Quite simply, Love Canal is one of the most appalling environmental tragedies in American history. But that's not the most disturbing fact. What is worse is that it cannot be regarded as an isolated event. It could happen again – anywhere in this country – unless we move expeditiously to prevent it.'

This very same EPA refused to test the soil in East Palestine directly after the chemical spill from the February 2023 train derailment. Stephen Lester, who has worked for the Center for Health, Environment & Justice for the past forty years and has supported communities affected by dioxins – including those in Love Canal – says that the EPA did not immediately test for dioxins in East Palestine because they didn't want to admit their presence at the site.

At a townhall meeting a few weeks after the disaster, Lester heard from residents who lived fifteen miles from the derailment describing burning ash on their property. Someone three miles away talked of 'a black cloud that completely smothered his property'. On 2 March 2023, Lester wrote in the *Guardian*:

no one has done any testing for dioxins anywhere in East Palestine. No one. And, it seems, that the EPA is uninterested in testing for dioxins, behaving as though dioxin is no big deal. This makes no sense. Testing for dioxin, a highly toxic substance, should have been one of the first things to look for, especially in the air once the decision was made to burn vinyl chloride. There is no question that dioxins were formed in the vinyl chloride fire. They would have formed on the particulate matter – the black soot – in the cloud that was so clearly visible at the time of the burn. Now the question is how much is in the soil where people live in and around East Palestine. Without testing, no one will know and the people who live there will remain in the dark, uncertain about their fate.

Eventually, the EPA did test the soil in East Palestine. Tom Perkins, writing in the *Guardian*, explained that newly released data showed that the soil there did indeed contain dioxin levels hundreds of times greater than levels of exposure known to pose cancer risks. Testing was done by Norfolk Southern and also by a private firm on behalf of the state of Indiana, who would be storing some of the waste in state landfills. The levels of dioxin found in two soil samples were up to fourteen times higher than dioxin soil limits allowed in some states. This points to the possibility of wider contamination, according to Linda Birnbaum, an EPA scientist and the former head of the US National Toxicology Program. The controlled burning of vinyl chloride possibly dispersed toxic chemicals further afield. Only more soil testing will tell. The state of Ohio is now suing Norfolk Southern for this derailment, calling it just one of a 'long string' of incidents involving the company.

I was thinking about this toxic legacy – such a familiar one, too – as I ordered a bagel and cream cheese with my coffee in the café in Lima, Ohio. The fresh-faced waitress with two long blonde plaits running down her back brought my bagel over on a Styrofoam plate, with the cream cheese in a small plastic tub and a plastic knife sheathed in a kind of cling film. Although I was eating in, my coffee also came in Styrofoam with a hard plastic lid. I couldn't help but draw a direct line between what lay on the table before me and the chemicals that had spilled in their tonnes onto land just east of Lima, towards the state line with Pennsylvania. What leached into the ground from those railway carriages was a carcinogenic soup not unrelated to the plastic buffet served up before me. Our dependence on this material is killing everything in its wake.

I boarded the bus in Lima at one o'clock. It was a very cold day, with an Arctic wind. We were due in Columbus, Ohio at 2.40 p.m. This bus was operated by Greyhound, although the actual vehicle was owned by Barons, an intercity bus company based in Cleveland, Ohio. Barons Bus operates a federally funded service in parts of rural Ohio and also has routes in Illinois, Indiana, Michigan, New York, Pennsylvania and West Virginia.

This particular bus was old and dirty. The seats were lumpy and encrusted with what looked to be solidified food (ketchup? Bubble gum? Cheese?). And it was crowded. People took their places by the window, stuffing their plastic bags and blankets onto the seat next to them hoping no one would ask them to remove them. Watching passengers board and scan the bus for a free seat, or even better a free pair of them, was a kind of anthropological study. Each person measured up who might be OK with taking their belongings off the seat next to them to make room and who might protest and cause a scene. You could see other questions and concerns flash across people's faces: Will this person talk to me? Will they be eating messy food? Will they be watching loud, violent films on their device without headphones? Will they shout or make odd noises? And, although this sounds cruel: Do they smell?

Unusually, no one took the seat next to me on this bus.

A woman across the aisle was laughing and calling out, 'Praise Jesus!' We passed the Allen County Fairgrounds on the outskirts of Lima, which at this time of year looked somewhat bleak. There were piles of scrap metal, yellowed fields, a white clapboard church of the Christian Assembly, small houses still displaying their off-season Halloween and Christmas decorations, now deflated and dirty. Steeples poked into the blue sky like giant needles. I didn't see any birds. We passed Rudolph's Pork Rinds, which was hiring at 'porkrindjobs.com'. I imagined what life would be like living in Lima, Ohio and working at Rudolph's. A large billboard brought me out of my pork rind reverie: 'ALL BABIES CRY. TAKE A BREAK. DON'T SHAKE.'

The passengers on this bus were quiet. Everyone just wanted to get where they were going. I dozed off and was woken with a hard lurch over a pothole. We arrived in Columbus, Ohio, where my journey would hit Route 66, spot on time. The bus depot consisted of a parking garage the size of a small airplane hangar. At both ends, electric doors opened and closed when a bus entered or exited. The concrete walls were lined with larger-than-life-size AI-enhanced photos of smiling customers. A small, tarmacked island, where passengers boarded or were disgorged, was wedged between two bus lanes – one going in, the other going out. On this island sat a chemical toilet, no drinking fountain and very few seats. The entire tunnel-like structure had no windows. The air was choked with exhaust. A police van was parked at one end of the tunnel and armed security guards stood against a wall facing us. If you had commissioned an urban planner to design the most hostile, uncomfortable and unhealthy environment for passengers, this would be the result.

I had a look at some online reviews of the Columbus,

Ohio Greyhound station. One of them summed it up perfectly: 'They are literally trying to destroy lives.' Another reviewer left a more detailed review: 'I am 76. There were other elderly passengers there, but also a few people with young children, including an infant and some toddlers. The porta-potties smelled so bad within 5 feet of them that only the desperate would dare open a door to one.... A week ago, when I was there, I was disgusted. Now I'm just saddened.' And another: 'Cold, no food, no bathrooms, no organization whatsoever. Not easy for someone that's hard of hearing to figure out where you are going.' It seemed I was not alone in my reaction to this horror show of a public space. But who are the people behind it? If you were to lodge a complaint via their online customer services form would the zeros and ones of your comment sit in a data centre built on melting permafrost in Iceland, unread until the end of time?

My bus was scheduled to leave for St. Louis at 3 p.m. I looked around at my fellow passengers, all of us stuck on the concrete island between bus lanes: one man sitting on the ground eating an orange; a couple pacing with a muzzled black Labrador; an elderly man with a walker and four large zip-up bags printed with 'Patient Belongings'; a woman with a child who sounded like he had croup sitting face-level to the exhaust pipes of the incoming buses. A couple travelling with a large fluffy blanket had set up a makeshift bed propped up against the porta-potty; a mother and her teenage son struggled with several large cardboard boxes. The sign on the empty Greyhound kiosk read: 'As of January 25, 2023 – you will need photo ID to buy tickets.' Yet another barrier separating those with no driver's licence, no fixed address, no passport, from those who can board a Greyhound – which is still the cheapest option for travelling around the country.

The sign added:

No Boxe's [sic]
No garbage bag's [sic]
No bikes

Sparrows had managed to find their way inside this exhaust-filled tunnel. The couple with the makeshift bed threw bits of bread to them. The Bed Couple were the John and Yoko of this bus garage, but with sparrows. People watched the tiny birds hop as the crumbs landed on the tarmac. A man arrived hugging a couple of worn plastic bags with broken handles. He spotted his bus just as it was revving up to leave. The door closed and the bus pulled out. He ran after it, but the driver didn't stop.

5 p.m. and still no bus. People were arriving with blankets and pillows, preparing for overnight trips. I caught the eye of a passenger who had been waiting as long as I had on this strip of concrete between the bus lanes. It turned out he was a university student from Hyderabad. Like me, he had been checking his app, which now showed that the bus had been and gone. How could we have missed it when we hadn't left this garage? Ruben, a young rosy-cheeked Amish man, approached us as we stared in shock at our phones. We told him what the app said and his face flushed. He looked stricken. I gave him my phone so he could tell his family he was stuck in Columbus. Nearby, a one-handed man in work boots, sportswear and a baseball cap chewed noisily on uncooked noodles he poured into his mouth from a pack of dried beef-flavoured ramen he held in his good hand. He asked us if we knew what was going on. We didn't. So we all introduced ourselves. The one-handed guy's introduction was, 'I just got out of a fourteen-month coma.' He

held up his stump. The student from Hyderabad wandered off at this point, but Ruben and I stayed transfixed.

'Yeah, I got electrocuted at work,' he added. 'My wife and baby both died of Covid and then I got electrocuted. I lost my hand.' He paused. 'And also seventy per cent of my tattoos got burnt off.' He pulled up his sleeves to show us the faintest vestiges of ink.

'Wow. You've been through a lot,' I said. Ruben looked shocked.

'But I found God, though.'

'That's good,' I replied. Ruben nodded and smiled vigorously.

'So, He is getting you through,' I added.

'Yeah. He kept me alive for over fourteen minutes while I watched my hand melt. My tooth exploded. It flew out of my mouth. My hair fell out.'

'You look really good for someone who has been through so much,' I told him, and I meant it.

'I paint a smile on in the morning. I cry every night.'

He filled in a few more details about the accident. His boss was a drunk and a meth head and would often get high on the job. It was during one such session that his boss didn't turn off the electrics on a building when he was meant to. This is when some very high voltage tore through him. When he woke up in the hospital from his coma and all the tubes had been taken out, his boss showed up and offered him $40,000.

'I told him where to stick it. Then he came back with $1.5 million and I didn't accept that either. I got some lawyers and I am going for $50 million.'

His hearing was set for 23 April – in about five weeks – and I told him I'd think of him on that date. My problems over a delayed bus suddenly paled in comparison.

The student from Hyderabad wandered back and the

four of us discussed how to get to St. Louis. We were looking up other buses, Amtrak trains and car shares on our phones when a Greyhound employee showed up and took a seat in the previously empty little kiosk on our concrete island between the bus lanes. Desperate passengers trying to get to bedsides, parole hearings, jobs and loved ones instantly swamped her. She looked utterly out of her depth. She was using the same app we were and the information it provided did not reflect what we could see in front of us.

At 5.30 p.m., our bus showed up, but we were further delayed while passengers getting off waited for their luggage. Apparently, a faulty hold had opened and bags had scattered along the highway. That was one story. Another was that their luggage was locked in the hold because the door got stuck. Yet another was that the delayed arrival was due to an oil tanker overturned on the highway. You never quite know with these tales from the bus. What happens on a Greyhound journey can take on a mythical dimension.

Eventually, we filed on and our driver was telling anyone who would listen that she had never done the Columbus–St. Louis route before. She was doing someone a favour, she told us, and she was already regretting it. When she looked at my ticket, she said, 'I wasn't meant to do this route, you know,' as if I were somehow partially responsible for this error.

The bus itself was falling apart. Some of the arm rests were missing, many of the seats were torn and tilted at odd angles. One whole row of seats had been ripped out, the floor was caked in something sticky, the luggage lockers above the seats didn't close properly and I just knew that every time we rounded a corner, the little doors would flap open and bang shut (they did). Of course, the

116

overhead lights didn't work. We aren't expected to read on buses anymore, unless it's from a backlit screen. The bus did not seem roadworthy. I took a seat, and as Ruben headed to an empty one towards the back he said he'd like to make a phone call. Once we got moving, he came up to get my phone so he could tell his family he was running late.

When he handed my phone back to me, he leaned over and whispered, 'The last time I came through Columbus a woman beat up the driver. The driver woke the woman up when we got to the station. When she got off the bus, she was so angry at him for waking her up that she pushed him to the ground and punched him. He was lying in a pool of blood. An ambulance had to take him away and the police came and took her.'

We had left Columbus now, but instead of the usual beeline to a highway, we were winding our way through unlit back roads. Passengers were calling out 'Take a left!' when we got to intersections or 'You're going the wrong way!', but the driver carried on, inexplicably using the satnav on her personal phone for about an hour. She must have had her directions set for 'avoid major roads'. People were getting louder; the atmosphere heavy and tense.

The sun had set and all I could make out was a featureless landscape, lit up every now and then by brightly illuminated petrol stations. The bus was jiggling like mad. The overhead lockers banged away. It was a terrible road. The plexiglass between the driver and the passengers was streaked with grease of some kind and the remnants of masking tape, no doubt the vestiges of old printouts telling us to wear a mask, disinfect our hands, keep our distance. The bus pulled up in the parking lot of the Love's Travel Stop in Springfield to let some people off. A few passengers headed to the front of the bus with cigarettes in hand, and the driver freaked out, 'This isn't a stop! We aren't stopping here! Stay on the bus!'

A woman called out, 'How much longer is this freakin' bus going to take?'

The driver replied, 'Do you want to stay here?'

'If I wanted to stay here, I'd get off the bus,' came the reply.

Then they shouted at each other. We were all tired and testy.

Finally, the passenger said, 'Look, I've been on this fucking Greyhound for three days and I just want to get going.'

The driver made a phone call. 'Yeah, in a black T-shirt,' I heard her say.

Then she announced, 'We're gonna be here for fifteen minutes until the police show up if y'all want to get something to eat.'

I got off to go to the bathroom but I was worried the bus might leave without me if I joined the queue to buy food. So I stayed close and watched the flashing lights of a police car approach. The woman in the black T-shirt got off the bus and got in the police cruiser.

Back on the bus, the driver did the usual head count. 'Is everybody here?'

Someone piped up, 'That dude in the front seat isn't here.'

'Nah, he ran off when he heard the cops were showing up.'

'How about those two brothers?' someone else called out.

No-one knew where the two brothers had gone.

We headed off into the night and a deaf woman looked over to the guy who had been signing for her the entire journey to keep her up to speed. 'I'm telling this lady that our driver keeps getting lost,' he told us by way of explanation, 'but hopefully we're on our way'.

The Marine behind me had been on the Greyhound customer services line for most of the trip – either on hold or giving them a blow-by-blow account of our journey peppered with expletives. We pulled out of Love's and once again ended up winding through back roads in the dark. The man signing to the deaf woman said, 'I'm telling her I think we're lost again.'

The driver pulled over on the side of the road. We were in a suburb and someone said, 'Hey, looks like we're in the 'hood.'

Another replied, 'Let's get comfy.'

The driver kept repeating, 'This isn't my normal route.'

The Marine who had been calling customer services finally snapped. 'Use my goddam phone,' he said as he ran to the front of the bus and demanded that the driver slot it in her phone cradle. 'My GPS actually works,' he said. 'Unlike yours.'

She put his phone onto speaker mode, and I heard the GPS say, 'Stay on highway 41 for 127 miles.' It was 9.15 p.m. and we were nowhere near St. Louis. We were still in Ohio.

Just as we were approaching Indianapolis, two Italians stormed to the front of the bus shouting 'Dayton! Dayton!' They didn't speak English and were trying to get the driver to look at their tickets.

'I'm driving, I can't look!'

A passenger got up to help. 'These guys were supposed to get off at Dayton,' the passenger said.

'Dayton? That's an hour behind us!' the driver shouted and brought us to an emergency stop on the shoulder of the highway. She got up and went to talk to the Italians. There were several of them, including a baby. There

119

was nothing else for us to do but drive back towards Springfield and let them off in Dayton. It would add over two hours to our journey.

'I wasn't supposed to do this route,' the driver repeated as she turned the bus around and headed back to where we had come from.

The Marine behind me was still swearing at the Greyhound customer services people: 'She's just done a U-turn on the highway!'

A woman across the aisle from me one row ahead was watching videos of a baby crying. She had the sound on. Was this her baby? Someone else's baby? Was it being looked after by relatives? Friends? Between bouts of crying there was the sound of shattering glass. Maybe it was some kind of game. Someone else was watching a violent film with the sound up. Gunfire rang out from his iPad. Crying, glass shattering, automatic weapons. We drove on. The sign language guy was keeping us informed about what he was telling the deaf woman. We approved of his running commentary.

Backtracking to Dayton, Ohio, the driver, despite using the Marine's phone, got lost again. She pulled into an unlit parking lot and, as we came to a stop, another car drove up alongside our bus. The woman driving the car honked and got out. She was a well-dressed, fifty-something Black woman in a red coat and high-heeled boots. She walked to the bus driver's window. I assumed she must be a Greyhound official or maybe an off-duty driver. 'Where you going?' she asked.

'Trying to get to Dayton, but I'm going in circles!'

'OK, follow me.' She got back in her car, and we followed.

'Is she a Greyhound employee?' I asked the driver.

'I have no idea.'

'She's a guardian angel,' someone shouted.

'Yeah, right,' the driver replied.

We followed the well-dressed woman to Dayton and our driver announced we could get off and get some food. I overheard the driver on the phone telling someone on the other end that she was quitting. 'OK, not until Indianapolis. I'll get them all there and then that's it.'

We arrived at Indianapolis around 2 a.m. Our driver got off and walked away. She quit, just like that, in the middle of her shift, but thankfully in the time it took for us to get from Dayton, Ohio to Indianapolis, a replacement driver had been found. While we waited for the new driver to get ready, there was a commotion in the station. A thin, nervous man was running around shouting 'FUCK, FUCK, FUCK, FUCK... I'm stuck here!' It turned out his phone had been stolen and his ticket was on it. He was wild with panic. His face was covered in open sores.

The harsh lights of the station, the crowds, the shouting, the late hour – I was starting to lose a sense of time and place. I was starting to feel deeply unmoored. A sentence kept surfacing in my mind, 'Something in the US has broken.' Everyone around me felt more desperate, more angry, more prone to violence. Even the crappy vending machines in the Greyhound stations were empty. The diners were closed. The telephones had been ripped out of the walls but their ghostly outlines had been left behind along with some of the wires sticking out of the walls like fingers, reminding us of a time when we didn't all have our own phones, when they were communal, when we could call 'home'.

The new driver was having trouble with the bus's hold. The Marine jumped up to show him how it worked. 'It's hydraulic,' the Marine said.

He took his place in the seat directly behind me again

and tapped me on the shoulder. 'Hey do you want to see that lady get arrested?'

'What lady?' I asked.

'That one who got arrested back in Springfield.'

'She really got arrested?' I asked. I couldn't believe what I was hearing.

'Yeah, handcuffed and everything. She's going to jail. Wanna see?'

'No thanks.' I could hear him watching it on his phone. The woman screaming. The cops telling her to do what they said. The desperation in the ether that night was palpable.

On my previous ride from Detroit to Indianapolis, I had not managed to get a seat to myself. A middle-aged man had plonked himself down next to me at our stop in Grand Rapids, Michigan. He immediately caught my eye and shifted in his seat to face me. My heart sank. On a bus there is no escape. He had just visited a 'woman friend'. She had written the book he held up for me to look at: *A Year in Saigon*. He had served in Vietnam and had over 2,000 slides from his time there. Now he was a consultant for the Ford Motor Company in Chicago. They hadn't hit their 4 per cent decrease in emissions, so they'd had to replant some forests. He'd got them to hire Native Americans and given the Ford Motor Company a list of twenty reasons why they had to hire minorities. Number 1 was 'Because it's the right thing to do.' He laughed. His real goal was to dig wells in Africa for communities who had little access to clean water. His phone rang and I took the opportunity to plug myself into my discman. Will Oldham's 'I See a Darkness' started as the rain hit the windows.

Ford Motor Man got off his cell phone and began

talking to me again. I didn't want to seem impolite, so I took my crappy little headphones off.

'That was a call from Wolverine Oil,' he paused. 'You gotta live life to the full,' he said, and then added, 'If you were to call up my kids right now, they'd tell you my favourite saying is, "Life's not a dress rehearsal." And I truly believe that.'

If I were Karl, I would be bursting with anger at how this type of middle-aged man always seems to take up one's time and energy. It never matters to them how non-committal or uninterested you sound, they always tell you about their son's success at college or their daughter's wedding or simply let loose a stream of non sequiturs. I was now hearing how Mr Ford Motor had changed careers four times. I wanted to scream; instead, I nodded politely.

I got my bread and hummus out at our stop in Fort Wayne, Indiana. The famous Art Deco 'Streamline Moderne' station clad in 'Greyhound Blue' enamel had been razed to make way for a parking lot in 1992. I had seen postcards of this building, which was designed by William Strudwick Arrasmith, for sale on eBay. I hadn't bothered describing the new station in my journal and I can't remember what it looked like, but I did note that a lot of people got on in Fort Wayne, many of them in sparkly clothing, as if they had been clubbing all night: enormous hoop earrings, sequinned skirts, high heels. Mr Ford Motor leaned over, 'You've got a whole rolling restaurant, there,' he said, pointing to the pot of hummus and slab of Turkish bread given to me in Detroit.

Then the entire bus was distracted by a woman who got on without a ticket. She wore a black tracksuit, large white trainers and huge sunglasses. Her mother's Sunday-best lilac dress matched a purple straw hat perched on her head.

'My mother is handicapped,' the woman shouted several times, to make sure we heard. The mother-daughter duo tried to sit behind the driver but couldn't fit next to each other with all their bags.

The woman moved across the aisle from her mother, 'I don't even want to go to Indianapolis,' she said loudly, and then proceeded to extract plastic plates from a Kentucky Fried Chicken bag. The plates were leaking coleslaw onto the floor. The woman tried to mop up the mess with a Kleenex, but the tissue quickly disintegrated into brown mush on the linoleum. She told her mother that they should have gone for a burger instead of the healthy salad plate option. She dropped a corn bun onto the floor, quickly picked it up and blew on it.

'I won't give this to you, Mom,' she said, 'It might kill you.' And then took a bite of it herself.

Mr Ford Motor told me that the last time he went through Fort Wayne, the Drug Administration people did a sweep of the bus. One guy was taken off, handcuffed, and whisked away in a cruiser.

The woman in the front row continued to open and close the plastic Kentucky Fried Chicken bags to extract bits and pieces from her salad tray. More liquid dribbled out. 'Sir,' she said to the driver, 'I think I've created an oil slick here with the mayonnaise from my salad plate. I'll clean it up when we get to Indianapolis, though.'

At that point the driver started his spiel: 'Your phone needs to be on vibrate. If I can hear it up here, it's too loud. Nail varnish and nail polish remover need to have their lids on so we can all breathe. And by the way, keep your shoes on.'

It had been a warm spring in 2006. Out the left-hand side of the bus, the sun was beating down, buffing the black tarmac. Out the other, low-slung charcoal-grey clouds hung like fat hammocks across the sky. The fields on either side of us were the colour of dry oatmeal, with vibrant green geometric strips appearing now and then. We had a fifteen-minute break at a truck stop in Marion, Indiana. The store there sold over twenty kinds of chewing tobacco in neat little tins stacked in floor-to-ceiling metal racks specifically designed for these containers. Next to the chewing tobacco was a concession stand. I asked the woman in a bright yellow top if I could have a cup of tea. I had spotted a metal urn with a spout just behind her along with some Lipton's tea bags.

She turned to look at the urn. 'No one has ever asked for hot tea before,' she laughed. 'I don't know how to do it.' I explained it to her and after looking around, she found some milk.

I wandered outside with my cup and Mr Ford Motor followed.

'I wanted to say goodbye to you,' he said. I had assumed he was going to Indianapolis, but he was getting off here to help a guy who had just been released from the state penitentiary. This young guy's mother had been dealing prescription drugs and he had been taking some and got the blame for her dealing. Twelve years ago, Mr Ford Motor had taken a vow of poverty. He had made a lot of money but gave it all away. He set aside a fund to help Black kids go to college and he gave money to people freshly out of prison. He handed me his card and said that if I ever got into trouble, I could call him. I glanced at the card. Clay Bryant lived in York, Nebraska, but had been born in Elwood, Indiana. He leaned down, kissed my cheek and placed his hand on my forehead to bless me. I felt terribly guilty for having been annoyed with him earlier. He was one of life's good people. He died, sadly, in 2022.

Back on the bus, a wiry young man in a blue chequered shirt and a red baseball cap sat next to me. When we started moving, he asked how long I'd been on the bus.

'Since Detroit,' I replied.

'Oh,' he said, clenching his teeth.

A young woman diagonally across the aisle from me was reading the Bible aloud very softly, almost in a whisper, to her daughter who looked about six years old. It sounded like music. Next to her a woman was crocheting a bedspread. We stopped in Anderson, Indiana to pick up more passengers.

The woman in the black tracksuit, who had created the oil slick on the floor, stood up to help a very large man heave himself up the steps of the bus. He was carrying a laundry basket full of clothes and a big black bin liner. As Tracksuit Lady lifted his garbage bag to put it on the shelf above his seat, she said, 'God, this is heavy! What have you got in here, a gun?' People laughed somewhat nervously. She and the large man with the laundry basket began chatting as he took a seat just behind her. His uncle was a pastor in Fort Wayne called Jimmy Clark. 'Hallelujah,' she replied.

A very handsome young Black man told the bus that he had quit drinking a few months ago. Tracksuit Lady said she'd never touched a drop and Mr Laundry Basket said that in all his fifty-one years, he still had no idea what alcohol tasted like. Mr Handsome felt better now that he was no longer drinking. Back when he was using alcohol, he would get angry and get into fights all the time. Track Suit Lady told him that if he lived where she did in Fort Wayne, he'd probably be dead by now. Mr Handsome said he'd lasted one year in Anderson, Indiana, but he was getting out because the cops were too heavy. Tracksuit Lady said they were nothing compared to the cops in Marion.

'They have a history,' she shouted. After a pause she added, 'A history of hanging people.' With that, the bus fell silent as we let her comment sink in.

On 7 August 1930, three young African Americans, Thomas Shipp, Abram Smith and James Cameron, were imprisoned in Marion, Indiana after being accused of raping Mary Ball, a nineteen-year-old white girl, and killing her fiancé. Shipp and Smith were dragged from prison by an angry mob, beaten, and then hanged in front of thousands of spectators who had driven to Marion to watch the horror. After the mob placed a noose around Cameron's neck (he was only sixteen at the time), Mary Ball appeared and is said to have shouted: 'Take this boy back. He had nothing to do with any raping or killing.' While Cameron was in prison awaiting trial, Mary Ball admitted that there had been no rape. Cameron nevertheless spent four years in an Indiana State prison, charged with being an accessory to the fact (meaning he was part of the planning but not present for the execution of the crime). After release, he went on to have an extraordinary life, working as the Indiana State Director of the Office of Civil Liberties from 1942 to 1950, organizing chapters of the National Association for the Advancement of Colored People (NAACP), founding America's Black Holocaust Museum in Milwaukee, and writing his memoir, *A Time of Terror*. In 1982, after years of rejection from publishers, Cameron remortgaged his house and self-published the book. He sold the first print run of 4,000 copies from the trunk of his car. Ten years later, the book was republished by Black Classic Press and went on to win an Independent Publishers Award.

In 1993 Cameron received an official apology and pardon from the state of Indiana and was given keys to the city of Marion. He died in 2006 – as I was passing through Marion on a Greyhound – just one month after his sixty-eighth wedding anniversary. He and his wife Virginia had raised five children. The hanging of his friends Shipp and Smith in 1930 was the last lynching of African Americans in the state of Indiana.

Mr Laundry Basket asked Tracksuit Lady if she had kids. Her youngest was forty, she replied. No one could believe it; she looked far too young. She pointed to her quiet, lilac-clad mother and exclaimed, 'She's ninety-seven and my aunt in Toledo is a hundred and eight and has all her faculties intact!' Then she told the young man that his perfect teeth could make him money in toothpaste commercials. 'In fact, you could be a model,' she told him.

'No, I couldn't.' he replied.

'Sure, you could. If you really wanted to. You could be anything you want.'

Tracksuit Lady pointed to me and asked why I had been taking photos of the Greyhound bus sign in Anderson. I told her that where I lived, in Britain, we didn't have Greyhound buses.

'Huh, that's interesting,' she said and then added, 'Well, welcome to the United States.'

She turned to face the front and a few minutes later, our bus came to an emergency stop on the hard shoulder of the highway.

The bus driver, in a deadpan voice: 'Is somebody blowing bubbles up here?'

Tracksuit Lady: 'Sorry sir, I was playing with my grandkids' toys and couldn't resist blowing some.'

'Well, not on my bus!'

We roared back into the traffic.

The woman reading the Bible to her child and Mr Laundry Basket were having a conversation about

Proverbs while Tracksuit Lady was looking for her mother's medication.

Red Baseball Cap next to me asked if I wanted to listen to the radio. I was confused. I couldn't see a radio. Sensing my confusion, he held out one of his earphones. 'We can share,' he said. I was reminded of the spaghetti scene in *Lady and the Tramp*. 'Thanks,' I said and smiled, 'I'm OK.'

I slipped *Blood on the Tracks* into my discman. We were all inhabiting Kerouac's *On the Road*, with the Greyhound full of 'crying babies, and hot sun, and countryfolk getting on at one Penn town after another, till we got on the plain of Ohio and really rolled, up by Ashtabula and straight across Indiana in the night.' It wasn't night, but it definitely was Indiana.

For most of Simone de Beauvoir's tour, she criss-crosses the United States by train, airplane and car to lectures, parties, tourist attractions and visits with friends – many of whom are the intellectuals, the 'beautiful people' Rorty disparages in *Where Life is Better*. The Greyhound bus trips she makes show a world that hasn't disappeared altogether but has changed drastically.

In 1947, segregation on interstate buses was still being inforced, despite the fact that the US Supreme Court had the previous year ruled that it was a violation of the law. This ruling came after Irene Morgan, a Black woman, was arrested in Virginia for refusing to give up her seat on a Greyhound bus. She spent time in jail and initially lost her case. It wasn't until the NAACP took her case to the Supreme Court that she won. Morgan had been riding the bus from Virginia after suffering a miscarriage, to recover at her family home in Baltimore. In 1947 – the year of de Beauvoir's trip – civil rights activists rode buses and trains across the US as a response to Morgan's win.

These acts of non-violent protest were called Journeys of Reconciliation. A song was written with the lyrics: 'Get on the bus, sit anyplace, 'cause Irene Morgan won her case.' Morgan died at the age of ninety in 2007, a year after my first Greyhound trip.

On her journey between Jacksonville, Florida and Savannah, Georgia, de Beauvoir noted that Natalie Sorokin, the friend she was travelling with (whom she referred to as Natasha),

> sat beside a young black man, since there was no other place. As soon as a seat among the whites became free, he pointed it out to her: "I imagine you would rather not stay here," he said dryly. She answered that she was quite comfortable where she was, and that she was French. Then he opened up and began to talk to her. He said that he'd entered the war as a volunteer in order to have the right, on his return, to the years of free study granted to veterans; now he's a scholarship student at a black university, where he's studying to become a lawyer. With bitter passion he explained why he so ardently wants to earn the right to plead cases in court: this is one of the only concrete ways to fight for the black cause. Behind all these docile faces – through discouragement, fear, or, more rarely, hope – revolt is always imminent. And the whites know it.

It wasn't until 1960 – thirteen years after de Beauvoir wrote about her experience and fourteen years after Irene Morgan won her case – that segregated waiting rooms, lunch counters and bathrooms for interstate passengers were outlawed. These rulings, however, were often ignored in the Deep South. The Greyhound bus was not only the most economical means of travel for people on low incomes – it also became a harrowing symbol of the violence meted out towards Black Americans in their fight for equality.

In the early sixties, the Congress of Racial Equality (CORE) began a racially integrated Freedom Ride through the South by Greyhound bus to verify whether buses and station facilities were complying with the Supreme Court rulings. Predictably, these journeys were often met with violence, which culminated in an attack on a bus on Mother's Day in 1961. This particular Greyhound bus was taking Freedom Riders from Washington, DC to New Orleans when it was mobbed in Anniston, Alabama by men wielding baseball bats, chains and iron pipes. Around fifty men slashed the tyres and battered the bus's metal siding before throwing a firebomb through a broken window. Fortunately, the passengers managed to escape the flames, only to be beaten up as they tried to flee. Some of this is captured in a series of anonymous photos showing smoke billowing out of the passenger door, creating a giant black cloud, like a deathly exhalation from the jaws of the racing Greyhound logo on the side of the vehicle. After six months of protests, arrests and press conferences by the Freedom Riders, discriminatory seating practices were outlawed along with the removal of 'Whites Only' signs from interstate bus terminals.

The egregious yet legally enforceable separation of African Americans from white Americans in the South disturbed de Beauvoir. On a bus from Houston to New Orleans, she wrote,

Our Greyhound is certainly different from the nearly empty one that crossed the deserts of Arizona and New Mexico. Now there are lines at the bus stations, which are all situated in the heart of town. The blacks, for whom there is often no

131

sheltered waiting area, wait outside, sometimes on benches but usually standing, until the superior race is settled in the bus; four or eight places on the back seat are reserved for them.

Very little of this segregation, and how these histories are reinforced or resisted, is touched upon in the Great American Road Trip books written by men driving their cars. In a car, the driver is removed from the communal, from difficult histories, from the people who, behind the scenes, are keeping much of the country going with little fanfare and very little money: the cleaners, care workers and manual labourers, or more precisely, anyone who isn't them.

On the final push to Indianapolis – a city I decided not to revisit in 2023 – I had watched a huge sun slowly lower itself from a bank of black clouds onto a horizon of ploughed, yellow fields. I had booked a room in Indianapolis from Detroit, as I knew we would be getting in late. As ever, finding somewhere to sleep within walking distance of the bus station was a challenge.

The first person I saw as I disembarked in the Indianapolis Greyhound Terminal was a guy wearing a T-shirt that said: 'I have the dick, so I make the rules.' Karl would be making a note of that in her journal. I asked a man standing behind an information desk if he knew where my hotel was. I showed him the address.

'That's miles away.'

'Can I walk there?'

He laughed.

I got into a taxi parked outside the station. He kept looking at me in his rear-view mirror. 'I'd like to take you out,' he said smiling. 'What do you like to drink?'

I couldn't think of anything to say. I spent the rest of the ride listening to him tell me about all the places we could go to together in Indianapolis.

The hotel was on a highway next to a rehab facility. The only place to eat required dodging fast-moving cars across several lanes of traffic. I told the people at the desk that when I booked my room, I had been assured that the hotel was a short walk from the Greyhound station and close to a couple of food outlets. They shrugged, uninterested, and told me that if I wanted to eat, I needed to hurry because the diner across the highway was about to close.

¶ As we sped through the Illinois night towards St. Louis with our replacement driver and the Marine behind me still complaining loudly to Greyhound customer services, I leaned my head against the window remembering that the last time I had passed through this landscape, it had been lush and green. Very close to the highway and clearly visible from the bus, I had noticed wildflowers and tall grasses in a meadow bordering a swamp where sandhill cranes were wading. I searched on a map for what small wetland I may have seen from the window of the bus, but I wasn't able to track it down. It's reassuring, in a way, that Google is not all-knowing and all-seeing. The scene now feels like a mirage. When they do come into view, cranes are so often like the ghostly apparitions described in Aldo Leopold's *A Sand County Almanac*. The 'high horns, low horns, silence, and finally a pandemonium of trumpets, rattles, croaks, and cries' of cranes, who 'emerge from the lifting mists, sweep a final arc of sky, and settle in clangorous descending spirals to their feeding grounds'.

These slate-grey creatures conjure a sense of the ancient – they have the oldest fossil record of any bird on Earth. Their enormous size and their bustle-like tails have something prehistoric about them, quite the contrast to the metal carapace of the bus that was whizzing me along the tarmac. Leopold describes the peat layers of their bogs that, since the Ice Age, have been 'laid down in the basin of an ancient lake', where 'time lies thick and heavy'. According to Leopold, cranes stand 'upon the sodden pages of their own history' like 'an endless caravan of generations'; they have built of their 'own bones this bridge into the future, this habitat where the oncoming host again may live and breed and die'.

What are the sodden pages of my own history? How many of us are aware of the caravan of generations and the bone bridges that have brought us to our present and will shuttle us into our future? These ancient creatures know precisely in the core of their beings the shape and texture, the give-and-take of a patch of Earth, and how to function within its cycles in a way that is alien to us. This profound knowledge is at odds with life on the road which seems to exist, as described by Leopold, as being in an ever-present now with 'no history, no shoals or deeps, no tides of life and death'. My fellow Greyhound travellers and I were on a tarmac sea sailing to ports known and unknown, unmoored from and unaware of the deep time that had shuttled us all into our present.

A Sand County Almanac first brought the idea of a land ethic to western readers. It is not in the canon of Great American Road Trip literature, but it does contain a chapter called 'Illinois Bus Ride' in which Leopold describes 'sitting in a 60-mile-an-hour bus sailing over a highway originally laid out for horse and buggy.' The 'ribbon of concrete', he wrote, had been 'widened and widened until the field fences threaten to topple into the road'. And in this 'narrow thread of sod between the shaved banks and the toppling fences grow the relics of what was once Illinois: the prairie'.

'No one in the bus sees these relics,' Leopold lamented. But I wondered, as we sped through Indiana, if perhaps my fellow passengers did see these relics of wildness creeping between the fences and the road, but simply didn't know how to make sense of them, how in fact to name or interpret what they were seeing. From the seat of a bus, the natural world outside is more of a blur than a reality, as you zoom past, unable to get out if the mood takes you. Yet, it also holds more weight – more reality perhaps – than the view from a car windshield because of the communal experience. On a bus, we are all members

of an audience. We know there are others seeing what we are seeing. What of all the sunsets, sunrises, buttes, cliffs, clouds, mesas, gulleys, gulches, ditches and bright red deserts like crazy dreams witnessed by every passenger just on the other side of the window – a pane of glass made, after all, of limestone and sand? Maybe if we knew that these windows had once been a beach or had come from deep inside our Earth, we would be able to see what was on the other side even more clearly, and that communal blur could take on the mantle of the real, a real we might have the names for.

5 a.m., St. Louis. An eight-hour trip had stretched into twenty-four. But, at least our replacement driver got us there. As I entered the station, a message came on over the intercom: 'For surveillance and security, please remove all hoods.' A Black teenager with his mum got off the bus just in front of me. He had his hood up and a guy yelled at him to remove it. The teenager immediately pushed his hood off his head. 'My bad,' he replied.

I walked out of the St. Louis bus station into a very cold, dark morning. The Marine was in the parking lot, still on his phone, still losing it with Greyhound customer services. 'The driver fucking walked off the job at Indianapolis. She quit. I mean, you guys need to sort your shit out.'

The new St. Louis bus station was cold, ugly and uninviting. The old one I had stopped at in 2006 had surprised me with its Corinthian columns, elaborate gilt balustrade and large rosette in the centre of a ceiling, like white icing on an upside-down cake. Its opulence was the result of having been built by the Cass Bank and Trust in 1927 – the same year the Ford Model A hit the streets. In the 1950s, a new road appeared in front of the bank and

the owners, putting speed, efficiency, money and cars together, set up the first drive-up bank in 1957. In 1991, the building, which had been sitting empty for three years, became the Greyhound station. Two years after Karl and I had passed through there, it closed down and, as far as I know, it's still vacant.

There was one taxi parked outside the new Greyhound station. The driver was asleep but woke up as I approached. He wasn't booked, so I got in. It was too cold and too dark to walk, and I was exhausted. The taxi brought me to a Four Seasons Hotel.

'This isn't my hotel,' I said. I had given him the address of my America's Best Value Inn and Suites at 1100 Lumiere Place – which was very close to the Four Seasons – but he had obviously thought this wasn't where a middle-aged woman would want to roll up to at 5.30 in the morning. I'd chosen this particular motel because in 2006, when it was an Econo Lodge, I had stayed here with Karl.

Back then, I had booked a room there from Indianapolis because it was cheap and walkable from the old Greyhound station. I had asked a taxi driver who was parked outside the station how far the Econo Lodge was. He told me it wasn't too far, but that he wouldn't let his daughter walk there on her own. So I got in his car, and when we got to the motel, he cheated me of my change by about ten bucks. I was angry that I hadn't noticed in time to challenge him before he sped off. I walked into the reception area and as I started speaking to the guy behind the large piece of streaky plexiglass, a couple of women came charging past me. I stepped back to give them space. One of them shouted, 'We want our money back!'

The guy behind the plexiglass stared at them.

'Do you know what man stains are?' the more vocal of the two demanded.

142

He didn't reply.

'They're all over the chair and the bed! I'm talking bodily fluids. Also, black finger marks all over the walls.'

The guy told her he could give her another room. She looked at her friend and they decided to accept.

Once they'd gone, it was my turn to get my room key. I tried to joke with the guy by telling him I'd prefer a room without 'man stains', channelling a bit of Karl humour. He didn't laugh, but the woman behind me who had also been privy to the confrontation did. We exchanged smiles and I took my key. When I got to my room, I dumped my backpack onto the bed and headed into the lobby to ask where I could get something to eat. The guy at the desk gave me names of places that were a ten-minute drive. I told him I was on foot, and he said, 'You want to walk around this city at night on your own?'

'Yes, I do.'

He looked at me with a worried expression.

'Is this plexiglass bullet-proof?' I asked.

'What do you think?' came the reply. 'This is St. Louis.'

I was getting the picture. But here's the thing: some places just give you a warm feeling. In this case, St. Louis, with its old industrial buildings, its tree-lined avenues and its wide river, enticed me. Maybe it was because on that first visit I had come upon it on a particularly glorious day. I had already decided I was going to make my journey without fear. I had realized when mourning my sister Mary, that fear could hold a similar grip to that of grief. Both can overwhelm you and I was going to resist this. I remembered C. S. Lewis's statement in *A Grief Observed*, which I read after Mary's death: 'No one ever told me that grief felt so like fear'. The anxiety that comes from loss, that seeps deep into us, the gnawing sense of foreboding

– I had experienced this after the death of my sister and my miscarriages. I would be open, and willing to hurl myself into the unknown on this trip. And, I had Karl with me who, as a teenager recently grieving her father, would be even more keen for experience. After years of looking after her dying father, Karl was owed some life, some adventure. She, too, liked St. Louis.

Karl and I wandered down to the river as the afternoon light began to slip away. My heart pounded a little faster when I realised this was my first sighting of the Mississippi. The Mississippi! Sal Paradise in *On the Road*: 'And here for the first time in my life I saw my beloved Mississippi River, dry in the summer haze, low water, with its big rank smell that smells like the raw body of America itself because it washes it up.' As it was spring, the water was high. I could imagine the logs that would have once travelled down the waterway, like the ones from my childhood clogging the Ottawa River. My mother would point at them, 'Men used to run these logs until a few years ago,' she would tell me. These bodies of flowing water, always being put to use like giant beasts of burden shouldering our ever-growing need for commodities, for wooden furniture and toilet paper and cardboard boxes. Sal Paradise again: 'We arrived in St. Louis at noon. I took a walk down by the Mississippi River and watched the logs that came floating from Montana in the north – grand old Odyssean logs of our continental dream.' This old river, this continental dream so steeped in a difficult history of commerce, industry and exploitation. The muddy banks I saw that day were littered with construction debris, plastic tubing, metal scraps and bits of heavy machinery. It looked like someone was planning to gentrify the area along the river, build some luxury condos

144

with gyms and wine bars, dog-grooming businesses and yoga studios, but hadn't quite got their act or their money together just yet.

The sun was sinking behind me and I watched it throw streaks of orange, yellow and violet into the water. The river was wide and high, undulating as if it were in slow motion. The casino lights on the other side of the Mississippi, in East St. Louis, Illinois, came on one by one as the sunlight disappeared and the water went black like a curtain going down after a show. In the darkness, the sound of splashing against the muddy banks got louder. I turned to walk back onto the main road and headed into town.

How different this Americas Best Value Inn and Suites, wedged between Interstate-44 and the Mississippi River, felt from its previous incarnation as an Econo Lodge. Same location, same building, but something about it had fundamentally changed. When I arrived at 6 a.m. to check in, the parking lot was empty, bar a few unhoused people wandering around the place. A man appeared in the small reception area as I entered, and I explained to him that although I had been supposed to arrive the previous night, my bus had been delayed by sixteen hours. I would, of course, pay for the room, but as a gesture of goodwill, could I check in early, if possible? The empty parking lot suggested that this wouldn't be a problem. The guy on the front desk didn't seem to understand and I had to keep explaining the situation. He finally got it. Despite booking my room in advance, the room rate of $120 I'd been given had mysteriously been upped to $180. The extortionate rate was because of ball games and conferences in town. I'd had trouble finding even one available room in St. Louis. There were none under $200. So, I was stuck.

And I was tired.

After handing over a fifty-dollar bill as a 'deposit', which I was told I would get back when I checked out, I headed to my room for a shower. Amazingly, it was the same room I had stayed in back in 2006 with Karl. But the place was in terrible shape. The carpets smelled, the room was dirty, and the TV didn't work – although the guy at the front desk did come and fix it for me when I asked. Cranes and bollards obscured the view of the Mississippi. The place was dismal.

After a short nap, I went out into the freezing cold, grey day to try and retrace the walks I had done the last time. But the city felt different. It was -5 Celsius with a terrible wind. I went to the riverfront district called Laclede's Landing, where seventeen years previously Karl and I had watched the Cardinals play the Chicago Cubs on a giant TV screen in a brewery. The name of the bar escaped me, but I had made a note of the name of the player who had hit a home run for the Cardinals, Juan de Dios Encarnación.

That March had been warm. I remembered walking under an overpass and gasping when, between a stand of darkened warehouses, the Mississippi came into view. 'I've heard Americans debate where the West begins,' writes William Least Heat-Moon in *Blue Highways*, 'Texans say the Brazos River; in St. Louis it's the Mississippi, and they built a very expensive "Gateway Arch" to prove it.' And there it was, Aaro Saarinen's 'very expensive' Gateway Arch rounding its back like a giant cat in the distance.

On that visit, the city seemed to shimmer around the black, slow-moving mirror of water. It all felt unreal. But on this trip the magic had gone. The brewery on a

little cobbled street where I had sipped on a Schlafly, the local St. Louis beer, while Cardinal fans cheered, had closed. Sundecker's, a much-loved St. Louis drinking spot in a handsome red brick building dating from 1914, had also closed. Gone was the music venue Mississippi Nights, which had opened its doors in 1976. This is where you would have gone to hear Sonny Rollins, Wynton Marsalis, Willie Nelson, Burning Spear, Jimmy Cliff, Roxy Music, Nirvana, Iggy Pop, the Ramones, the Red Hot Chili Peppers, the Pogues, the Flaming Lips, Hole – the list is absolutely endless. The entire riverfront area was deserted. Bollards and fences prevented me from going down to the river. Private security cars patrolled the area, diligently moving people on even though they had nowhere to go. The number of homeless people had increased despite the freezing temperatures. The 'very expensive' arch was still there, however, watching over everything.

As I wandered around taking photos, hoping to find somewhere for coffee and breakfast, a security vehicle started following me. Those on foot in the US are considered suspicious unless they are on officially pedestrianized roads. The driver looked at me through his reflective sunglasses but slowly crept past, not bothering to stop. He did get out when he spotted a Black guy standing outside the Four Seasons Hotel and told him to move along. A man wearing Spongebob Squarepants pyjamas and wrapped in a blanket walked past me. He looked lost. It was too cold to be outside in pyjamas.

I headed for the Metro as I wanted to revisit the University area – the Delmar Loop – which I remembered well. I had bought *Actual Air* by the poet and musician David Berman at Subterranean Books, where

149

I'd had a conversation with a woman working in the book-shop. She told me she had left Austin as it was 'exploding' and moved to St. Louis in the early 1990s when it was 'imploding'. Everyone I met then in St. Louis seemed to allude to problems in the city in the late 1980s – problems that were still simmering away. In 2023, the problems seemed to have intensified.

I tried to buy a ticket from a machine in a downtown Metro station which would get me to the Delmar Loop. I couldn't find a machine or a human working there. The subway was empty except for dozens of people in vari-ous stages of getting high and coming down, waking up or going to sleep. It was still -5 degrees Celsius. Standing outside for a long period without warm clothes could literally kill you. I looked on my phone for information of how to get to Delmar. 'All passes and tickets for Metro Transit can be purchased at any time via the easy-to-use Transit app.' I tried downloading the app but my fingers were freezing. The app was complicated and I didn't want to hand over my debit card details to make one return journey on the subway. I got an Uber.

The beautiful 1920s Tivoli Cinema in the Delmar Loop area, around the University where in 2006 I'd watched Jonathan Demme's film *Heart of Gold*, about Neil Young, was now a giant meeting place for the St. Louis-based One Family Church. The student cafés and Subterranean Books were still going strong, which cheered me up. After coffee and a browse in the bookshop, I got another Uber back to Laclede's Landing. I decided not to go to Soulard, the French area of St. Louis which had been blossoming with cherry trees on my last trip. The pavements then were carpeted in pink and white petals and birds were frantically singing in the treetops. The imposing red

brick houses and apartment buildings in Soulard, like those I had seen in Detroit, were the colour of Edward Hopper paintings, but these ones were lit from inside. This spring was too cold to go exploring on foot. It was walking to Soulard all those years ago that I'd found myself in a gumbo restaurant with a live band. The place was loud and the crowd was composed mainly of old hippies. I ordered a Schafly just as some very fast Bluegrass started up. Older couples got up to dance. The music worked on me like a heartbeat. In this moment, away from anything and everything familiar, was where I wanted to be. I didn't really know where I was, but I wasn't lost and I had Karl with me.

During her lecture tour of the US, Simone de Beauvoir met Iris Tree, the English poet and artists' model who posed for Amedeo Modigliani, Augustus John, Duncan Grant, Vanessa Bell, Roger Fry, Man Ray and the sculptor Jacob Epstein. Federico Fellini cast Tree as a poet in *La Dolce Vita*. She had the money and social rank to be a classic bohemian. She was the daughter of the actor Herbert Beerbohm Tree and the mother of Ivan Moffat (who was married to de Beauvoir's friend and travelling companion Natasha Sorokin). De Beauvoir writes of a party at Iris Tree's house in Ojai California: 'America is nowhere. But music escapes the limitations of time and space. It can capture something out of thin air and give it to me. At least that's what I think tonight.' Nights like this are gifts.

As I sipped my beer, a man caught my eye and smiled. He looked like the energetic dancing type. Long ponytail, cowboy boots and a shirt open to reveal a chain with a dangling silver marijuana leaf. Before he could ask me, I left the bar in search of food.

There was no dancing or music for me on this trip. I ended up eating ravioli and ice cream alone at the Old

Spaghetti Factory in St. Louis and then walking the short distance back to my America's Best Value Inn and Suites.

The following morning, when I checked out, the man behind the counter asked if he could keep my fifty-dollar deposit as a tip. 'Um, no,' I replied. He dangled it in front of me, 'Are you sure?'

'Yes, I'm sure. I've already paid 360 bucks for two nights when I only slept here for one.'

He reluctantly handed it back.

I didn't bother telling him that on my way down the stairs from my room to the reception, I had seen someone trying to force a door open with a metal bar. The parking lot was still empty. I was ready to leave.

When I returned to London after my Greyhound trip, I discovered that the St. Louis Best Value Inn and Suites had helped themselves to an extra \$415 from my debit card in addition to the \$360 I'd paid on the spot. It took weeks of emails (that mostly went unanswered) and letters to the St. Louis Better Business Bureau to get the stolen money back. The owner eventually called my mobile number in London to ask for my address. Apparently, he owns a business in Reading and visits the UK often. Maybe we could meet up, he suggested. I did not volunteer my address.

The motel's one saving grace was that I had been able to tune into Turner Classic Movies. In an act of divine providence, George Stevens' *Giant*, with Elizabeth Taylor, Rock Hudson and James Dean, was on. The screenplay for *Giant* was co-written by Ivan Moffat. This brought to mind one of the strangest details in de Beauvoir's Greyhound trips. Her companion, Natasha Sorokin, is described throughout as simply a 'close friend'. In fact, Natasha was the woman with whom de Beauvoir began an affair in 1939 when the girl was just seventeen and de Beauvoir thirty-one. In 1943, Natasha's mother complained about this affair to the Lycée where de Beauvoir was teaching. The author was charged with the 'corruption of a minor' and her career as a teacher ended abruptly. In her letters, de Beauvoir mentions her affection and tenderness for Natasha (who was a virgin before their affair). As with every sexual triangle she and her lover Jean-Paul Sartre orchestrated, it was complicated, at times manipulative and often subordinate to the primary relationship between the two philosophers. In an act of sexual and emotional curiosity, Natasha went to bed with Sartre in order to 'find out what sort of person' she 'was up against'.

By the time de Beauvoir met up with Natasha in California, the young woman was married to Ivan Moffat, the British aristocrat, screenwriter and notorious womanizer with whom she had a daughter. Moffat was working with the director George Stevens at the time and later co-wrote *Giant* as well as *Shane* and *A Place in the Sun*. He lived a fast Hollywood existence, hanging out with James Dean and having an affair with Elizabeth Taylor. Natasha and Ivan's relationship didn't last long. Natasha, de Beauvoir's Greyhound companion and Moffat's wife, died in 1967 at the age of forty-six.

Indulging in this Technicolor epic rather than exploring the city was research, I told myself. As I lay on the thin, damp polyester sheets in my dank room in St. Louis watching this Technicolour dream, I could think about de Beauvoir and the parties she went to and the people she rubbed shoulders with – some of whom were acting in *Giant*. It was the perfect film to watch the night before heading west – properly west, to Tulsa, and then onto Amarillo, Texas.

¶ Seventeen years ago when my miscarriages were still fresh and the sadness over the death of my sister Mary still very much alive, travelling alone on a Greyhound bus across the United States took me out of my mourning and placed me squarely 'in the moment', in seats with their sticky upholstery and dirty windows looking onto landscapes, horizons, farms, suburbs, gas stations and parking lots. I could spend hours listening to other people's stories and losses and not have to think about my own. I was running away from grief, from my body's inability to hold onto a growing child and from my sense of failure as a woman.

In *Travels with Charley*, Steinbeck, like many chroniclers of the road, was searching for something outside of himself. He was trying to 'rediscover this monster land'. His 'tough, fast, comfortable vehicle', with its 'camper top – a little house with double bed, a four-burner stove, a heater, refrigerator and lights operating on butane, a chemical toilet, closet space, storage space, windows screened against insects', was called 'Rocinante', after the emaciated old horse in Cervantes's *Don Quixote*. (He was disappointed that no one he met on his trip ever asked him about the name.) 'You do not take a trip,' he wrote in *Travels with Charley*, 'a trip takes us.'

'Takes us *away*', I'd add. And the reasons for allowing a trip to take us away vary wildly.

When Steinbeck packed up his truck, friends and neighbours stopped by. 'I saw in their eyes', he wrote, 'something I was to see over and over in every part of the nation – a burning desire to go, to move, to get under way, anyplace, away from any Here.' Steinbeck saw this restlessness as an American affliction. 'They spoke quietly of how they wanted to go someday, to move about, free and unanchored, not towards something but away from something. I saw this look and heard this yearning everywhere in every state I visited. Nearly every American hungers to move.' A desire to be unanchored and in a state of constant movement has plagued me my whole life and yet is manifest within me alongside a paradoxical but equally profound desire for 'home'. The two seem to need each other like demanding co-dependent siblings.

James Rorty was propelled by yet a different impetus. One *New York Times* critic compared Rorty's reason for writing *Where Life is Better* to Walt Whitman's 'intent, to see, if possible to sing, America'. But Rorty doesn't so much 'sing America' as shout in its face, grumble, proselytize, and then, once exhausted, whisper his love for it into her ear. He despised 'the intellectuals, the "beautiful people"', whom he saw as 'irrelevant, adventitious and meagerly parasitic'. Rorty's trip 'was an attempt to substitute physical motion for motions of the mind'. Rorty tried to leave 'confusion and nonsense behind' by performing the 'one and noble function of the time', the function to '*move*'. Movement for Rorty is akin to being rocked in a cradle. It is capable of soothing the internal turmoil, the insomnia, the sadness. This seemed to be the motivation for many of the Great American Road Trip books, a feeling I understood after my own losses – and yet how much more powerful it is to *move* alongside others, in a communal space.

Every one of the Great American Road Trip books expresses – albeit in very different ways – a desire for movement, for a certain kind of freedom. Where Kerouac seeks transcendence, Steinbeck is going after the zeitgeist, or in his words, 'What are Americans like today?' In *The Great American Bus Ride* Irma Kurtz, who has been living outside of the US for decades, is also searching for an America she no longer knows. But where she speaks to people who come into her orbit on the bus, in stations, in diners and walking along pavements, Steinbeck can be choosier as he decides where to stop and where not to. A bookseller in Fargo, North Dakota says to Kurtz, 'You've got to remember that by and large towns in America are places being passed through. Most of America is being passed through or flown over most of the time.' Not so on a Greyhound. Whether you like it or not, there will be unintended stops. There will be no flying over anywhere.

Henry Miller jumped headfirst into exploring the elusive American dreamscape in his three-year journey across the United States, which culminated in *The Air-Conditioned Nightmare*. Miller's reasons for his trip were similar to Steinbeck's and Kurtz's. He had been living in France for ten years and felt out of touch with his home country. So, in 1940 he got in his car, with 500 bucks given to him by his then-publisher Doubleday, Doran and headed out of New York accompanied by his friend Abraham Rattner – Anaïs Nin having turned down the invitation to accompany him. Doubleday, Doran rejected the manuscript, but it was eventually published in 1945 by New Directions. Like all the major travelogues written by men about crossing the enormous expanses that make up the United States, Miller's journey was taken in a car, a 1932 Buick. Like Steinbeck after him and Rorty before him, Miller was critical of what he saw: 'What have we to offer the world beside the superabundant loot which we recklessly plunder from the earth under the maniacal delusion that this insane activity represents progress and enlightenment? The land of opportunity has become the land of senseless sweat and struggle.'

Throughout *America Day by Day*, de Beauvoir repeatedly voices her loathing of the 'superabundance' of American shops, restaurants and homes – a word used often by Miller. She also complains about the air-conditioning and the antiseptic packaging of experiences for human consumption, echoing Henry Miller's thoughts on the preference in the United States for the artificial over the natural, and its associated human cost. Here is de Beauvoir at the Grand Canyon:

> I find the same atmosphere as at Niagara Falls: the most ingenious efforts have been made to transform a natural marvel into a kind of amusement park. The tourist is plied with various attractions.... The tourist is offered every possible artificial means of taming this exuberantly natural spectacle. In the same way, people in America consume "conditioned" air.... Americans are nature lovers, but they accept only a nature inspected and corrected by man.

At the parties de Beauvoir frequents, people are talking about Henry Miller's trial, relating to the 1934 publication in France of his autobiographical novel *Tropic of Cancer*, which was banned in the United States on charges of obscenity. It wasn't until Grove Press published *Tropic of Cancer* in 1961, that these charges were tested in court. The State Court of New York ruled the novel obscene in 1963. But in the following year, the Supreme Court ruled that the book was a work of socially significant literature and was not, in fact, obscene. This set a precedent for the publication of future sexually explicit novels. In California de Beauvoir writes, 'I squint my eyes to see Big Sur, where Henry Miller lives, and I see nothing but a little log inn flanked by a gas station.'

Out of altruism and perhaps from a desire to hear some great stories, James Rorty picked up hitchhikers as he travelled. His project was to reveal the politics behind environmental extraction and the exploitation of human labour in the name of progress. In *Where Life is Better*, he rails against capitalism, the inhumane living conditions of the poor and the misplaced optimism of his fellow Americans. Most drivers just want to motor along safely in the bubble of their car, admiring the scenery, listening to NPR or a custom-designed 'Road Trip' playlist streamed from their phone. They are happy to drive by the poverty just outside the window, unbothered by the scent of other people's skin and aftershave, the sound of someone's breathing or a child crying. They are not there to witness the unmistakeable body language, when a passenger stretches their legs into the aisle of the bus, desperate to lay their body out for the night in a comfortable bed. And they will never have the sleeping head of a stranger bounce onto their shoulder, so close you can smell their hair. Where a car driver can select where they stop and who they speak to and whether they want to speed past the homeless guy with the cardboard sign or stop to put a few dollars in his can, the Greyhound passenger has no such luxury. The outside world is inside the bus. It strikes me as odd that there has been so little written about this, about the collective, about those who don't have cars or can't drive or have woken up in strange cities after a night of meth or booze or incarceration or honest bad luck.

A Greyhound bus is its own fragile and fluid ecosystem. In many ways you do not exist when you travel without a car. You can disappear, or simply not be found. You have no license plate, no autonomy and very little agency. Until recently, you did not need ID to ride a bus, and in some cases you still don't – if the driver doesn't ask for it, which most of the time they don't – yet. There is a camaraderie among Greyhound travellers that I have not felt on trains or airplanes. The camaraderie of people who know that if they could, they would be elsewhere,

161

living another kind of life, but who are making the most of this one, and perhaps even enjoying this brief moment of communion.

On my recent trip, I found this camaraderie – while it did still exist – had worn thin. There were fewer conversations and far less humour in our exchanges. No one bought food for others or offered cigarettes – vapes can't be shared, nor can you ask for a match to light one. There were few, if any, maps or timetables on station walls. The apps we are told to check do not reflect what we can see with our eyes: the empty space in place of a bus, the closed-up station, the non-existent amenities, the lack of help with luggage or access. This space between what we can see and what we are told we are seeing is where we dwell, and it also dwells inside us. This is how we travel and exist now, in a physical space made less real by its online shadow. The machine is taking over.

On both of my trips, I found a strange sort of transcendence on the Greyhound. The shared experience of a group of humans, all of them wanting to get where they needed to go, hoping for some kindness, some love, something that might be just out of reach or remembering something they had left behind and were regretting. I felt buoyed by the feeling that I was not alone, that there were others around me grieving, missing loved ones, wishing life had turned out differently or heading towards something beautiful and exciting. And then there is the fact that you are not in control; this is something everyone on a bus feels, which is absent in one's private vehicle.

Cars offer a promise (or mirage) of freedom. They also contain a political and racial dimension. There has always been a disparity along the lines of race and class between those with vehicles and those without; those who have the freedom to move when and where they want to and those who don't.

Before the 2008 financial crash, 93 per cent of White American households owned at least one car. The figure for African American households was 76 per cent. African Americans were also six times more likely to use public transport. This was a statistic I saw reflected around me on the Greyhound back in 2006. In 2023, the racial mix on the bus seemed more balanced. To move around America in the privacy, comfort and safety of your own car is, in effect, a privilege. Those who are higher up in the social order can 'move fast and freely, in and out as they wish, across and beyond borders in pursuit of their interests, while the others are stuck, blocked, hemmed in,' writes Andreas Malm in *White Skin, Black Fuel*, which he wrote with the Zetkin Collective in 2021. He goes on, 'The history of race in the US is one long history of differential mobilities.' Getting to work or college on time when you are relying on a crumbling transport system can be the difference between having a job and an education and not.

Michel Butor's *Mobile*, the avant-garde author's visionary novel describing his journey across the US, approaches this same theme but in a very unorthodox way. The work reads more like a prose poem than a straightforward narrative. Dedicated to Jackson Pollock, Butor's travelogue of his six months driving America's newly built and interconnected highways is a verbal collage of road signs, town names, catalogue listings, newspaper clippings, historical texts on Native American cultures and treaties, overheard snippets of dialogue and passages from speeches by American politicians. It is like a patchwork quilt made by a preacher, a prophet and a novelist on LSD; it is almost more Beat than the Beats. Written in

1959, it was published in France in 1962, and an English edition came out in 1963, translated by Richard Howard. The critical response was not favourable. It was called 'ugly', 'stupid' and 'unreadable' by some French critics. One British reviewer called it a 'bloody mess' while in the United States, it was accused of being 'impenetrable ... doggerel.' In the words of the essayist John D'Agata, who wrote an introduction to *Mobile*, it is a European's view of 'what happens to European civilization when it arrives in a landscape that permits it to develop on a larger scale.' It is, in other words, a very different kind of Road Trip.

If there is a narrative to it, it is one imposed by facts outside of the text: this is an America as seen by a Frenchman driving, as everyone seems to, from east to west, but organized on the page alphabetically by state name, starting with 'WELCOME TO ALABAMA' and ending with 'WELCOME TO UTAH'. The linguistic and formal contrasts and the upending of linear movement echo the upheaval in the US during the period when Butor was travelling. He was going in a straight line, but his text is circular. The Korean War had ended four years previously, the Cold War was in full swing and the idea of progress, of moving up and forward, of capturing the better job just around the corner – that pay rise, the starter home, the kids, the bigger car, was everywhere in the ether, and yet not available to everyone.

The connection between car and road as symbols of American domination over the land was not lost on Butor. By 1959, the year of his cross-country travels, 90 per cent of the American population lived within five miles of the new Interstate Highway System. Instead of settling along rivers, Americans settled along highways. Their canoes were now cars, their waterways were shiny tarmacked roads. These new highways occupied the popular imagination, not just as a means of escape and a cultural symbol of freedom, but as symbols for something much darker with the potential for violent destruction. By 1956, of the 185 targets identified as possible sites for nuclear strikes from the Soviet Union, 126 were highways. D'Agata writes,

> the initial blast from such a strike would occur in one-millionth of one second... it would expand into a fireball ten miles in diameter... it would travel at a speed of 758 miles per hour. And ... its temperature, according to a study by the Department of Defense in 1953 entitled The Effects of Nuclear War, would be five times hotter than the sun.

The 90 per cent of the population living near these highways added up to roughly 160 million Americans. They would be incinerated by such a nuclear blast so fiercely and so quickly, that they 'would literally not know that they were being destroyed until sixteen-hundredths of one second after they had been'. In President Kennedy's speeches on the campaign trail, he spoke of the death toll from nuclear war with the Soviet Union. It was ironic that the highways that had been built to get Americans moving had become potential targets of atomic attack. Looked at through this lens, Butor's strange, disjointed, fluid and circular text appears like a verbal spaghetti junction. Rather than the failed literary experiment described by its critics, it functions precisely as the representation of a confused, terrified and fragmented nation

Cars, along with the 4 million miles of roads built for them, are such an integral part of the story of the United States that it is impossible to imagine the country without them. Without cars, there would be no Detroit, no suburbs, no parking lots, no giant box stores, no urban sprawl, and our reliance on Big Oil would be a fraction of what it is today. 'Our cities,' said a report from President Eisenhower's administration in 1955, 'have spread into suburbs, dependent on the automobile for their existence. The automobile has restored a way of life in which the individual may live in a friendly neighborhood.' 'Friendly' here can mean many things.

He was born in Sarnia, a small town in Ontario, in 1925. His father had made some money in the shoe business and then the insurance business. In the 1940s, this man worked as an aeronautical engineer for the Canadian government in Ottawa, although at heart, he was an artist. His photos were exhibited in one-man shows that travelled across Canada, published in art magazines, and he managed to get policies changed for low-income housing through his documentation of people living in the poorest parts of downtown Ottawa. He conceived and designed the international exhibition of photography, *The Camera as Witness*, at the 1967 Montreal World's Fair. He hankered to do more photography but he also needed a job. In 1949, he met a young and very pretty woman who was working in the parliamentary library in Ottawa. She had emigrated from the United Kingdom as a child and had grown up in Montreal. They married in 1950, and their first child was born the following year. Their small downtown apartment rapidly became too small for the three more children born in quick succession. In 1955, with the help of an architect friend, this man and his wife began designing a modern house in a suburban area of Ottawa called Alta Vista. It was completed in 1957. As the man liked to say, "No idea why they called it that as it wasn't 'Alta' and there was no 'Vista'." Three more of Jasmine and Philip's children were born there. I am the youngest.

166

The story of Philip and Jasmine is a common one. Their choice to settle in the suburbs, where they could buy a cheap piece of land, construct a house with enough space for a bunch of kids was – and still is – a choice being made by millions of North Americans. In 1955, Alta Vista still had a few of its old, timber farmhouses among the mainly empty lots being divided up and sold by property developers. By the time I, their seventh child, came along in the mid-sixties, the suburb was full of L-shaped bungalows, mid-century modern houses with exposed brick chimneys, driveways lined with colourful flower beds and ridiculously green, chemically enhanced lawns. Alta Vista was like thousands of other suburbs and subdivisions across North America. You could easily exchange the name 'Levittown', a suburb on Long Island, for 'Ottawa' in this description from 1950: 'Above all there is the uncluttered bowl of the sky – a great, clean, blue presence coming down all over Levittown. On a clear, bright day Levittown is brilliantly etched in blue and green and is close to the sky. Only the houses reach toward it. Everything else is young, growing, and close to the ground.' The words 'clean', 'clear', 'bright', 'young' are key.

Apart from cheaper land and more space, people moved to the suburbs in pursuit of healthier lives in a cleaner, brighter – and whiter – environment. There is often the mistaken view that life outside downtown is also somehow closer to 'nature'. In *Topophilia*, the geographer Yi-Fu Tuan makes a direct link between the American suburbs and the agrarian ideal fostered by Jefferson: a vision of virtue in small settlements and independent family farms. 'Popular names for suburbs characteristically recall some aspect of nature or country,' he writes, 'this may be taken as one more evidence of America's

167

nostalgia for rural ways. The front lawn and the back garden take the place of the farm, and pets the place of livestock.'

Suburbs are environmental cosplay for folk who want to imagine themselves as farmers (those flower beds!), landowners (those decorative architectural and lawn ornaments!) or even hunter-gatherers (those steaks on the barbecue!). There is a fakeness to the architecture of North American suburbs which is expressed in the non-weightbearing plaster Corinthian columns on either side of the garage doors, the Juliette balconies overlooking the driveways – balconies that have never supported a human being, the wrought iron railings that were originally designed to deter burglars or invite large trailing grape vines into their curly cues, but have seen neither criminal nor vegetable.

The suburb I grew up in didn't have pavements or shops within walking distance. Eventually we got streetlights, but I preferred it when the streets were pitch black because I could hear more birds from my bed. Alta Vista was closer to a David Lynch film or a Richard Yates novel than an idyllic Eden of plenty and pleasure. My father, who had moved his growing family there, had a complicated relationship to it. He rejected many of the expectations of life in the suburbs. We never mowed our lawn, for instance, and sometimes angry, anonymous letters of complaint would slip through our letterbox decrying the dandelions and the grass that reached our knees. Our front door was not at the front, but at the side of our house. People couldn't make sense of it, but more importantly, it was something the suburbs didn't like: our house was not only *modern*, it was *modernist* and very, very *different* from anything else around. While it was under construction, a petition circulated to have it stopped. The

168

house, the neighbours said, was hideous. Who would want to live in 'an ugly box on stilts'? Once, I caught my father shouting at a neighbour who was on his hands and knees meticulously clipping the edge of his lawn with nail scissors: 'You'd complain about the marks left on your lawn if Jesus Christ himself were dragging his cross over it!'

My father was an artist who read and thought about life constantly. I think he sometimes felt stuck in this landscaped terrain of sunken living rooms, soft beige carpeting and green lawns.

> When people seek to realize some of the small-town and rural values in the suburb, the intellectuals ... are not happy with the result. Many have shown their disapproval by calling suburban living "escapism", "nostalgic impotence", and, at best, a kind of "sadness", or "unpleasure". Like all human creations suburbia is flawed and criticisms are often justified. But it did and does represent an ideal, one which only developers and housing agents can now praise effusively,

writes Yi-Fu Tuan. If he were still alive, my father would be nodding in agreement.

In 1925, the year my father was born, the pastor and sociologist Harlan Paul Douglass wrote of suburbs:

> Formed out of the dust of cities, they wait to have breathed into them the breath of community sentiment, of neighbourly fraternity and peace. They reflect the unspoiled and youthful aspect of urban civilization, the adolescent and not yet disillusioned part of the city, where, if at all, happiness and worthy living may be achieved as well as material well-being.

169

This was the dream, and like so many dreams, it fell far short of the reality. In many respects these car-dependent oases became nightmares that fed not only our loneliness and atomization but our dependency on fossil fuels.

The four 'natural environments' which Yi-Fu Tuan believes 'have figured prominently in humanity's dreams of the ideal world' are 'the forest, the seashore, the valley, and the island'. Although suburbia tried to combine the forest, seashore and valley, it ended up recreating only the island. In the case of Alta Vista, one that was cold, empty and isolated.

Just after the Second World War, when my parents made their move to the suburbs, the United States Congress authorised 37,000 miles of new highways. Then came the notorious 1956 Federal-Aid Highway Act which initiated, in Andreas Malm's words, 'the largest single construction project in human history: ribbons of highways or "freeways" – roads exclusively devoted to cars – laid out between states, within cities and to new neighbourhoods around them. A smooth way was paved to suburbia, where whites could isolate themselves from black masses.' Over the next twenty years, cities across North America were to experience White Flight to the suburbs, where for every two people of colour who moved into cities, three white people moved out. And to compound matters, Malm explains,

[t]o clear the way for the roads, bulldozers and wreck-
ing-balls smashed into African American districts, bisected
them, reduced them to junkyards – later to be filled with
incinerators and dump sites – and accelerated the vicious
circle that constituted the black ghettos in the post-war era.
As affluent whites withdrew into monochrome serenity,
they left behind the urban rot from which the image of the

171

menacing black man could grow, the one space inconceivable without the other. Suburbia became the prime site of twentieth-century American whiteness, literally a location where light skin denoted the "world's highest standard of living" and a safe distance from squalor and crime.

Not only do cars function as machines for acts of removal and separation, but so do the roads they drive on. Roads and highways, while so often being seen as modes to connect us, as avenues to take us towards 'Freedom', also allow for a subtle segregation, a quiet death for those seeking the utopian ideal far from the sometimes imagined, sometimes real squalor of the city. For others, suburbia becomes an opiate, a gateway into a world unharmed by poverty and extremes of any kind. 'White flight from urban centres', writes the sociologist Paul Gilroy, 'was not just accomplished by means of the automobile, it was premised on it.' These machines burn carbon-producing fossil fuel and keep us distanced from and blind to the very ground this fuel has destroyed, either through its extraction or its combustion. Those of us who grew up in the suburbs never saw the oil fields, the devastation caused by leaking pipelines and grounded oil tankers. No one told us that the fuel needed to prop up our lifestyles was destroying the Earth.

I can remember as a teenager watching Orson Welles' *The Magnificent Ambersons*, based on the 1918 novel by Indianapolis-born Booth Tarkington. We are not supposed to like the character of George Minafer, the coddled, conservative son of the wealthy Isabel and Wilbur. We are instead supposed to back the handsome, progressive widower and automobile manufacturer Eugene Morgan, played by a young Joseph Cotton. When Isabel's elderly father, Major Amberson, asks Eugene

172

whether he thinks his 'devilish machines' will 'change the face of the land', Eugene replies, 'They're already doing it. They can't be stopped.' George then interrupts saying, 'Automobiles are a useless nuisance.' Everyone around the supper table goes quiet and then Eugene Morgan delivers his famous speech:

> I'm not sure George is wrong about automobiles. With
> all their speed forward, they may be a step backwards in civ-
> ilization. It may be that they won't add to the beauty of the
> world or the life of men's souls. I'm not sure. But, automo-
> biles have come. And almost all outward things are going to
> be different because of what they bring.... And I think men's
> minds are going to be changed because of automobiles.

Everyone who grows up in a place like Alta Vista either learns to drive or leaves. I left on a Greyhound bus at the age of seventeen, as soon as I graduated from high school, without a driver's license. My choice to live somewhere with metros, tubes, subways, buses, trams and shops within walking distance aligned with my desire never to have to funnel gas into the tank of a car. The romantic view I had of my adult life merged seamlessly with my mistrust of Big Oil and the car industry – perhaps the result of growing up not far from Detroit and Canada's own car towns, Hamilton, Windsor and Oshawa. I felt that somehow life in a big city could be greener, that ditching the car, walking to the local art house cinema and book-shop might be the answer. Maybe communal gardens and orchards could be involved.

These were my thoughts as a teenager before I had heard of urban planners of the 1920s like Clarence Perry and his radical Neighbourhood Unit concept or the New Urbanism movement to promote walkable cities in the

1980s. These were both precursors to the more recent urban planning movement known as the '15-minute city'. This concept proposes that the basics needed by the inhabitants of a city, such as employment, food, health-care, education, parks and cultural activities should all be found within a fifteen-minute walk or cycle ride from their front door. One of the great benefits of 15-minute cities is that they cut fossil fuel emissions massively. The idea went global when, in 2020, Paris's mayor Anne Hidalgo made it part of her election platform – and she won. Milan, Ottawa, Edmonton, Seattle, Oxford and cities around the world are trialling the idea – or at least iterations of the idea. Melbourne, for instance, is imple-menting a 20-minute city.

But there is resistance to the idea. A powerful coun-ter-movement has sprung up – backed by fake news on social media and misreadings of the *Global Report on Urban Health: Equitable, Healthier Cities for Sustainable Development* published in 2016 by the World Health Organization and the United Nations. The authors of this report state that

> [t]he urban environment itself plays an instrumental role in health because it affects the way we live our daily lives.... Cities can and should be planned for people in order to optimize the health of their residents, and maintain their economic and cultural vibrancy... One key principle for making cities healthier for their residents is to make their daily needs accessible by a combination of walking or cy-cling and public transportation.... One of the ways that city design can promote physical activity is through ... relatively high residential density ... – the things people need and the places people need to go are close by.

Opponents of the 15-minute city cite this report as an example of state overreach by the 'elites' of the UN and the WHO and an assault on car-owners and rural communities. Their fear is that this movement is being designed as a form of population control and that they will be forced to live in planned urban environments. Where there is control, there is the potential for the abuse of this control by global bodies and western governments. Viral campaigns against 15-minute cities are flourishing and moving from the online sphere to the streets. Protesters are claiming that walkable urban centres will become 'concentration camps' or 'open-air prisons'. Some conspiracy theorists describe a *Hunger Games*-style situation, claiming that residents of these walkable urban centres will be forbidden from leaving or entering their 'zones'. In a debate on 3 February 2023 in Britain's House of Commons, the Conservative MP Nick Fletcher called the 15-minute city an 'international socialist concept', adding that they 'will cost us our personal freedom, and that cannot be right'.

The idea of settling in the city as a way of being 'green' hadn't just been the wild imagining of a 1970s suburban teenager – there is data to back it up. For instance, we know that New Yorkers pollute far less than those in the surrounding suburbs. Supporting the auto-dependent lifestyles of those in their detached suburban homes requires more gasoline, more electricity (for heating and cooling), more roads, more pipes and utility lines, and more energy is used to supply these large homes with water. Not to mention the giant, thirsty lawns covered in chemicals and sprinkled with fresh water throughout the summer months.

My desire to live in a city was not simply one of seeking like-minded people (other writers and artists, perhaps) and creating a smaller environmental footprint. I was also running from the lifeless suburbs of my childhood and what lay just beyond them: the dreaded *sprawl*.

David Cieslewicz, before becoming mayor of Madison, Wisconsin, taught university courses in urban studies. He wrote about cities as 'the antidote to sprawl', that they are 'on balance, good for the environment'. And, in his book *Urban Sprawl*, the sociologist David Squires also sees sprawl as the evil protagonist in the story of America's increasing hunger for gas-powered vehicles. He continues Cieslewicz's point: '[W]e will not solve the problems of sprawl until we resolve the contradiction and we learn to embrace city life – living in places of real, compact urban form with all of their advantages and disadvantages – as the most positive environmental choice an individual can make.' When I left the suburbs for Toronto and then London, with brief flings with New York and Boston, was I making the 'most positive environmental choice' I could? I don't think so; but I was trying to aim for some kind of harmony with the Earth and I was struggling to see how to make it a reality.

When you think about sprawl, as I did growing up in what felt like the tarmacked addendum to a city, you realize, as Cieslewicz writes, that the 'problems of land use are not just problems for land. Land use is the key factor behind remaining water and air quality issues we face.' Why is it that so much environmental writing and thinking is centred around the concept of 'wilderness' or national parks or land that is seen to be empty? Why do nature and environmental writers feel they need to go to Alaska or the Hebrides or the Himalayas in order to tackle the subject of how humans are negatively affecting our planet? A puddle in a casino parking lot in Vegas or a bed of vegetables grown in a scrubby patch of communal land

176

next to a block of flats in Ankara or Detroit or Dakar can tell us just as much about our relationship to the Earth as any other location. Cities and roads and highways and council estates and terraces and gated communities and every other kind of dwelling, and the means by which we inhabit them and move between them, should be equally ripe for greening and rewilding and should be seen as opportunities for ecological improvement.

Greyhound buses feel like part of an overlooked ecosystem. One that uses less fuel and spews less CO_2 into the air than individual cars. The space they create is a rare one: an environment where strangers are connected by the simple need to get somewhere. You can't buy anything on a bus (like you can on a plane or train), you can't upgrade either – you're all in it together. As more and more public places become privatized, I feel there is a fragility to this sort of space. The Greyhound is more library than shopping mall, more community centre than curated retail space. In our post-Covid world, these vehicles also remind us of a before-time when we could sit maskless in our Greyhound bubbles, rubbing shoulders with strangers, safely breathing alongside each other without fear. They might yet become symbols for a way we once lived in each other's presence.

In the late 1940s when the wildlife ecologist Aldo Leopold wrote about his ideas of a 'land ethic' in *A Sand County Almanac*, he advocated for humans to include plants, soil, water and all living creatures into our idea of what might be termed an 'ethical community'. Surely all ethical and ecological communities should include the roads and byways that bring us together and keep us apart, the parking lots and box stores on the outskirts of towns, the inner cities and the sprawl, all of the built environment – even the ugly and awkward parts that are so

177

often ignored.

Since I cannot drive, I have had to be a passenger all my life. In order to cross the United States on my own, I was always going to have to do so as part of a group rather than as an individual. Simply by eschewing the car, one becomes a communitarian, a fly in the ointment of modernity and progress, however short-lived. The fact that most of the Great American Road Trip books are written by men driving cars (or trucks) while letting their fancies, their desires and their needs dictate their routes only serves to make the writings of Irma Kurtz, Ethel Mannin and Simone de Beauvoir more radical.

De Beauvoir first boarded a Greyhound with Natasha Sorokin in Los Angeles after they'd done some car travel together. Natasha was a nervous driver, having only just got her licence, and de Beauvoir was a reluctant navigator. They'd already got dangerously lost a couple of times, so they decided to take the bus to Santa Fe. 'On the road we often envied the swiftness of these large gray buses, which passed us easily, despite our sixty miles per hour. We thought it would be relaxing to entrust ourselves to them while travelling thousands of miles through the deserts', de Beauvoir wrote. They boarded in downtown Los Angeles where the bus station was 'dreary, like a subway stop in the early morning'. But it was a 'real station with a buffet, a cigarette kiosk, newspaper vendors, a luggage room, a ticket office, and numbered doors that open onto different platforms alongside the Greyhound'. In other words, there were people there, small businesses, places to sit and read and get a cup of coffee. This station, which opened in 1939, is the same one that stands today – the very one I was headed for. De Beauvoir's excitement is palpable:

We settle in the front of the bus with our books and cigarettes, and we feel quite comfortable.... The bus is nearly empty. Americans never use buses for touring, only for transport, and again, only if they are people of modest means. They consider it a slow and tiring way of traveling. This relative slowness will allow me the leisure to really see the regions we cross, and I, at least, find this day most relaxing. I read, I look, and it's a pleasure to give myself over from morning to night to a long novel while the landscape slowly unfolds on the other side of the window.... Every three or four hours we stop at a gas station. You can eat and drink there.... These stops are brief celebrations, allowing us to get out of the bus and leave the desert behind. I'm especially enchanted by the jukeboxes.

Later on, she adds: 'It's so easy to travel in this part of the country! The buses are always empty. When you get to the station, there's a cloakroom that's open day and night with little lockers stacked on top of each other like boxes in a columbarium.' Columbariums! The novelty soon wears off, however: 'We are beginning to hate these bus stations where you eat charred meat, where the jukebox plays Frank Sinatra and Bing Crosby'.

Much has changed since 1947. The rest stops are McDonald's, there is no charred meat or jukeboxes, nor do the stops feel in any way celebratory. Later still, de Beauvoir writes:

Even the gas stations contribute to the monotony of the landscape; we know all the songs on the jukeboxes by heart, and the stuffed animals are no longer amusing. We read. But when evening falls, reading becomes impossible, since there's no light inside the bus. We're relieved to see the lights of Pecos. Some passengers are already settled for the night, their heads on their pillows; we wouldn't like to be in their places.

De Beauvoir enjoyed her bus travel as an experience, but was happy to book herself and Natasha into Santa Fe's Hotel La Fonda which she exclaimed was 'the most beautiful hotel in America, perhaps the most beautiful I've ever seen in my life'. The adobe hotel is still there, and for 359 bucks a night, you too can 'Step into the past and experience the splendor of the American Southwest at La Fonda on the Plaza™,' where 'tasteful, modern conveniences blend with the warmth of authentic New Mexican style'. The Santa Fe de Beauvoir fell in love with is not the Santa Fe™ of today.

The connection between cars and suburbs, between cars and the destruction of the planet, between cars and Big Oil, between cars and individualism, between cars and racial segregation, between cars and dominance over the land has been well researched and recorded. In *Urban Sprawl*, Squires writes,

> Virtually every new development since World War II has been designed for ease of auto travel. By strictly dividing land into vast large-lot, single-family-home subdivisions connected to ever larger shopping malls and business "parks" by wide highways and streets, we have made driving mandatory in virtually every new development built in America in the last half of the 20th century. In fact, this development pattern means even short trips demand auto travel. One in four automobile trips is less than one mile in length.

180

It's not just suburbs and the exurbs beyond them that require car travel, but many American cities – even in their downtown cores – have no form of public transportation, nor are they accessible on foot or safely navigable by bicycle. When I was planning both bus trips, I tried to find motels and hotels to stay in that were walkable from Greyhound bus stations. This was almost impossible for two reasons: firstly, the stations were often in dodgy neighbourhoods and the hotels were essentially flop houses or crack dens. Secondly, the walk between station and motel was often too far or unsafe at night. In 2006, I relied on the kindness of cab drivers, which for the most part seemed inexhaustible. In 2023, there were fewer taxis, so I relied on Ubers.

When you travel by bus, you still need a car to get you to a bed, a diner, a bar, to that part of town with a bookstore. Life in America without a car prevents you from fully taking part in education, work and leisure. It is not just a physical barrier, but a temporal one. Those who rely on public transport to get to school or work are at the mercy of shifting schedules, late drivers, the inability to change their route in the case of road works and construction, causing yet more division between the car-havers and those without.

We've come to expect sprawl as an inevitable consequence of cities, and cars as a simple extension of this inevitability. This is a problem of imagination which illustrates so perfectly the disassociation we have created between our very bodies and the material world we inhabit.

We can't divorce our dependence on cars from our dependence on oil. Cars have created sprawl and oil is the lubricant. David Cieslewicz again:

> To take the measure of environmental problems caused by
> sprawl, we need to follow the cars. The dramatic increase in
> driving caused by our sprawling, auto-dependent develop-
> ment patterns force the exploration for oil into increasingly
> environmentally sensitive areas. The attack on biological
> diversity in Prince William Sound caused by the *Valdez*
> can be traced back to our need for gasoline to power the
> vehicles that we must drive to get around the places we have
> built thousands of miles away. The *Valdez* sailed for us.

The *Exxon Valdez* oil spill was one of the first oil spills
to be documented at length in the media. On 24 March
1989, a tanker with 53 million gallons of crude oil in its
belly left the port of Valdez, Alaska, en route to Long
Beach, California. Just after midnight, the tanker rammed
into Bligh Reef, a well-known hazard in Alaska's Port
William Sound. The collision tore a huge hole in the
ship's hull, which then dumped 11 million gallons of oil
into the sound. The oil slick poisoned 1,300 miles of
coastline and took the lives of 250,000 seabirds, almost
3,000 sea otters, 300 harbour seals, 250 bald eagles, 22
killer whales and billions of salmon eggs. Populations of
pacific herring, a cornerstone of the local fishing industry, collapsed. This was the worst oil spill in US waters
until the Deepwater Horizon oil spill in 2010. Images of
birds whose feathers were cemented together with sticky,
black oil were printed in magazines and newspapers. It
was later discovered that the captain of the *Exxon Valdez*
had been drinking that evening and had allowed an unli-
censed third mate to steer the ship. Even today, remnants
of oil from that tanker can be found along the coastline.

¶ I got an Uber to the bus station in St. Louis at 7 a.m. for my 7.45 a.m. bus, which was scheduled to arrive in Tulsa, Oklahoma at 3 p.m. My Uber driver was chatty and very happy to tell me that he was now retired and made over $100,000 a year as a driver. He got healthcare from his wife's job. 'What's everyone complaining about?' he asked and looked at me in his rear-view mirror. 'I work full-time. I treat this as a proper job. If you work hard, you'll be OK.' I thanked him, got out and added a tip via the app.

Several buses had been cancelled and the station was heaving. The vibe was nervy and angry. People were sleeping on the floor. Some sat on the bolted down chairs in the narrow eating area, their heads resting on the similarly bolted down tables. The food counter was open – the first I had seen on this trip so far. The guy working there had his AirPods in. I ordered a coffee and a bagel with cream cheese. He seemed in a good mood, smiling and nodding along to his music. He was moving at half normal speed. I watched him as he slowly extricated a bagel from a bag, stood for a moment, then opened a fridge very slowly, found some little tubs of cream cheese, and then exceptionally slowly brought them to the counter, still nodding along. Then he went to pour a cup of coffee from a flask.

'Oh, I forgot to put any water in here!' he said a bit too loudly, presumably because of the AirPods. He disappeared into a back room to find some hot water.

'Oh, that's OK. I don't need the coffee,' I called out after him. He couldn't hear me. He was gone for some time.

Next to me at the counter was a tall, good-looking man, about my age, waiting for the nachos he'd ordered. I sensed it might be a while yet before they appeared. We smiled and made small talk. Behind us in the main hall of the bus station a commotion erupted. A skinny guy, tattooed all over, front teeth missing, a couple of dogs with him, started shouting. It was something to do with his phone. It was missing. His ticket was on it. This was the second such commotion I'd seen. Another reason to bring back paper tickets.

The man was still shouting and running around desperately with his dogs. His eyes were wide with panic, drugs, sleeplessness, terror. A security guard, a tall blonde trans woman with long eyelashes and shiny black nail polish, calmly walked over to him. The guy next to me at the coffee counter nudged my arm and pointed, 'Her revolver is the same as my grandad's,' he laughed. 'It's old. Probably doesn't even work.'

'That guy seems really upset,' was all my un-caffeinated brain could formulate. He was now pounding the wall with his fist while the security guard kept one hand on her holster.

'The problem is, it's all digital now. They just look at their computer,' the man said miming someone typing officiously on a keyboard. 'They say "Sorry I can't help you," if it's not right there on their screen. Nobody cares. My dad was a trash collector. Me and my brother used to ride on the back of the truck when we were kids. Now the guy doesn't even get out of the truck and you only need one person to drive,' he paused. 'All you need to know about this digital stuff and robots is that they're making people lose their jobs. So many jobs lost. If you work with your hands, you have no hope.'

The man told me he was a master carpenter. His fingers were long, almost delicate. I could imagine them making a perfect dovetail join.

'I'm fifty-seven now and just waiting until I turn sixty-two so I can retire. Although they're trying to change

186

that, too.'

'What happens when you're sixty-two?' I asked.

'I can stop working.'

'What about healthcare?'

'That's when the state takes over.'

'Is that good?'

'I'm not too sure. Probably not good. I see on my pay-cheque every month how much I give the state and yet they always say they have no money. They have money, they just mismanage it.'

The guy at the counter reappeared with the nachos. 'Oh, I forgot the water for the coffee,' he said.

'That's OK. I'll just have the bagel.' I was grateful for his oversight as I had over seven hours on the bus, and I was watching how much liquid I drank so as to avoid having to use the onboard bathrooms. I was sticking to my semi-dehydration diet.

The man collected his nachos and I headed with my bagel to join the queue for Tulsa. Around me people were on hold to Greyhound customer services. I knew the sound of that 'on hold' jingle like it was my own heart-beat. A TV was on in one corner of the station, the sound turned down and subtitles running along the bottom of the screen. The talk was all about Donald Trump. It was interesting how on every TV I'd seen in public spaces on this trip there were men and women, most of them alarm-ingly coiffed and made-up, shouting hysterically about Trump. On this TV, a man with bright pink foundation was saying that the former President was being arrested on Tuesday, 21 March. 'That's right. In downtown New York City, he's going to be handcuffed and put away. That's right,' ran the subtitles. It was now 19 March. No one was watching the TV. Not one person. I had yet to hear anyone in real life so much as mention Donald

Trump on this trip. Their concerns were not about him; they were about whether they could get from A to B, look after their kids, get a meal and find a job.

My conversation with the man at the deli counter reminded me of a passage in Ethel Mannin's *An American Journey*. She had a similar conversation with her friend Rickey, whom she had gone to visit in California. Rickey described in 1967 what I was sensing around me in 2023,

> Art as we know it is on the way out.... Painting, music, literature, poetry, as we've understood these things, are finished. Because human beings as we've known them are on the way out. Automation is here, and the machine has no use for people. Not people as we've known them. And not many people anyway – not more than are needed to press the buttons of the machines.

I looked around at the people in the queue with me:

A woman on the phone was telling the person on the other end that she'd had three back surgeries. Her daughter, maybe seven years old, tugged on her mother's sweatshirt, 'Four surgeries, Momma.'

A nervous young woman kept asking everyone if this was the line for Tulsa. She had told us all repeatedly that she REALLY NEEDED to get to Tulsa.

A blind man stood quietly with a young woman. His carer? His daughter? A friend?

An old hippy in crocs and socks, a chequered shirt and well-fitting jeans sat with his phone plugged into the wall, a bottle of water and a stack of books (I couldn't make out the titles). He'd made this station his office for the day.

A very chatty young man who was overly enthusiastic about everything was telling us all how great it is that there are phone chargers on buses now.

The driver on this bus was the first who seemed happy with his job. The bus was full and once we'd all taken our seats, he did his little spiel. In his lovely, soft Spanish accent he said, 'Please don't smoke or drink alcohol. If you use the toilets, please hold the handrail. Respect your fellow passengers. Keep your cell phones on silent and use headphones! At 11.30 there will be a smoke stop in Springfield. At 12.50 a food stop in Joplin. We will be arriving in Tulsa at 3 p.m. Please sit back and enjoy the ride.'

Although this bus wasn't as filthy as the others I'd boarded, my window was so dirty that everything outside appeared smudged, like a Gerhard Richter painting. We pulled out of St. Louis to a perfect sunrise transforming the sky's pinks to blues.

We passed fields and giant, sprawling manufacturing plants. It's impossible to understand the place of manufacturing in the American economy without seeing these vast buildings and their parking lots full of cars. When you are drinking your skinny latte in New York or tucking into your acai bowl in San Francisco, it's easy to forget how many Americans rely on manufacturing jobs, some of which are precarious, and how huge swathes of the population are just a paycheque or two away from economic breakdown. Those whose lives had collapsed were on the bus or hanging out in the stations – that is, the stations that hadn't yet closed. I was starting to realize that Greyhound bus stations – even the beautifully designed sleek Moderne ones – were no longer seen as important cogs in a public transportation system or necessary places for bus passengers to sit, get a coffee, wash their hands, have a drink of water. They are now earmarked as prime real estate for developers who are buying them up and

190

turning them into hotels, luxury apartments and office blocks. Once again the forces of capital are removing those with little disposable income from one of the few public spaces left in the centre of towns and cities.

On this trip, I saw many more sunken faces, saucer eyes, bruised arms, weeping sores, sobbing adults and people who seemed shocked into silent desperation than I had ever seen in my life. Once all the Greyhound stations are sold off, these same people will be lining roads on the outskirts of cities where they will have no amenities whatsoever. FlixBus, the new owners of Greyhound, are in the process of introducing the jaunty-sounding 'curbside pick-up', which entails waiting by a large road possibly for hours, come rain or shine, with your luggage and not so much as a bench to sit on. In a 2021 article in *TechCrunch*, the journalist Ingrid Lunden wrote,

> This is also where Flix's tech comes into play. Like other transportation startups such as Uber ... Flix's approach has been to take a legacy service – in this case buses (it also operates trains) – and apply better algorithms to determine pricing and routing and timing for the different buses on the network. Indeed, it has often been referred to as the 'Uber of buses'.

I remembered the previous St. Louis-to-Tulsa trip when I met a guy called Benny Decker. He had been sitting in the seat in front of me and as soon as the bus started moving out of St. Louis towards Tulsa, Benny turned and introduced himself. I couldn't imagine anyone doing that today – times have changed and so have I. He was stocky and handsome in a cocky sort of way. Big smile and large hands that looked like they'd worked hard. He was from West Plains, Missouri but had lived in Chicago for a long

192

time. The bus stopped for a break at a McDonald's in Rolla, Missouri. We both got out to stretch our legs. He was getting a burger and asked me if I wanted anything.

'I'll just have a coffee,' I replied.

He gave me a hard stare, 'Hey, this is the States,' he said, 'You never turn down food because you never know when you'll get your next meal.'

Chastened, I walked towards the McDonald's with him and clocked the Marlboro he was smoking. I bummed one and when he asked again what I wanted to eat, I told him I was a vegetarian, but that I was in his hands.

'That's good,' he replied, and then added, 'wait here and I'll get you something.'

I stood outside in the parking lot. The sun was beating down hard. It had been a while since I'd had a cigarette and my head felt light. Bennie returned holding up two burgers, 'I know you don't eat beef, so it's chicken or fish.' He was sweetly excited at this version of vegetarian food. It would have been churlish not to have accepted one.

I chose the fish.

It was time to climb back on the bus. Benny asked if he could sit next to me and I felt guilty even thinking about saying 'no'. He asked where my husband was and I laughed and told him that Americans seem obsessed with my lack of husband. 'I have one,' I told him, 'but he's back in London, working.'

Bennie's reasons for travelling were complicated. For the past thirty days, he'd been in jail in Cook County, near Chicago. He'd been done for drunk driving. This was something I heard often. When he got out of jail, his car had been towed and he had no money to get it out of the pound.

A bunch of squaddies got on at Fort Leonard Wood, home to a large army base. Then, just outside Lebanon,

Missouri someone at the back of the bus announced they could smell burning. All of us could smell it: burning rubber. Sparks appeared outside one of the back windows. The driver calmly pulled over and told us all to get out. The transmission had gone and sparks were flying because the metal fender was dragging along the highway. I made a note of the last sign I'd seen: Interstate 44 at the exit for Pomme de Terre Lake, Mile 129.

Now we were all standing in a field of tall grass next to the highway, the bus still smouldering. I sat down and Bennie came and sat next to me, offering me a cigarette, which I took. He told me about his life in a gang in Chicago and then lifted his T-shirt to show me his bullet holes and the marks left from a few stabbings on his stomach and chest. It made me think of the Denis Johnson story 'Steady Hands at Seattle General', where a guy in rehab tells the protagonist, Fuckhead, that he's been shot twice.

'Twice?' Fuckhead asks.

'Once by each wife, for a total of three bullets, making four holes, three ins and one out.'

The story ends with the guy telling Fuckhead to 'Talk into my bullet hole. Tell me I'm fine.' I couldn't stop thinking about this as I looked at Bennie's bullet-ridden torso.

He told me that one of his lungs had been pierced, and then added that when it happened, he was going out with the gang leader's sister. His chest was a map of violence.

'Were the stabbings and shootings to scare you or kill you?' I asked.

'To kill me,' he replied. 'Yeah, they wanted to kill me, but you see I am just too stupid to die!' and then he laughed.

His daughter's name, 'Amber', was tattooed on his arm.

194

As he started telling me about her, a guy in huge running shoes and a too-large tracksuit jumped up and shouted, 'I just got a tick on my arm!' Everyone else stood up and started inspecting their arms and legs for little black dots. Bennie told me to let him kill any ticks I might get wherever they were on my body. I did an internal eye roll. I would be forty-one in a month's time, and when I had set out on this trip, I hadn't known what it would be like to travel as a woman alone. I had been so consumed with grief over my sister's death and my inability to carry a child that I hadn't been thinking about my body as a locus of desire. There is something about desire sneaking up on you unexpectedly – and about being desired – that can bring you back to life.

After the tick scare, most of us sat back down. It was hot and we had no idea when the next bus would be showing up. Every now and then the sound of cars and the rattling of trucks along the highway would die down and the chirping of crickets and the buzz of cicadas would emerge. I was enjoying being out of contact and this strange reclaiming of joy must have shown. The bus driver called me 'Buddha' because, according to him, I'd been 'smiling too much on his bus'. Greyhound riders don't smile, he told me. He handed us all complaint forms to fill out so we could try to get our money back for this leg of the journey.

'You're not American, are you?' the driver asked me as he handed me a form.

'No, I'm Canadian.'

'I knew it. You're just way too happy to be American.' He paused and looked around as if wondering whether to carry on. 'This breakdown is all the fault of a Canadian company called Laidlaw,' he said. Greyhound had been bought out by them and since then, according to this driver, 'They don't care about the passengers, they only care about the shareholders.' I apologized on behalf of my birth country and he laughed, 'It's not your fault.'

A woman called Marianne joined Bennie and me for a cigarette. In her early sixties, with long white hair, she was a chain-smoking ex-hippie who turned out to be both a devout Catholic and an astrologer. 'Hey, there's my man,' she said, waving at a guy who had pulled up behind the bus. She had phoned him to tell him of the breakdown.

'See those overalls?' she asked, pointing to her husband who was chatting with the bus driver. 'There's nothing on under them!' she laughed. 'The funny thing with women is that we don't need to have orgasms to keep the species going and yet we have them anyway. I've never figured that one out.' And with that she got up to greet her husband. 'Adios amigos,' she called out as she got into the truck.

Next, Bennie's brother Larry came to pick him up. Bennie invited me to come with them and stay with his family. I would like them all, he promised. I politely declined and told him I had more travelling to do. He shook my hand and said farewell. As he got into Larry's car, he turned and waved. More and more passengers were being collected by friends and family. An Amish couple were sitting like little bowling pins in the grass. Earlier, Bennie had asked them where they came from. 'Humansville,' they had replied in unison. I wasn't sure I'd heard correctly, so I asked them again. 'Humansville,' the woman repeated, 'like where humans come from.' As they walked towards a white van, the guy with the tick called out: 'Hey, I didn't think you guys were allowed motorized vehicles!'

It had been several hours now since we had broken down. We were sharing out what food and water and cigarettes

we had left. I was madly making notes for the sake of Karl. She would be smoking and listening and thinking about her mother and what she would say to her. She had to get it right or she might lose the house in Napanee. One guy, whom Bennie had called the Unabomber because of his long dark coat, black gloves and large bag all taped up, which Bennie was convinced held a gun, was still with us in the field. He hadn't said a word. A woman in her thirties, dishevelled and nervous, was asking everyone if she could buy a cigarette from them. No one took her money; everyone gave her a smoke. Another woman with a disabled son was getting seriously worried about his medication running out.

I lay in the grass looking up at the clouds, smoking the cigarette Benny had given me 'for the road'. Then my mind wandered to Bennie Decker and how easy it all felt here on the road with all these complete strangers. Bennie had told me to watch my back, to be careful about being ripped off. I'd replied that I'd never had anything stolen and he replied that the US was the right place for it to happen for the first time. I looked Bennie up recently and found out that he died in 2020.

After five hours in that tall grass watching the hot sun cross the blue sky, the handful of us who remained got on a new bus. I had realized that my journey of choice and escape was not the same journey that so many of these passengers were on. The driver said, 'Hopefully none of you have any hot dates lined up. But if they love you, they'll wait!' as he pulled onto the highway. An older Amish woman sat next to me with a bundle on her lap wrapped in fabric and tied with string. She asked about my family and I told her I was one of seven children, avoiding the usual question about how old my own non-existent children were. Talking about my mother and all her kids made this woman smile. She told me about her five children and she didn't ask anything more about me, which was a relief.

The trees outside were turning black against the streaks of mauve, pink and blue. Birds of prey circled overhead. The Amish woman fell asleep and her head in its lace bonnet bobbed like a little doll. I'd taken music with me that related to the cities I'd be passing through. I listened to Gene Pitney's 'Twenty-four Hours from Tulsa', taking in the words for the first time. What an absolutely devastating story. I got out some baba ghanoush and bread and although the baba was warm, hadn't seen a refrigerator in over 24 hours and contained mayonnaise, I was too hungry not to eat it. I called the hotel in Tulsa. Whispering into my phone as quietly as I could, I told the guy who ran the improbably named Savoy Hotel that I would be getting in late. He said he would hide the key for me and described in detail where it would be.

It was just before midnight when we rolled in. Tulsa was deserted. I stood outside the station wondering which direction to walk in when a cab approached and slowed next to me. The driver asked why I was standing on the side of the road so late at night all alone. I told him my bus had only just got in and I was working out which way to walk to my hotel.

'There have been twenty-seven homicides so far this year in Tulsa,' he told me, which I guess was his way of saying, 'Be careful'.

'How far is the Savoy Hotel?' I asked.

'Not too far. Maybe a thirty-minute walk, but I'm free if you want a lift.'

The driver was listening to Bill O'Reilly. I tactfully kept my mouth shut until he asked me where I was from. I told him I was Canadian. He looked at me in his rear-view mirror and said he had married a woman from Toronto and had lived in Woodstock, Ontario. He'd liked living up there but found crossing the border from Canada into the US to visit his family got too stressful. So, he moved back to the US. The last time he had taken the Greyhound from Toronto to Tulsa, he realized when he got to the border that his wallet had been stolen in the Toronto bus station. He had no money and no ID. He was held in a room as he tried to convince the immigration officers that he was an American returning home. After about forty-five minutes of questioning, they asked him if there was anything at all that might be in their computer system that could verify his identity. So, he told them about his criminal record from his days in Pennsylvania. 'When I was just a normal guy trying to get home, they didn't want me, but when I was a convicted felon they took me in with open arms. Welcome to America!' he said, pounding the steering wheel to emphasise his point.

He dropped me at the Savoy Hotel and the key was hidden where it was supposed to be. I flopped into bed.

Leaving St. Louis in 2023, I was still angry at the motel employee for dangling my fifty-dollar deposit in front of me as he asked for a tip. (I had yet to find out about the extra $415 they would lift from my bank account). I focussed instead on the sunrise and the scenery.

We passed the hangar-like Living Word Church.

Then Country Bob's Café.

CBD Outlet.

St James water tower.

The First Assembly of God Church.

Old signs on buildings telling us we were on Route 66.

Crumbling houses with falling down signs also telling us we were on Route 66.

Billboard: 'AFTER YOU DIE, YOU WILL NEED GOD.'

Signs for Meramac Caverns.

John Deere dealership next to a church, next to a huge billboard saying 'Pleasure Zone'.

THC dispensary: 'No ID Required'.

At La Rolla the land was still flat. It looked dry but conifers and a few hills appeared. The colours were muted: shades of grey and creamy yellows.

A sign reading 'Lion's Den Adult Super Store'.

A 'Uranus Fudge Factory' billboard with a drawing of an old-fashioned delivery man.

Hours of leafless trees, dry ground, no wildlife to be seen, only cows.

Acres of storage facilities.

'Den of Martial Arts'.

Towering motel and gas station signs.

10.53: the Niangua Conservation Area, post oaks, white oaks, sycamores.

More trees.

Parking lots, auto repair shops, truck stops, 'Your Wick's Trailer Expert', Wick's Truck Centre.

At Springfield, the Robert W. Plaster Center for Advanced Manufacturing, part of the Ozarks Technical Community College.

We stopped briefly in Springfield. The driver showed us the places where we could smoke. Even outdoors you can't light up just anywhere these days. A young woman appeared as we were reboarding and pleaded with the driver to let her on. 'Please sir, I just want to go home. Just let me on the bus so I can go home. Please, sir.' She was crying. He said he couldn't let her on. Her ticket wasn't valid. I'd lost count of the number of adults I'd seen crying in public on this trip. Someone asked if we were going

202

to Wichita. For my sake, I hoped not. No one answered the Wichita guy. The blind guy sitting kitty corner to the driver turned in my direction, as if sensing my anxiety over where we were headed: 'If you ever want to know where you're going, ask a blind person. They will be the person to be able to tell you.'

I spotted a falcon.

An LED sign on the side of the highway flashed: 'WE'LL BE BLUNT, DON'T DRIVE HIGH.'

Then a billboard: 'Ozarkland! Lots of Taffy!'

The soil was becoming rocky. Shades of red appeared.

1 p.m.: We stopped in Joplin. The shop there was run by a South Asian man. He had a large warming oven full of deep-fried everything. I bought some battered mushrooms and okra. He served his food in small paper bags. I was getting a headache, possibly from dehydration. I hadn't had any luck finding my go-to Greyhound drink: V-8. No one seemed to sell it anymore. Even in Indiana, where they make the stuff, the gas station fridges were heaving with purple, pink, green and orange energy drinks. I refilled my water bottle. Just then my phone vibrated. My hotel in Amarillo was asking me to check in, the way you might check in for a flight. They wanted all my information confirmed via their app. I declined the opportunity.

Back on the bus I spotted another falcon. The culverts and ditches we sped past were bone dry. In the spring, shouldn't water be flowing? In the distance, a huge black plume of smoke billowed up into the sky. I took to Google to see if there might be news about this black smoke. There was no mention of it. Cows grazed. I saw my fourth hawk. I got a better look at it. With his white breast feathers, I think it was a red-tailed hawk.

Just on the outskirts of Tulsa, we crossed the Verdigris

River, a tributary of the Arkansas River and part of the Mississippi watershed. Its water was copper-green and I wondered if that was how it got its name. Trees along the highway were in blossom, some of the flowers were lacy and white, perhaps dogwood or serviceberry. Our arrival in Tulsa was uneventful. Spring was in full flow and the sky was bright. I had paid extra to stay in a hotel walkable from the station. Once I'd checked into my room at the La Quinta, I went to Tulsa's artsy area, which since my last visit there had become an Arts District™ with a Woodie Guthrie Museum, expensive restaurants, shops, galleries and a First Fridays evening. The old red brick warehouses were now occupied by businesses.

In 2006, it had felt somewhat dusty and off the beaten track. I remember it being a cloudy day in April when I found myself wandering through Tulsa looking for something to eat. After a while, I found Phat Philly's, which specialized in hoagies, giant submarine sandwiches. Eric Clapton was on the radio. The guy who made my sandwich asked how many chillies I wanted. Apparently seven was the norm. I told him I was good with one. Then the usual question: where was my husband?

'Home.'

'He must really trust you.'

'He does.'

'What you need is a boyfriend for two days to show you around Tulsa,' he offered.

I laughed. 'Maybe you could just tell me where I can find a nice bar to get a beer and listen to some decent music?'

He drew me a map.

Would Karl have taken his offer up? I don't think so. I think she would have taken the map and run as I did.

That's how I found Caz's, which filled the ground floor

of a handsome nineteenth-century warehouse down by the train tracks. The only brightness in the place came from fairy lights. At the back of the large room was a pool table; over the bar, a boar's head sported a clown hat. A large sculpture of a fish, made out of folded beer cans, stood on the wooden counter, bras hung from the ceiling, and neon signs advertised domestic and imported beer. On a wall of graffiti near the bathroom, someone had written SLAYER in that recognizable font with its pentagram. The Doors' 'People are Strange' greeted me as I walked in. I took a stool at the bar and ordered a Rolling Rock. You could smoke here (the smoking ban only came into effect in 2021). Karl, with her love of Slayer, cigarettes, alternative music and short bleached hair would be a regular here. And she would find the bartender, a young woman also with bleached blonde hair, very cute.

In the dimness I could make out a table of drinkers beyond the pool table. With their tie-dyed clothing, sandals and long hair, they were vintage Woodstock. They were saying they wanted pot and mushrooms, not more beer, and then they were onto movies. I heard one of them mention *Apocalypse Now*. The bartender was telling the young woman sitting a few stools away from me that the first film she ever saw was *Tommy*. She loved The Who and all that British stuff. Her friend, looking at the table of Baby Boomers said, 'God, I'm so glad I wasn't alive in the sixties. I hate all that natural shit.'

This was where I met Earl Spann, the silver-haired out-of-work actor who seemed to appear from nowhere to occupy the stool next to mine. He immediately launched into a story about being in Alan Parker's *Mississippi Burning* with Gene Hackman. He'd done the whole Hollywood thing, lived next to Bob Hope and then tried to sue United Artists for something that was

206

far too complicated for me to follow, but I remembered the punch line: he lost his case. He still knew everyone in the business, though. As he talked, his cell phone kept ringing.

'That person really wants to talk to you,' I said.

'I never pick up my phone.' He then scrawled his number onto a piece of paper and handed it to me.

'But you never pick up,' I said.

'I do sometimes,' he smiled.

When I told him I was heading to New Mexico and then Vegas he took my journal and began writing down names of people he knew in those towns. His aunt, Margaret Kerekes, lived in the Anabella Mansion on Paleras Street in Las Vegas, but I never was able to find it on a map. It was near Wayne Newton's estate Casa de Shenandoah, he told me. Margaret was good friends with Wayne Newton – Mr Entertainment, Mr Las Vegas, The Midnight Idol.

While we drank and talked, a woman kept putting money in the jukebox. She was dressed for a night on the town. She'd inexplicably gone from Aretha Franklin to Coldplay. Maybe that was to be the trajectory of her night out. Earl was trying to convince me to go to his home state of Alabama. He had so many friends there who could show me a good time. He jumped off his stool and performed a double act of someone from Alabama meeting me for the first time:

Alabaman: 'Where you from, honey?'

His version of me: 'Canada.'

A: 'Canada? You're from Canada? Is that near Tallahassee?'

H: 'No, it's a whole 'nother country.'

A: 'Oh, a country outside of Alabama, huh? Ain't that something.'

He was a convincing actor. Apparently, if he took me with him to Alabama, people would be amazed by my teeth.

'If I introduced you to my friends in Alabama, they'd look at your teeth and then ask me if you bathed. If I said "yes", they'd say, "Damn, she's got teeth and she bathes! Marry her!"'

Earl grabbed my journal again and wrote down the names and numbers of all his friends in his home state. One of them, Lesley Vance, worked in a funeral parlour. He was also a member of the Alabama House of Representatives (in 2010 he left the Democratic party and became a Republican; he died in 2015). Earl called him up and left a message on his voicemail telling Lesley that a Canadian woman was coming to visit him. He then called Bill Richardson, the Democrat Governor of New Mexico who was also a good friend of his. He handed the phone to me. When Mr Richardson picked up, I stuttered something about how it was nice to 'meet' him over the phone. He seemed confused but when I mentioned the name Earl Spann, he laughed. I don't remember our conversation. It was all so bizarre and I'd had one Corona too many.

Earl said he had noticed me walking around Tulsa earlier and he was glad to end up in the same bar. Everything was beginning to feel slightly surreal. He was trying to convince me to go to Alabama and make a documentary about it. He hated Oklahoma and he knew I would love Alabama. The beer was beginning to talk and I took my leave, wandered across the train tracks and back to my hotel, wondering how much of what Earl Spann had said was real and how much was made up. I have since found out that there was a woman in Vegas called Margaret Kerekes who was well known for owning 65 vintage cars.

The Savoy, where I had stayed on my first night in 2006, didn't have an available room for my second night in Tulsa, so I booked into a corporate hotel downtown. I looked for it on this second trip and couldn't find it. Maybe it had been torn down or taken over for offices. It was in that faceless hotel whose name I have forgotten that I turned on the TV and stumbled upon a documentary. I immediately recognized the soulful face of John Trudell, the Native American activist, musician and poet. It brought me back to my childhood in Ottawa: I recalled one of my sister's boyfriends, a Native Canadian himself, talking about John Trudell in our kitchen. I remember the feeling of being opened up to a way of thinking about the world, one that was hidden away out of sight in the suburbs. Like many stories told by adults within earshot of a child, some of them stick for life. This was one of those.

Trudell had been one of the main occupiers of Alcatraz in 1969, where he set up Radio Free Alcatraz. Throughout the seventies, he was a chairman of the American Indian Movement. I was fourteen in February 1979 when his mother-in-law, his pregnant wife Tina and their three children died in a mysterious house fire. Tina had been working at the time on water rights at the Wild Horse Reservoir in Nevada. Only twelve hours before the house fire that killed his family, John Trudell had set an American flag alight in Washington, DC to protest the treatment of Native Americans by the United States government. Trudell, who died in 2015, never believed the fire was an accident. To him, and to many others, it would always be an act of arson and murder. The film ended with Trudell talking about his grief after his family was killed. 'This thing about falling apart, it doesn't go away. Time doesn't have that magic. Distance is one thing, but magic is something else. And with some falling aparts, there is no magic to fix it,' Trudell says in the film. What kept him going was his poetry and the lines of verse that came to him from Tina after her death. Tina 'gave me the lines to follow', he said. I have since tracked down the film. It's called simply *Trudell* and was made by Heather Rae in 2005.

Time. Distance. Grief. How to recover from centuries of abuse. The signs of this abuse are still there for anyone to see. But do we really see it? This disconnect is one I often feel in Canada and the US: a disconnect between the veneer of contemporary comfort and the violence of the past.

In Ethel Mannin's *An American Journey* there is a chapter called 'The Indian Tragedy'. Born in 1900, Mannin was a surprising champion of Indigenous rights. A prolific author, she wrote six autobiographies and over a hundred works of fiction and non-fiction. Married twice, she had one daughter, and famously had affairs with W. B. Yeats and Bertrand Russell. She crossed the United States twice by Greyhound – from New York City to Los Angeles and back again. The reason for her trip was to research a novel 'which demanded a non-European setting'. Mannin's descriptions of riding the Greyhound are suffused with her horror at the racism she witnessed and the devastating effects of European settlement on Native Americans. She writes:

> It is time to look more closely at the American Indians, not as picturesque adjuncts of the Grand Canyon, and the Indian country of Arizona generally ... but to consider how they came to be there on their reservations, like a rare species of animal being conserved in wild-life parks. Why did they settle there, on those mostly desert lands? The answer to that is simple: they had no choice when their lands were

210

expropriated by the white settlers.

Mannin continues:

> If all the plans for bettering the economic conditions of
> the Indians everywhere in America, through industriali-
> zation, materialize and the payrolls of the Indians increase
> throughout the reservations, it will be in a sense all part of
> their defeat, for it will mean that the old tribal culture will
> have gone forever; the machine will have taken hold of them
> as it has of the white man; what, then, becomes of those
> spiritual values ... that have been part of their lives all the
> days they have known?

Time and history have given us the answer to this
question.

Tulsa's very first oil strike took place in April 1897, when
an explosive was dropped down a hole which turned
out to be the first commercially successful oil well in
Oklahoma, the 'Nellie Johnstone Number One'. This
was forty-five miles north of Tulsa, in a place called
Bartlesville. It gushed fifty barrels a day but back then
there was no means for it to be shipped or transported,
so the well was capped. The capping was rudimentary,
and as the perfect portent of the oil industry to come,
Oklahoma's first oil strike also became its first oil disaster
when the well began leaking.

Throughout the early 1900s, as more and more oil was
discovered in and around Tulsa, it was dubbed the 'Oil
Capital of the World'. By 1920, Tulsa was a thriving city
of 100,000 with 400 oil companies, 200 law offices, 150
doctors and two daily newspapers.

All of this 'progress' and digging for oil was taking

place on what was called the Indian Territory, which was comprised of modern-day Kansas, Nebraska and Oklahoma, minus the little panhandle jutting out of its northwest corner. These millions of acres of pristine rolling prairie, meandering rivers, fruit groves and ancient forests had originally been home to the Apache, Arapahoe, Comanche, Kiowa, Muskogee, Osage and Wichita, among others.

President Andrew Jackson, in an aggressive and brutal act of deracination, passed the Indian Removal Act of 1830. The first nation to face eviction, the Choctaw, were forced to leave their lands in 1831. Over 14,000 left what is modern-day Mississippi to begin their walk during a particularly harsh winter. In 1838 and 1839, Jackson forced members of the Cherokee nation along with the Creek, Chickasaw and Seminole tribes to surrender their lands and move to Oklahoma. This migration has become known as the Trail of Tears. It was so named because of the thousands of people who died from hunger, disease, malnutrition, exposure or simply exhaustion. Of the estimated 15,000 Cherokees who walked this path, over 4,000 of them perished on their journey – a journey of several weeks that covered thousands of miles.

The French writer Alexis de Tocqueville, who had witnessed some of this forced migration in 1831, described these evictions as so 'evil' that he 'would find it impossible to relate' them to his readers – but relate them he does. He describes the Choctaws leaving their lands 'in the hope of finding a retreat which the American government had promised them'. This was in the 'depths of winter and the cold was exceptionally severe that year; the snow had frozen hard on the ground; the river was drifting with huge ice-floes.' Tocqueville continues,

213

The Indians had brought their families with them and hauled along the wounded, the sick, newborn babies and old men on the verge of death. They had neither tents nor wagons, simply a few provisions and arms. I saw them embark to cross the wide river and that solemn spectacle will never be erased from my memory. Not a sob or complaint could be heard from this assembled crowd; they stood silent. Their afflictions were of long standing and they considered them beyond remedy. Already the Indians had all embarked upon the boat which was to carry them; their dogs still remained upon the bank. When these animals finally saw that they were being left behind forever, they raised all together a terrible howl and plunged into the icy Mississippi waters to swim after their masters.

When those who survived got to their new 'homelands', the suffering did not end. They had been severed from their lands which had provided them with their myths, their food, their clothing, their shelter and their long histories, and their new Indian Territory was rife with smallpox.

¶ Back in 2006, when I was travelling with Karl, I got progressively nervous as I got closer to Vegas, where her mother lived. Karl's meeting with Jean was to be the climax of the novel. I would be checking into the hotel she stayed in, scoping out the bar where Jean worked and looking at the city through the eyes of a young woman whose meeting with her estranged mother would not give her the love and certainty she was looking for. Tulsa had felt like my entrance to the West; just beyond it lay deserts, mountains, space and Las Vegas.

The downtown hotel in Tulsa where I'd stayed offered a shuttle bus to the Greyhound station, which seemed like luxury after all my schlepping down dodgy streets from motel rooms carrying a heavy backpack. As I waited for the shuttle, I made a list called Tulsa Memories:

Wide streets. Four lanes wide in many places.
Empty downtown.
Strong wind.
Long shadows.
Every denomination of church: Church of Christ the King, Seventh Day Adventists, Unitarian, Methodist, First Church of Christ the Scientist.
Very good bar
Earl Spann (what a name)
Chillies
You can smoke everywhere
Empowering graffiti
Art deco everywhere!
Trail of Tears
Trudell film

Sitting on a sofa in the lobby of my Tulsa hotel waiting for this mysterious shuttle bus was a Greyhound bus driver

217

in his crisp uniform. I asked him if I would get to the station in time to get my bag tagged for the bus to Amarillo. He said he'd ticket it himself to make sure I made it.

The shuttle bus stopped en route to the station to pick up two more passengers: a Texan train engineer who was heading for his shift on the freight trains and a guy who worked in the Great Western Hotel on 7th Street – a 'fine' hotel, he told the Texan as he dropped into the seat next to him. I stared at the backs of their heads as they talked about the gangs in North Tulsa which were, apparently, getting out of hand.

'And it's so crazy that they're fighting over turf!' one of them said.

'I know. It's weird that they would stab each other over a field. "Hey, get off, that's my grass!"' They both laughed.

One of them said, 'Every time I fly back home to Oklahoma it hits me that I live in a great big field.'

One person's field was another person's home.

The driver looked into his mirror and asked me where I was from.

'Canada,' I said.

'You know it's illegal to give tattoos in Oklahoma,' he told me, sounding like he was giving me a warning. 'This is the centre of the Bible Belt. Prostitution is illegal and abortions are frowned upon.' He sounded proud of these laws. I didn't have a tattoo, but Karl was designing one: a mountain lion on her belly.

I asked about all the stencilled graffiti I had seen around Tulsa. I'd noticed 'Faith', 'Ability', 'Understanding', 'Compassion', 'Generosity', 'Goodwill' and 'Determination' on pillars, concrete walls and buildings.

The guy who worked in the Great Western Hotel piped up, saying that all the hurricane victims from nearby states were coming to Oklahoma and covering the place with graffiti. 'The mayor who has just been re-elected is cleaning up all the filth. It makes me happy to see this. I hate graffiti.'

On our final stop before we got to the Greyhound station, we picked up a guy who took the seat next to me and introduced himself as Miguel. He had a tattoo on his arm: MADE IN MEXICO, which obviously he hadn't had inked in Oklahoma. He saw me clock his tattoo and told me he was actually born in California, then added, 'And I was arrested in Indianapolis for PI.'

I had to ask him what that was.

'Short for Public Intoxication.'

He took off his cap and rubbed his bald head with thick fingers. He was a trucker and during his 36 hours off, he had gone to a bar with one of his work buddies. He hadn't been sure about this bar and when I asked him why, he ran his forefinger up his forearm as if to point out the colour of his skin. His work buddy, who was white, said he would look after Miguel, but after a few beers, Miguel woke up in a cell in Tulsa with his hands cuffed to his ankles. His friend had taken off with all his stuff and left him only with his ID and enough money to get a bus ticket. He was heading to Phoenix, which if all went to plan he'd get to by 10.55 the next morning. He hoped he'd still have a job.

At the station, the Greyhound worker I'd met in the hotel lobby took my bag and rushed me to the right line and tagged it for me. Before I was able to thank him properly, he was gone. In front of me in the line was a Kurt Cobain look-alike. Shoulder-length blonde hair, loose T-shirt, pearls, skinny, cute and slightly lost. He told me how much he loved travelling on the bus.

'You can see more of the world travelling through the US than anywhere else on earth,' he said. Someone had told him that and he truly believed it. But he was in the wrong line. He was meant to be heading for Idaho and sprinted off when I told him he was in the line for Amarillo.

Our first stop was Oklahoma City. I spotted a large billboard: '"As my apprentice, you're never fired" – God.' Then a dark-haired woman got on with a T-shirt that read: 'Blondes are cool, but brunettes are HOT!' Pulling out of Oklahoma City, I started to notice how much the bus seemed to be tilting to one side. I figured maybe the luggage in the hold was unbalancing it. The luggage was fine. The driver was not. We got pulled over at a gas station and he was arrested. A replacement driver arrived quickly.

Caz's in Tulsa was still in business but it was too packed for me to enjoy this time. Post-Covid, I still wasn't able to embrace jostling, loud-talking crowds. And the bar seemed to have lost some of its grungy charm. I went to an outdoor Tiki Bar instead which was playing Hawaiian freedom songs. I drank a cold Mexican beer looking out onto a parking lot and the Tulsa high-rises beyond. Where were the Earl Spanns, Clay Bryants and Benny Deckers – the visionaries, the outsiders, the people who wanted nothing more than to tell you their stories and who would enrich your travels? Had they all been silenced by the indifference of a population hooked to their iPhones? Or was it perhaps that, once you hit your fifties, the stories are no longer handed out to you?

Certainly, the attention from men doesn't flow in quite the same easy way – which comes as a relief. As an older woman, I now have a solitude that I never had as a young woman. Until this Greyhound trip, I had never been able to travel on my own without regularly being

taken out of my own thoughts, without having my journal grabbed and written in. What I had now was a new kind of solitude and freedom, but it came with the heaviness of knowing I was leaving something precious behind that I would never have again. In 2006 I was escaping grief; in 2023 I was looking to rediscover the places I had been, to gauge my reaction to them, to inhabit a strange landscape of alternating recognition and surprise. One trip was about fleeing; the other was a pilgrimage of sorts.

I hadn't had any conversations with people in Tulsa this time. I ate on my own, drank on my own. Walked around without speaking to another soul. On the morning I left, the sun was bright, the streets were empty and I was full of conflicting thoughts. At the Greyhound station, the TV was on. The news reported that a man in Tulsa had been struck by a train. I had seen a tent pitched perilously close to the tracks as I had crossed a bridge the previous night while walking back to my hotel. Could this have been him?

The station was in chaos. The buses to Dallas and St. Louis had been cancelled. A woman sitting near me was on the phone to Greyhound customer services. Her phone was on speaker on her lap with that familiar jingle playing endlessly on a loop. Her head was in her hands. It looked like she might be crying. A Greyhound employee behind a counter faced with a queue of people called out to ask if there was a bus on Detroit Avenue (the address of the station). A guy looked out the window, 'No, ma'am. There is no bus.' The Greyhound employee rubbed her eyes. She looked utterly defeated. She knew that today, like most days, she would be talking to hundreds of people who risked losing jobs, who would be missing important occasions and appointments and would be put in terrible situations because their bus hadn't shown up. Oprah was on the TV talking to Alan Ruck, an actor from *Succession*. The canned laughter was like an insult. Nothing around us was funny.

Our bus left at 10.30 on a beautiful sunny Monday morning – about an hour later than scheduled. Our driver, who looked like Don Rickles, gave his spiel in a loud southern accent, without using the P.A. As he ran through the no smoking, no drinking, be respectful list, I noticed a cat in the parking lot. A man who looked like he hadn't eaten in days was kneeling next to it scooping some tinned food onto a plastic lid. The woman across the aisle from me told me that five or six kittens had been born in the parking lot. 'People look after them,' she said.

We were due in Amarillo at 16.20. I was looking forward to this drive because I knew what I was in for. The earth would be turning ochre and red, the light would travel for miles, illuminating telephone poles and creosote bushes and cottonwoods and farmhouses, draping everything with golden light. I was heading west, with its mountains and mesquite, its seemingly endless horizons and Kerouac's 'cool purple airs', the 'transmuting clouds of gold'.

So many of the Great Road Trip Books trace the author's journey from East to West, mimicking the history of European settlement. In doing so, the West becomes the destination, the dream, the candy-coloured future – both destiny and destination with its abrupt Pacific boundary. William Least Heat-Moon, who bucks this trend by hugging a circular route around the Lower 48, writes that,

> The true West differs from the East in one great, pervasive, influential, and awesome way: space. The vast openness changes the roads, towns, houses, farms, crops, machinery,

politics, economics, and, naturally, ways of thinking. How could it do otherwise? Space west of the line is perceptible and often palpable, especially when it appears empty, and it's that apparent emptiness which makes matter look alone, exiled, and unconnected. Those spaces diminish man and his constructions in a material fashion, it also – paradoxically – makes them more noticeable. *Things show up out here.* No one, not even the sojourner, escapes the expanses.

His use of the word 'apparent' with 'emptiness' is important. Least Heat-Moon is very much aware that these lands are not empty. In deserts, life can be difficult to observe because in order to survive, it has learnt how to hide. Against the odds, animals and plants thrive in deserts – it's just that most of us don't know enough to see this. N. Scott Momaday, the late Kiowa novelist and poet describes this sense of space in his 1969 Pulitzer Prize-winning novel *House Made of Dawn*:

In the morning sunlight the Vale Grande was dappled with the shadows of clouds and vibrant with rolling grass. The clouds were always there, huge, sharply described, and shining in the pure air. But the great feature of the valley was its size. It was almost too great for the eye to hold, strangely beautiful and full of distance. Such vastness makes for illusion, a kind of illusion that comprehends reality, and where it exists there is always wonder and exhilaration.

'A kind of illusion that comprehends reality' – how perfectly this describes the vastness of the West. Both Momaday and Least Heat-Moon express how the immense landscapes in this part of America make you feel at once smaller and more noticeable, a paradox that is perhaps part of the pull westwards so many of us feel.

224

These spaces ask questions of us; they demand that you work out your place on Earth, your relationship to the land, and how much or how little of it you will occupy, use or travel across. And there is a relief that comes with feeling we are not the centre of things; we aren't even close to it. This draw towards clarity and smallness, towards the deep geological time of a place stripped down to its essence, is an invitation to feel desire for a narrative of how to live on this planet. Deserts, like outer space, are places where time and space collide. The scrubby mesquite you see before you might only be three feet tall, but its roots have travelled down eighty feet under the ground and are sucking up water that fell in the form of raindrops 2,000 years before its seed had taken hold in the ground. No wonder deserts are where the mystics, visionaries, ascetics and searchers go to wander, to lose themselves and to find answers.

Least Heat-Moon writes that most people see desert 'as barren waste when they cross it' – it is what they might later describe at the motel bar as 'nothing'. But in the desert near Eldorado, Texas, the author gives himself the challenge of listing these great 'nothings' around him, from mockingbirds and mourning doves to coyotes and catclaws. He manages to name thirty living things in his direct line of vision. 'Had I waited until dark,' he writes, 'when the desert really comes to life, I could have done better.' So much for these 'empty' spaces we call deserts – spaces that are under threat from Lithium mines and solar panel arrays designed to preserve our lifestyles in an ever-expanding trajectory of consumption.

When I look out at the desert, I see a landscape I want to understand but for which I do not possess the vocabulary. When I read writing by people who are from the desert, I am made aware of my lack of connection to a

specific place. Scott Momaday writes, 'Not only did I discover an incomparable landscape in all of its colors and moods, but I discovered myself within it. From that time I have known that the sense of place is a dominant factor in my blood.'

Looking out of the Greyhound onto the mesas, buttes, canyons and riverbeds, I was aware that there is transcendence to be found here, that there are stories, myths and direct links between those living on this land and their ancestors. Where my suburban history is fragmented, my sense of belonging to a land non-existent, I have had – in material terms – a relatively comfortable life. But how important is comfort when it relies on extraction and exploitation for its existence? And how much more important is the meaning that stems from the knowledge of a land, the reassurance that comes from living in kinship with all living beings?

On the bus from Tulsa to Amarillo sat a Greyhound driver who'd just come off her shift. She was sitting diagonally opposite our driver, the Don Rickles lookalike. He pointed to a woman we passed as we pulled out of the kitten-strewn parking lot. 'See that woman with the two-wheeled trolley? I've taken her on my bus lots. She rides everywhere! Dallas, El Paso, everywhere!'

'Yeah, I've taken her to Mexico,' the off-duty driver said.

'Yup, she rides all the time. Everywhere.'

'Hey, didn't you drive to Abilene to pick up a cat?'

'Yup, my girls wanted it. Once they closed the station, I knew that cat would need somewhere to go.'

Meanwhile, two girls behind me who were also watching the parking lot cat being fed sang out in unison, 'Bye kitty, bye kitty.'

I was fascinated by the two Greyhound drivers talking shop. They both agreed that the showers in Amarillo stink. 'It's dirty'.

'Where do you stay when you're in Amarillo?' Don Rickles asked.

'In the dorms. You're not supposed to, but...'

'They kind of turn a blind eye?'

'I don't even know about that. Maybe they just don't notice.'

The two girls behind me who bade farewell to the 'kitty' were making friends with another child on the bus, maybe five or six years old, who was sucking on a baby bottle.

'Do you have a cat?' they asked her. She shook her head. 'You should get a cat.'

The girl with the baby bottle said, 'No way. They smell.'

'Not as much as a dog.'

As we approached Clinton, still clinging to Route 66, hills emerged and iron oxides in the soil began to glow under the bright sun. Dark clouds suddenly rolled in and rain began to lash the window. It all happened so quickly.

Don Rickles' phone rang. It was another driver warning him of upcoming weather.

'Yeah, we're being battered here too by the wind, bro.'

We pulled up at a Sayre Travel Stop. It was one of those indiscriminate places built to service the most basic needs along with the extraneous ones we've come to expect, like those ubiquitous walls of refrigerated, brightly coloured variations of water, sugar, food colouring, chemicals and caffeine wrapped in plastic bottles. Although we were in Oklahoma, we could have been anywhere on the continent. There was a Denny's and an array of cheap fast-food options. Lorries were parked next to a sign which outlined the rates for showers and overnight stays for truckers.

I bought an orange juice and got back on the bus. Sitting there watching the rain and the cars come and go, I got that sense of being suspended that sometimes hits me, as if I am separated from reality. It's akin to that sensation when you wake up and it takes a while to realize where you are. It's a feeling I have always loved and one that is increasingly rare in our hyperconnected world. Thankfully, I was out of cell phone service, so I could revel properly in this sensation of being slightly lost, uncontactable, weightless.

We got back on the highway and the two drivers continued their chat.

Don Rickles: 'Half my family is in the funeral business. The other half are in transportation.'

'Interesting.'

Don Rickles: 'So I grew up doing both. I had to spend twenty minutes cleaning my windshield before I could get this bus going. Those guys who work in the stations, I love the lot of them, but my grandfather would have fired them. I mean look at this dirt. It's nasty! El Paso is great though. They clean your gears for you. Amarillo is OK.'

'Yeah.'

'So I got my new contract. I read it upside down and sideways and it didn't make sense. I signed it anyway and realized I got sold down the river.'

'I'm glad we got a union. They serve their purpose. You got a union rep in Tulsa?'

Don Rickles: 'No! There's only three of us.'

'Did you hear about that driver who was three and a half hours late because people kept smoking on her bus? She had to keep pulling over. They had her crying. It was terrible. A few of the passengers had just gotten out of prison and wanted to get home.'

The rain continued and the dry ground looked grateful for it. Wind farms started to rise up on the horizon as well as those iconic, old-fashioned windmills. We'd passed the Oklahoma–Texas state line and more clouds gathered. Giant, 3-D ones.

I knew we were getting close to Groom, Texas because I could just see hovering on the horizon, the 60-metre cross erected by The Cross of Our Lord Jesus Christ Ministries. As we drove past, no one commented. I remembered on my previous trip how a passenger had exclaimed, 'Sheesh, look at that!' which got me looking out the window. 'We must be gone to heaven,' someone said. To which a guy sitting near me replied, 'If this is heaven, then I got on the wrong bus!'

These somewhat anarchic, communal bus-wide conversations had lessened over the years. Most people were now plugged into their devices, barely aware of the passengers around them.

Dark brown earth spread out before us, parting like a sea for the bus to sail through. The rain continued. Train tracks appeared as we approached Amarillo. We pulled into town on the dot of 16.24. Our driver had made up the time from our late start. He was a pro. It was 20 March, the vernal equinox, but there would be no moon tonight. The wind had risen, clouds had formed. The swirling dust in the air obscured the sun. In my three-minute walk from the bus station to the Downtown Marriott I saw more homeless people than I had during two days in Tulsa. One man was rolling around on the sidewalk, oblivious. His trousers were down to his knees. The combination of bad weather and the boarded-up shops meant the streets were almost empty. The wind had deposited plastic bags in the branches of street trees. Bits of metal had dislodged from the streetlights and were clanging in the wind, adding an eerie soundtrack.

I had decided to splurge on an expensive hotel in Amarillo – my room at the Courtyard Marriott was $125 – which astonishingly was $55 cheaper than the horror show of a motel in St. Louis. When I'd booked this one, there wasn't much choice available unless I wanted to stay on the edge of town. Once you added the price of a taxi to the cost of a motel room on the outskirts, you might as well just stay somewhere a bit more expensive within walking distance of the Greyhound station. The Marriott had taken up residence in the ten-storey Gothic Revival Fisk Building. Built in 1928, it was one of many handsome brick and stone buildings constructed from the spoils of the petroleum boom. Like Tulsa, Amarillo gave off a feeling that it had once been seriously lubricated by a combination of the extraction of raw materials and oil, along with a newly built railway to distribute these commodities.

After dropping my bag off in my room, I walked across the road to a Mexican restaurant. A waiter approached, 'For just one?'

As we were having this short exchange a young woman reared up from behind me, in her early twenties with a slender frame, false eyelashes and heavy make-up. She was getting stuff out of her pockets. 'For my ID, I have this,' she said slurring her words. Bits of paper helicoptered to the ground as she retrieved her ID. She fell over while trying to pick them up. She got herself up and the waiter looked confused. She held a scrap of paper in front of him, 'It's a police report,' she said. 'You can use them for ID.' I had noticed some of her cards were still on the floor. I collected them and handed them to her. It took her several seconds to focus on what I was holding in my

hands. 'I was here before you,' she said.

'Yes, I know. These are yours,' I held them out.

'That's my ID.'

As I turned to leave, the waiter shouted over the woman's pleas for alcohol, 'You're not staying for supper?'

'Um, I might be back.'

I couldn't find anywhere else open downtown, so I ate in my hotel. I was the only person there. Back in my room, Josef von Sternberg's *The Last Command* was just starting on Turner Classic Movies. A momentary escape I was grateful for. I was exhausted and fell asleep before the final credits rolled.

In the morning I found a little café called the Palace Coffee Shop. As I ordered a coffee, the guy behind the counter asked me what I was doing in Amarillo. I told him and he replied that he'd never ridden on a Greyhound bus.

'Oh, you should. You'll see a whole other side of the US.'

I noticed that all the plates, cups and cutlery were either made of crockery or metal. My scone was served on what looked like a vintage tray from an Easy-Bake oven. I commented on this. The server, whose name was Jayson, replied that they were trying to be plastic-free.

The sun appeared despite huge panhandle clouds scudding along in the wind. Jayson told me I had to go to Aunt Eek's on 6th Street in the San Jacinto District, which was full of small independent businesses. Confusingly, 6th Street (which on the map is called 6th Avenue) is part of the old Route 66. There was no public transportation to get me there, so it would have to be another Uber. It was only 9.15 when I got to San Jacinto and many of the shops hadn't opened. Patty, my Uber driver, wasn't comfortable letting me off as there were people wandering, stumbling

and weaving their way down the middle of the road and along the sidewalks. It was bright and sunny and I didn't feel in any way in danger, but Patty wouldn't hear of it. She drove me around and we chatted while waiting for the shops to open.

Apparently, Amarillo has a crime problem: incidents of assault, murder and rape are much higher than the national average – almost double, I was told. For the past few years, those figures have been falling, but I could understand Patty's reluctance to let me out on an almost empty street with my backpack. Once we saw a shop put out its sandwich board, Patty was satisfied that I would be fine, so I hopped out at the 6th Street Mall where I met the owner, Chip Hunt, who on top of running the largest store in Amarillo was also running for local councillor. Chip compensated for the lack of conversation on this trip. She was keen to share stories from the hunting excursions she'd been on with her ex-husband. Once, while hunting with him and some of his buddies, she saw them train their sites on a fawn. Chip was in the car and honked the horn so hard it scared the animal away. A bullet grazed its shoulder but it managed to escape unharmed. Chip was banned from hunting with them ever again. She was crazy about animals.

'My strangest encounter was at the vet's,' she told me. 'I was sitting in there with one of my dogs, Doctor Schultz, and a guy was in there, all tattooed and pierced. On a leash he had an ocelot. It was maybe six months old. It came over to me and put its paws on my shoulders and started purring. I looked into those eyes, I can't even describe it. They were so beautiful, the colour of celadon. That fur was softer than the silkiest satin made by human hands. It was life-changing.' She paused. 'Apparently the ocelot came from some people who were "eccentric,"' she said, making quotation marks in the air with her fingers. 'By that, I mean they were actually crazy but rich enough to be called "eccentric". They also had camels and zebras, all kinds of wild cats. Anyway, the guy in the vet's was trying to get the ocelot off me and I kept saying "No, it's fine. The cat is beautiful."' He then told her that he'd had the ocelot defanged and declawed. 'You should be shot!' she told him. 'I mean, who does such a thing?'

I said goodbye to Chip and wandered down 6th Street, which was lined with tattoo parlours, a derelict gas station, the Broken Spoke Bar, a pottery shop, a bakery, housewares, diners and shops selling potpourri and scented candles. Many had the 'Route 66' sign in their windows. The vibe was 'crafty biker'.

My energy was flagging. It was getting warmer and I had too much to physically carry. I had travelled 1,300 miles with over a thousand to go. I was also interrogating my intentions. What was I doing? Why was I here? On my previous trip, I had the sadness of my losses, I had a novel to write which persuaded me that I needed to keep going for the sake of the story. The book's first title was *Slow Road*, but my agent at the time thought it sounded too negative. 'Who wants to read a book with "slow" in the title?' he asked me. It didn't matter that I did. Then I changed the title to 'The Great Tulsa Coin Toss', and then eventually to 'Tulsa' which Karl liked because it was 'a slut' backwards. Several agents had shopped it around. No one bit. So, the manuscript went back in the drawer, where it still sits.

On this second trip, I became acutely aware that moving from one place to another was becoming less of a possibility for many. The appification of society is forcing a shift towards online ticket sales and queries. Many Greyhound stations do still exist, and in some you can purchase a ticket from a human without showing ID, but this is changing. Stations, now seen as prime real estate, are being sold off, transactions are being encouraged via the Greyhound app, and those who cannot afford a smartphone or who struggle to navigate mobile banking will be left behind. All this combined with the increasing closures of public spaces, a lack of public transport, a diminishing of affordable amenities, the non-existence of drinking water and clean bathrooms – or in many places, any bathrooms at all – is yet more evidence that the material world is being supplanted by the digital. Around me, so much seemed to be crumbling – not just the people but the physical spaces around us. Why, for instance, when the Greyhound stations ripped out their telephones, did they leave the ghost prints of the old one, the wires, the holes in the wall? Couldn't they have painted over those ghostly markings? Maybe put up a poster? Why, when they removed the vending machines selling microwave-able food, did they leave the microwaves in place, sitting broken, with their doors hanging off? Why had they ripped out so many water fountains and replaced them with half-empty machines selling overpriced coloured drinks and water bottled in plastic by PepsiCo and Coca-Cola? Why had most of the diners in the stations closed? Why did it feel like the whole Greyhound enterprise was coming to an end? And, why were there so many people lying on the ground?

¶ I got to the Amarillo bus station early. My bag was heavy and the constant hum of despondency all around me was wearing me down. My lips were chapped and dry from the sun and wind and I was relieved that I could indulge in a large drink of water before the measly four-hour ride to Albuquerque.

When I walked into the bus station, I was hit by a foul smell. A woman with half a dozen carrier bags seemed to be the source. I imagined something dead in one of her bags. It had to be; this was the stench of death. I turned and walked out, hoping selfishly that these bags were not coming with us to Albuquerque. I wandered around downtown taking photos, feeling unmoored, and not in a good way. Amarillo was getting me down. Outside, the only people on the street were looking for a fix. The old restaurant in the bus terminal was closed. Cupping my hands around my face, I pressed my nose against the glass. At one time, this had been a classic streamlined mid-century modern diner with Formica counters and booths. Anything nice or functional seemed to be out of bounds now, forbidden, broken. Let everyone sit on the curb or the floor. Don't allow them the dignity of a chair or a glass of water or cup of coffee. It's cheaper to let everyone fend for themselves. The material world where most of us dwelled was being ground to dust or turned to shit right before our eyes.

Much of the hope I had seen in 2006 had evaporated. Worsening climate disasters, a global economic crash, meth, fentanyl and every other opioid, Covid, zero healthcare, the relocation of human transactions and experiences to the digital sphere, all of it felt like a tsunami that had been gathering in size and strength for months, years, decades. We were now living in the devastation

left in its wake. I was beginning to see the United States as a failed experiment. I had grown up loving the place, I had lived in New York, Boston and Missoula, Montana. I have as much family and as many friends in the US as I do in Canada. So many places are like home to me there. But I was starting to lose faith in the whole project, in the adventure called 'America'.

I noticed Carrier Bag Woman had left the bus station. I went inside and spotted a box of donuts on the counter with a hand-written sign, 'HELP YOURSELF'. Behind the counter was the pony-tailed manager in a smart Greyhound shirt, jeans, a goatee and John Lennon glasses. He came out from behind the counter and picked up a pair of boots next to where I was sitting.

'These yours?' he asked.

'Nope. They're really nice boots, though.'

'Yup. But gotta send them to Dallas where everything goes that gets left behind.'

I asked if he knew when my bus would be showing up.

'It's running late,' he said. Apparently, it needed a service.

'They're always late, it seems.'

'Let me tell you, the company is falling apart. They're being taken over by FlixBus', he added, referring to FlixMobility, the parent company who bought Greyhound from FirstGroup in October 2021, who had previously bought it from Laidlaw – all of them running into financial problems. 'FlixBus are European', the manager told me. 'They don't understand ticket counters and the size of the US and the like.'

'Are they taking over all of Greyhound?'

'They're not changing the name. That's iconic. It's so American.'

I told him that on my travels many of the employees

seemed at the end of their tether. He nodded.

'You know, I suffer from social anxiety. I'm an intro-vert. I applied for a job working at this counter and they promoted me to manager two weeks ago. I feel blessed to have this job.'

He continued to tell me about his family. His mum had worked in an IHOP but quit because the boss had been hitting on her, so she went and waitressed at a Waffle House. 'That's where she met my stepdad. He used to sit in her section. And, well, that's how it happened.'

'Like a movie,' I replied.

'Yeah, except she was married.'

'Even more like a movie.'

He laughed. The whole time we'd been chatting, he was cleaning the station, sweeping, picking up rubbish, wiping the seats with a cloth.

'The station is so clean,' I said.

'Yeah, it's about taking pride in it and dealing with the people as people, being one of them. I wouldn't want a dirty station if I were a passenger!'

My bus was the last one scheduled for the evening. The station would be closing for the night once it had come and gone. The manager went over to a guy sleeping on a row of seats. He crouched down to his level and spoke to the man gently.

'Hey, sir, you can't stay here all night 'cuz I gotta close the station.'

'I know,' the man replied, his eyes still closed.

'But I can help you get to the Salvation Army. You can at least get a coffee.'

'No, it's OK. I'll just go outside when you close.'

'You're just going to go outside?'

'That's right.'

The tenderness of the manager and the acceptance of

the man on the row of seats that he'd have to just go and sit outside touched me. I could feel tears rising.

I took a break to go to the bathroom. This was where I was confronted with shit smeared on the walls. The place stank of human excrement. It was shocking and depressing. I wasn't sure whether to bring it up with the manager, but then again, I sensed he would rather know. I went over to him and told him in a very apologetic way.

'Oh, man,' he said looking genuinely upset. 'I'll get it sorted. It's not the first time.'

'Why would someone do that?' I asked.

He shrugged and went off to get gloves and cleaning supplies. A few minutes later he came over to where I was sitting. 'All done.'

'Oh, God,' I said. 'You shouldn't have to do that kind of thing.'

'It's part of the job.' He asked me about my trip. Why I was travelling. How I found the Greyhound buses these days.

I told him that one of the hardest things was organizing my trip so as not to arrive super late in the downtowns of cities. Bus routes didn't line up like they used to and there were no longer any cross-country passes.

'I hear you,' he said. 'So, did you spend the night in Amarillo?'

'Yes,'

'Why would you do that? It's the murder capital of the country!'

I had heard this a few times although I wasn't sure it was true.

'Well, my bus got in around 4.30 yesterday and it just made sense to get some sleep and leave today. I wanted to see a bit of Amarillo.'

'But it's a dangerous town.'

245

He told me about his half-brother who worked at the Tyson processing plant.

'What do they process?'

'Beef. And sometimes pigs and chickens get trucked in. At twenty-six, he was making $28.50 an hour. They sent him to college to study engineering. Now they've offered him a permanent job. He'll be thirty-one in July and he's got a good job.'

On my previous trip to Amarillo, the wind had been blowing in just the right direction for the town to be permeated with the smell of cow shit from the nearby feedlots. I had booked myself into the cheapest motel within walking distance of the station: the Civic Center Inn. My room was 40 bucks and it was only much later that I was able to find accurate feedback for the motel on TripAdvisor: '1 star. We got robbed it was horrible. Some dude took our money and tried to beat us up.' (The Civic Center Inn has since closed.)

During the short walk to my motel, I had tried to ignore the stench, but it was overwhelming. I could smell it inside my room. I could smell it inside my bathroom. I could smell it everywhere. Amarillo sits right in the middle of the Texas Panhandle, which produces a fifth of America's beef supply. In this part of Texas, cows outnumber people by 40 to 1. That smell, which is a well-known 'thing', seeps into Amarillo from 45 miles away where the notorious Southwest Feed Yards hold 45,000 head of cattle captive in bare-dirt pens.

Cattle in this part of Texas are force-fed as quickly as possible until they are fat enough to be slaughtered. It used to take a cow five years to grow large enough to be sent to the abattoir. Now, with antibiotics, growth hormones and a sedentary existence in a small pen, a calf

can go from 220 to 590 kilos in a mere six months and be ready for slaughter in 18. What I was smelling in Amarillo was not simply the manure from these intensively raised animals, it was 'faecal dust' – tiny particles of cow shit that get swept up and carried on the wind. As drought in the Southwest intensifies, so does the dust. It sometimes gets so bad here that the sun is subsumed into a giant brownish grey cloud and motorists use their headlights to see the lines on the road even in the daytime.

Between 2008 and 2017, over 100 complaints were lodged with the Texas Commission on Environmental Quality (TCEQ) about the smell and the dust from these feedlots. It's not just the odour that is a problem; there are associated health risks with industrial-scale cattle farms. Breathing in ammonia and other chemical particulates in cow manure is known to contribute to asthma, lung disease and heart problems. From 2014 to 2019 – despite people getting sick – the TCEQ took no action against any large feedlots in the Panhandle, issued no warnings and handed out no fines. Meanwhile, more facilities are being built.

The scale of these feedlots is hard to imagine. Harder so because, in 2013, legislators in Texas passed a bill that made it illegal to photograph them from the air. A trip via Google Earth to Hereford in Deaf Smith County, which lies to the west of Amarillo and is known as the 'beef capital of the world', gives you some idea of the scale. The hundreds of cattle pens that make up a feedlot are giant brown strips, like lined-up boxcars or shipping containers. The organic shapes around them are pools of manure – millions of tons of the stuff. These shit lagoons come in all shapes and colours. The shades of emerald, maroon, turquoise and oxblood come from the composition of the various chemicals used by the cattle farmers to break down the urine and manure as it drains into creeks, rivers, soil and groundwater. According to the Food and Environment Reporting Network, one feedlot can produce over a ton of manure in a year. Some of this is stomped on by hooves and machinery and then baked in the Texas sun to a fine powder. This is what I was smelling in Amarillo. But this is also where it gets complicated. You can be resolutely against the mass manufacture of animals, the cruelty and the ecological devastation are inarguable – and yet when the manager of the Greyhound bus station in Amarillo told me about his half-brother getting a job in a place that processes this stuff, a job with healthcare (the Holy Grail for millions of Americans) I felt genuinely happy for him. Very few of us can escape from participating in a society that has been built upon extraction and consumption if we want to survive in it.

In the 1960s and 1970s, when feedlots began operating in the Panhandle, the Ogallala Aquifer was seen as an almost inexhaustible source of water. Spanning eight states – Texas, New Mexico, Oklahoma, Kansas, Colorado, Wyoming, Nebraska and South Dakota – it provides 82 per cent of the drinking water for the 2.3 million people who live in the High Plains. If the water from it were spread across all 50 states, it would come up well past your ankles. It is indeed enormous, but like all earthly resources, it is finite. It is full of geologic water – fresh water found in the Earth's crust – meaning that when it's gone, it's gone. If emptied, it would take 6,000 years to replenish. This giant underground water reserve is one of the most depleted groundwater sources in the country. The tens of thousands of cattle squeezed into Panhandle feedlots suck 8.5 million gallons of groundwater from it per day. As the West gets drier, as wildfires get more extreme, as previously snow-capped mountains now display bare rock at their summits, fresh water is more precious, and it will become even more so in the future. The ground here is being poisoned with hormones from cattle feed and the run-off from chemical-laced manure, all to keep America in hamburgers – that's the smell of Amarillo. It is the smell of Big Ag, intensive cattle farming and unfettered greed.

Like many issues around land in the United States, the people backing destructive practices are livestock lobbyists like the Texas Cattle Feeders Association (TCFA). They oversee 6 million head of cattle in Texas, Oklahoma and New Mexico, which adds up to 28 per cent of the beef eaten in the US. Not only does the TCFA donate to political parties, they also sponsor academic research while aggressively attacking scientists who don't agree with their findings. Their most famous attack was in 1998 when, bizarrely, they went after Oprah Winfrey. She had aired a piece on her TV show about food safety in which her guest, Howard Lyman, a Montana farmer, vegetarian and animal rights activist, spoke about Mad Cow Disease in the UK and added that it was a matter of time before bovine spongiform encephalopathy reached American cattle. Winfrey's response was to state that she would never eat another hamburger. This was enough for the TCFA to sue her for $10 million in damages, because her statement on live TV contributed, they believed, to a drop in the price of beef. In February 1998, Winfrey took the witness stand in a packed Amarillo courtroom along with members of the public, journalists and her friend Maya Angelou. In the crowd outside, people sported T-shirts reading: 'The only mad cow in Texas is Oprah.' Despite concerns that the jury would be stacked with beef-supporting locals, they voted unanimously in her favour.

Then, in 2016, two scientists from Texas Tech University in Lubbock discovered antibiotic-resistant bacteria in some of the faecal dust being blown from feedlots. *Texas Monthly* reported that the TCFA allegedly went after these scientists by first requesting that they keep their research to themselves and then eventually attempting to get them fired. Writing in the *Texas Observer*, Christopher Collins added that, 'Cattle feedlots, along with poultry and pork megafarms, are protected by a "right to farm" law, which shields them from legal action that might be taken against them by neighbors. Ostensibly enacted to protect family farmers from urban sprawl, the laws instead disenfranchise rural people in favor of big agribusiness.' When it comes to the beef industry, very few people can stop cattle farmers from spewing tons of chemical-laden manure into the water table, nor can they be prevented from allowing the wind to spread toxic faecal dust across 'cattle country'. All the while, in the background, these hundreds of thousands of cows do what is asked of them and suck the little remaining water from an aquifer that should be treated as the miracle it is – a body of pure water lying under land that is drying up, losing its topsoil and becoming infertile at an alarming rate.

We boarded the Albuquerque-bound bus in Amarillo at 6.50 p.m., only 90 minutes late. I got a seat by myself, which is as close to comfortable as you can get on a Greyhound. My window, however, had been smashed. Normally there are two layers of glass in a bus window, but mine had only one – the outside one. All that was left of the inside pane of glass was a necklace of pointy shards sticking out of the rubberized edge of the window frame. A blue-grey sky, mostly overcast, revealed tiny strips of pink and orange on the other side of the single pane of glass.

Two teenagers sat across the aisle from me. The girl asked the guy what the smell was.

'It's the cow shit,' he replied.

I hadn't noticed it on this trip, but perhaps they'd been to a part of town I hadn't, where the wind had carried faecal dust in their direction.

A woman sitting in front of them turned to face them, 'My dad worked with cattle.'

The teenager replied, 'I couldn't do it. When the smell gets bad, I throw up.'

We headed off westwards, the horizon darkening as it filled with cattle.

I remembered this landscape: the black dots huddling in groups that eventually turned into giant smudges against the pale, trampled ground. On my last trip, the bus was packed. Three small kids got on the bus trailing after their mother like ducklings down the central aisle. Their mother, who used a walking frame, placed their bags on the shelf above their seats, but every few minutes one of the kids would ask for something to eat or play with. The mother kept having to stand up and was clearly in pain, but her kids didn't stop asking for stuff. She begged them to be quiet while simultaneously handing them enormous bags of Oreos and cans of soft drink. We were all listening to the sugar bubble up in them as their energy levels teetered on manic.

As we passed a cattle ranch as long as a freight train, the mother with the small kids said, 'Hey, look kids, that's where they make meat!' As one of her daughters stood up to stare at this gigantic beef factory, I noticed her T-shirt:

252

The light dimmed over the dry ground of the plains. I watched through my broken window as every now and then a canyon appeared like a mirage, a hallucination. A disembodied voice behind me asked what all the windmills were for.

The teenager said, 'They're for power.'

'That must be expensive for the farmer.'

'They don't pay for it, the taxpayers do,' he replied.

There is so much sky here. When it's overcast and leaden it feels oppressive, like someone shouting in your face. I was happy to be getting out of Amarillo.

We were motoring along Route 66 and, as we passed a ghost town called Boise, the sunset lit up the horizon like an explosion. The slanting sun, the red earth as we headed west. It was astonishing. As soon as we crossed the border from Texas into New Mexico, my cell phone lost reception. This felt right. I remembered that it was here at Tucumcari, just beyond the Texas–New Mexico border, that our driver had reminded us to turn our clocks back an hour. They don't do that anymore. I guess they assume we all have phones to update the change automatically. By Santa Rosa the ground had morphed from flat prairies to rocky, scrubby land.

The lights on the bus didn't work (of course) so I plugged myself into some Townes Van Zandt and watched the sky darken. We stopped at an inspection station. The disembodied voice again: 'They're looking for drugs. It would be hilarious if they found crack on this bus!' No one laughed. No drugs were found and we went on our way.

The landscape was changing. My journal notes from

2006 start to fall apart somewhat: 'Buttes and mesas rise like magic. Sagebrush. Creosote. Slabs of rock. Solitary mountains appear every now and then. Bushes. What are they? They look like little Christmas trees: bushy at the bottom and tapering towards the top like tear drops. There are stepped buttes here. As the sun dips, they turn purple. They are evenly spaced as if they know just how much room they need, as if they are each other's perfect neighbours. Beautiful mountain at Tucumcari. The highway has narrowed. The road is bumpy. Neck-jarring potholes. There is NO suspension on this bus. The bumps are insane! There is a small, solitary cloud.'

Because of my broken window and the single pane of untinted glass, I could watch the stars as they appeared. One by one and then suddenly millions of them, as if someone had turned on a switch that sent them scattering all the way down to the horizon. I looked out the window on the other side of the bus, and it was so much dimmer. All this time, I hadn't noticed how the darkened glass on a Greyhound cuts out an incredible amount of detail and brightness. As I admired the brilliance of the stars and counted myself lucky to have chosen the seat with the broken window, I thought, 'Ah, well, at least we haven't screwed *them* up.' And then I remembered all the space junk and Elon Musk's SpaceX programme and the 60 Starlink satellites he launched in 2019. It is getting increasingly difficult for astronomers to study space with all the light and debris up there. Musk is planning to launch 42,000 more satellites into orbit, making the study of the cosmos even more difficult. Nothing seems out of reach of our greed.

As we crested a hill, the lights of Albuquerque appeared in the distance. At that moment, the Handsome

Family's 'A Beautiful Thing' came up on my playlist. I'd been to a record shop on Central Avenue when I was last in Albuquerque. I had had a chat with the guy behind the counter. He is described in my 2006 journal as 'friendly cute'. Like so many people I was meeting back then, he wanted to talk, and began with the usual preliminaries: where was I from, how long would I be in Albuquerque, what was I doing here. It was my turn to ask him something: 'Why are there no Handsome Family CDs in the store when they live in Albuquerque?' It turned out that Brett, who was half of the Handsome Family, had lived for a while in this shop and knew the owner. But Friendly Cute Guy told me that 'Americans like their folk-country gritty and real, and by the way, they're not *from* here, they're from Chicago.' Just as I was thinking about this exchange, their song, 'The Giant of Illinois' came on.

In my 2006 journal, I find a list.

GREYHOUND BUS ETIQUETTE
AS OBSERVED IN APRIL 2006

Lights off at night (however dim they may be).
People need to sleep.
[In 2023 there are no overhead lights, so this is
no longer a problem.]

Share your cigarettes and carry spares for others.
[People rarely smoke now. It's too expensive and
vapes have taken over.]

After you chat, say, 'Well, it was nice meeting
you.' If you've been chatting with a middle-aged
woman wearing sensible shoes and dangling earrings, be prepared for a hug.
[Not anymore. Many of the niceties seem to have

fallen away. There are fewer conversations between
strangers and definitely no hugs or touching.]

If the driver pulls out quickly or makes an errat-
ic move and a passenger is standing up, shout out
to them to 'Be Careful!' and hold your arms out
in case you need to catch them. There is a passen-
ger-driver dynamic based on a low-level animosity
from the passengers towards the driver.
[Most people are staring at their devices and
don't notice the other passengers.]

If you stop at a McDonald's and a young woman is
travelling with a kid and doesn't buy anything,
you buy a snack and give it to them and you say,
'A little something for your kid'.
[This was once true but seems to be no longer.]

Also if a woman is travelling on her own with a
kid, play with the kid to give this woman a break.
Get out a pencil and play tic-tac-toe or whatever
and if the woman falls asleep, someone else will
take over when you've had enough. Basically, pass
the kid around. I never saw men travelling alone
with kids.
[I didn't see this on my recent trip. I wonder
if one of Covid's many lasting legacies will be a
reluctance to touch others or get physically close
to them. Or maybe it's now seen as suspicious to
take an interest, however well-meaning or innocent, in other people's kids.]

Do not talk on your cell phone. No one does this.
[Yes they do, but not too often, thankfully.
However, games and films are played with the sound
up. If you complain, you might get a tirade from
an angry gamer.]

¶ We got into Albuquerque at 10.30 at night. I breathed in the crisp desert air and remembered how much I liked this city. The last time I was here, I arrived on Good Friday and walked to the Hotel Blue, which at 69 bucks a night was more than I had been spending on motel rooms that trip. But after my sleepless night in Amarillo and the constant smell of shit, I had wanted a good night's sleep. I also needed to process what I had seen outside Amarillo: the feedlots, the dry ground, the pens full of cows tortured and hidden from view, the obvious severing of our connection to the non-humans we share the land with – land that had been stolen and was being trampled, sucked dry and poisoned.

This time, I wanted something different from Albuquerque, though I wasn't sure what. Or maybe I didn't want much at all. I wasn't writing a novel. My days of miscarriages were over. The jagged edges of my grief over the loss of my sister had been worn smooth. I was moving through time and space as an older woman. I realized this trip had become more of an observational journey. As a fifty-something female I was near invisible. And in retrospect I was so shocked by the state of the people among whom I was travelling that any search I thought I was undertaking was subsumed by the existence of so much suffering around me. It was difficult to see beyond that.

The Econo Lodge in downtown Albuquerque was on Central Avenue (AKA Route 66), tucked under the raised lanes of the I-25. It was far from fancy and when I told a friend of a friend who lives in Albuquerque where I was staying, she was alarmed. I was greeted by Bobby, a man in his seventies, working the night desk. He asked where I was from and when I said London, he told me that his surname was Lovelace and that his ancestors were from Kent.

'Like Ada Lovelace?' I asked.

'Oh, yes and the poet Richard Lovelace. I have some of his books of poetry. I'd like to get over to Kent to visit but I'm too old now. I wish I'd been able to go when I was younger.' He paused while I signed the hotel's admission form. 'But that Ada Lovelace, she was a smart girl. She really put women on the map.'

We chatted a bit more about Ada and the first computers and Babbage and how maybe he could get himself over to Kent. And then Bobby told me where my room was. 'You were originally way over there,' he said pointing across the very dark parking lot with the ubiquitous human shapes huddled in shadows. 'But I've moved you closer to the front desk. You're travelling on your own, so you'll feel safer in this one.'

I thanked him and we said our goodnights. Bobby was the reason you stayed in places like this, although the Bobbys were becoming rarer.

I opened the door of my Econo Lodge room to that familiar cheap motel smell: part bedbug spray, part Lysol, part old carpets. I thought about the bumps on the road and the enormous star-filled sky and how the Handsome Family songs had come on just as Albuquerque appeared on the horizon and how it all felt timeless somehow. This is the feeling I get whenever I pass the 100th longitudinal meridian – the light changes, the horizon retreats, the emerald greens turn minty, and my heart opens a little. At the Texas panhandle, the ground takes on a deep red hue, and by the time you reach New Mexico, the colours have become psychedelic. You've arrived in the West. Even at night, in the dark, you can feel this expansiveness. This is why I'm here.

I woke the next morning after terrible nightmares. In my dreams a woman fell from the top step of the bus and her head smashed on the pavement. Jason was travelling with me in the dream and I was telling him about what had happened, that this woman was dead. 'Her head was flattened!' I repeated. He wouldn't believe me. The women in the dream, both the Cassandra figure and the one with the flattened head, were me. The Cassandra in me was seeing things that most people do not see or do not want to see: the desperation, the sheer volume of people with nowhere to go, the lack of hope, the 'progress' being trumpeted at us from our phones (*You're almost there, just give us a few more details!*), from posters on walls (*Check us out online or download our simple app!*) and the utopianism beamed from the TVs (*And, you too can make money, lose weight, overcome your addiction; just call this number or download our app!*). The other woman in my dream, the one with the caved-in head, was the woman I once was when I last passed through Albuquerque. She was the younger, more naïve, more open, and perhaps freer version of me, but she was no longer.

Wandering outside my motel room that morning, I looked around to get my bearings. There was an empty swimming pool in the parking lot. The sun was harsh; the shadows hard-edged. The little lobby was also the breakfast room with cereal, milk, juice and the ubiquitous waffle-maker of many American motels. Like the elderly guest sitting on his own, I opted for the Bran Flakes. A young woman appeared with a stuffed animal. She placed the little dog on a chair and went and made herself a waffle. Every plate, bowl, cup and utensil was plastic or Styrofoam. My mind went to the fiery toxic blast in Ohio and the many toxic spills that never get reported.

264

A TV blared in the corner. It was 22 March, the day after Trump – according to other TV news shows I had glimpsed on my travels – was supposed to have been arrested. The people on the morning news in Albuquerque gesticulated madly and spoke like cult-leaders trying to rally their followers. But we all just ate our breakfast, watched the dust motes, and thought quietly about our day ahead. Wondering what the real world would be bringing to us today.

I was running out of clean clothes so I decided to revisit the laundromat I had been to on my last visit. Karl washes her clothes there before spending the night in a hostel near the Hotel Blue with Ben, a guy she had met on the bus. He tries to steal her stuff to buy meth but she rumbles him. They travel together to Vegas where they end up sleeping together in the Bridger Hotel. Karl, unsure of her sexuality, had been a virgin until their night together in Vegas. He leaves early the next morning on a bus to Phoenix and Karl begins to understand that she is attracted to women more than men. In small-town Ontario, you are expected to go to prom with a nice boy and then marry him. This will not be Karl's trajectory.

The Hotel Blue, where I'd stayed before, was now closed. It had this message on its sign:

```
EDDIE
  THE WORD
     IS
     *LLUVIA*
```

This was most likely a reference to the salsa song 'Lluvia', meaning 'rain', which was famously interpreted by the Puerto Rican singer Eddie Santiago. Beyond that, I had no idea why it was there in huge letters outside a

266

closed-down hotel in downtown Albuquerque. In the park across the road from the Hotel Blue, a man had constructed a shelter out of two shopping trolleys, rags and boxes. It looked like it was about to rain. I wondered how well his shelter would hold if a storm were to hit.

The Wash Tub laundromat hadn't changed. Still sparkling clean with magazines laid out for customers, huge washers and dryers and a cheerful woman running the show. With my backpack full of clean clothes, I went off to see if Java Joe's was still there. It was. I got a coffee and took it outside to a table on the pavement.

Two young guys were sitting at another table. They were the outdoorsy type, all checks and Carhartt and North Face. One of them called out to me, 'The coffee's great here.'

'Yes, I've been here before.' Then I recognized him. 'You were on my bus yesterday!'

He blinked at me wondering if I might be a little weird. His friend tapped him on the arm and added, as if to remind him, 'The Greyhound that got in at 9.30.'

'It was supposed to. It actually got in at 10.40.' A detail I added to let them know I wasn't making it up.

The guy who'd been on the bus was called Scotty, his friend was Jonathan. Scotty said, 'Yeah, I'm never doing that again. Too many crazies.'

'That was actually a good ride. No drama. Only an hour and ten minutes late. No breakdowns.'

'Yeah, I guess it wasn't too bad. But all those dogs!'

'I only saw one. That huge one.'

'There was also a chihuahua in a little basket.'

I laughed. I hadn't seen the chihuahua.

'From now on, it's Amtrak or flying.'

Jonathan asked me what I was doing in Albuquerque.

He had grown up here. 'People are always complaining about the city, but it's got the same problems as everywhere else,' he told me.

'Like what problems?' I asked. He stayed silent. I carried on, 'Drugs? Poverty? Not enough jobs?'

'Yeah, that kind of thing.'

He then leaned forward and told me I needed to monetize my trip. 'I mean, that's a nice backpack. If you went on TikTok and told everyone you were from England and here you are at Java Joe's in ABQ and you love this backpack, you could get followers and sponsorship. You'd go viral.'

'I'm not sure about that.'

Jonathan added, 'You've gotta work with what you've got in front of you.' He was making money selling western wear. 'From the *Wild* West,' he added, pronouncing the word 'wild' with sarcasm. 'Seriously though, you should promote brands on TikTok. You can make thousands. They send you stuff and you take a picture and post it. Take this advice from a twenty-six-year-old.'

On my last trip to Albuquerque, I'd had a strangely magical time. It was the long Easter weekend and the sky was an enormous polished blue dome. It was a time I would not be able to repeat. That Good Friday in 2006, I had walked down Albuquerque's Main Street noticing how the reddish-pink Sandia mountains hugged the east of the city. 'Sandia' is Spanish for 'watermelon'.

As I walked along Central Avenue (AKA Route 66), I had noticed a poster for a Jean Renoir double bill at the University of New Mexico: *Une partie de campagne* and *La règle du jeu*. I checked the map in my Lonely Planet guide. The route looked pretty straightforward, so off I went. As I approached a pedestrian tunnel under the train tracks, I

could just make out a huddle of silhouettes obscuring the light at the other end. Some were standing, some sitting, all of them blocking the footpath. I've always hated that rising fear, that slight panic that shows up when you have to ask a man to move out of the way so you can pass. It is so often accompanied by a subtle straightening of their back, an almost imperceptible hesitation on their part, often presented as a joke, but it's really just a reminder that if they wanted to stop you they could. I decided to forgo the Jean Renoir double bill and stood at a bus stop watching the sky darken. Little birds – I think they were swallows – swooped as the streetlights blinked on. It was then that I spotted a microbrewery called Chama River, named after the Rio Chama, which feeds into the Rio Grande.

In the Tewa language, spoken by the Pueblo people of New Mexico, the Rio Chama is known as 'Red River' because the Rio Grande once ran red for a few miles just below its confluence with the Chama. The word 'Chama' or 'Tsama' in the Tewa language means 'where they wrestled'. Thinking about these names, the realization hit me then that perhaps my difficulty in understanding maps is less to do with my dyslexia and more to do with a kind of stubbornness, manifested also in my refusal to learn to drive. On some profound level, I don't want to take part in a culture where rivers are straightened to increase their productivity and where mountains are often named after people who dominated, destroyed or never even set foot in the places carrying their names. 'All the greatness of any land, at any time, lies folded in its names,' writes Walt Whitman in *An American Primer*, 'I say nothing is more important than names... Names are the turning point of who shall be master.' Names can be useful. We need them to collectively talk about a landscape. They also encode

272

our shared memory of a place. The question we should be asking is what memories do we want to collect as we orient ourselves?

Maps, like names, are also useful, yet they reflect landscapes as solid and unchanging. They so often feel wrong to me, as if they are giving an approximation that doesn't correspond accurately to what I am seeing. Just as there were once no wild animals, because all animals were wild, landscape was also once wild, and existed outside the realm of the documented. With the online world being our guide and our trusted representation of the real, embodied world, it becomes more obvious to me that the map is absolutely not the territory – despite the best efforts of Silicon Valley to try and tell us otherwise.

When Simone de Beauvoir was in the navigation seat while Natasha Sorokin drove, they got lost. On their journey from Sacramento to Reno, the two women found themselves on snow-covered tarmac where they could no longer see the edge of the road and their tank was running low. 'I looked at the map as if it reflected a world submissive to the reign of man,' de Beauvoir wrote, 'with distances convertible to hours and exact gallons of gas.'

It was Easter Saturday. I took a seat at the bar of Chama Brewery and ordered a pint. A guy came in shortly after and sat two stools away. I noticed his height, his sandy blonde hair, blue eyes and wide-open face like a prairie. He and the bartender were chatting about a Bob Dylan gig they'd both been to. The guy turned to me and asked if I was a Dylan fan. I told him I'd just seen him play at the Brixton Academy in London last November, which would have been in 2005. Dylan seemed to enjoy taking apart his songs and playing them in a way that made them unfamiliar. He undermined our expectations. People in the audience shouted out requests and when something like 'Blowin' in the Wind' started up, it would take me several seconds to recognize it. I loved him even more for that. He didn't give us what we wanted; he gave us something else entirely.

It turned out that Jake, like me, was one of seven kids, raised a Catholic, lost a sister to breast cancer and had a birthday three days before mine. Chatting to him was like chatting to a long-lost brother. Our beer morphed into dinner at a tiny Mexican restaurant, where we sat outdoors under fairy lights drinking cheap cans of Tecate. Then against both of our better judgements we headed to a dark, student bar for a nightcap.

There comes a point when, as a woman travelling alone, you will meet someone who invites you to spend the night with them. I was learning on this trip that even when you hit forty and are travelling by bus in a pair of dirty jeans and a smelly T-shirt, this rule still applies. Usually, it's easy to brush off the advances, to make a joke of them, to say you have a partner, that he trusts you and you trust him and you are not willing to break that trust. Every woman has an armour they bring out to deflect unwanted attention. I usually resorted to humour. I've always thought that it's fine for anyone to declare an interest; it's how they react to your 'no' that marks out the good from the bad. If I had met Jake in another life, I most certainly would have said yes. I am greedy for other lives. Who is ever happy with just the one?

Irma Kurtz described this beautifully when she was invited to join a group of women, laughing and having fun trying on hats in Melrose, Minnesota. 'Come on and join us,' one of the women shouts to her as she watches from a doorway. Kurtz writes,

274

No sooner had she spoken than I felt a shift within my mind, and a crack opened between what was and what could yet be. It is through just such sudden fissures in reality that urbane women have been known to leap into the arms of Neapolitan fishermen, or ride off on camels into the Sahara. Before me was a glimpse of a whole new tempting invention: Life as a Lady of Melrose, Minnesota.

These fissures seem to be more common while riding the Greyhound because you so often end up in places you didn't expect, where your guard is down and the road feels so open you could disappear down it. But these fissures become much rarer as one edges into one's fifties.

The following morning, despite the gargantuan amounts of alcohol Jake and I had put away the previous night, he picked me up early from my hotel. He had wanted to show me Georgia O'Keeffe's Ghost Ranch near Abiquiu, about a two-and-half-hour drive from Albuquerque. We headed out of town and drove north. N. Scott Momaday, who grew up in northern New Mexico describes this place as a 'landscape full of mystery and life'.

I had never seen such a place. Such light. Such red earth. What Willa Cather describes as 'a sweep of red carnelian-coloured hills'. Where these reds met the blue on the horizon was a shimmering line, an almost imperceptible now-you-see-me-now-you-don't ribbon of violet, almost white. The magnetic pull of this land was powerful. What writer or artist with the means would not want to move here forever? 'During these last weeks,' de Beauvoir wrote while in New Mexico, 'I've seen so many landscapes, but this one touches me – I'd like to live here.'

New Mexico was where D. H. Lawrence started writing *The Plumed Serpent*. His views of the Indigenous people of New Mexico were highly romanticized, but he nevertheless claimed that his two years there changed him 'forever':

> You can feel it, the atmosphere of it, around the pueblos.... Come riding through at dusk on some windy evening, when the black skirts of the silent women blow around the white wide boots, and you will feel the old, old roots of human consciousness still reaching down to depths we know nothing of: and of which, only too often, we are jealous. It seems it will not be long before the pueblos are uprooted.

Sadly, he was right on that last point. Lawrence made another prediction which perhaps reflected some of what I was seeing around me on my most recent journey:

> But there it is: the newest democracy ousting the oldest religion! And once the oldest religion is ousted, one feels the democracy and all its paraphernalia will collapse, and the oldest religion, which comes down to us from man's pre-war days, will start again. The skyscraper will scatter on the winds like thistledown, and the genuine America, the America of New Mexico, will start on its course again. This is an interregnum.

Perhaps we have entered the era of skyscrapers scattered on the wind.

New Mexico has always attracted writers and artists for its light and the desert's spare beauty. The Ghost Ranch, which is about twenty minutes from Abiquiu, is where Georgia O'Keeffe lived from 1929 to 1984. It was closed on Easter Sunday, so Jake and I could only look at it from a distance. I could clearly make out beyond it the flat-topped Pedernal mountain O'Keeffe painted so often and the colours she captured. It was all there across this intensely quiet desert landscape. The only sound was the wind, which rose and fell, taking little swirling clouds of sand and sun-dried sage leaves with it.

Abiquiu is a tiny, dusty town of 230, lying eighteen miles west of the confluence of the Chama and Rio Grande rivers. It is on a small hill overlooking what Scott Momaday describes as a 'various landscape – grassy banks, rolling plains, bluffs of red and rose and purple and blue'. He goes on to say that Abiquiu was an old Penitente village, the Penitentes being 'a religious society composed of men who scourged themselves to blood and carried heavy wooden crosses on the Fridays of Lent and especially during Holy Week'. But when Jake and I wandered around the small outpost, there wasn't another soul around. The heat intensified and by midday, the buzzing of cicadas filled the still air and the mint green sagebrush barely cast a shadow. Everything looked, in that desert way, just as it should. There was nothing extraneous, nothing missing; it was like all deserts. It was perfect.

Momaday was fortunate to meet Georgia O'Keeffe in the early 1970s, when she was in her eighties. He describes her wearing a black suit and white shirt with her hair swept severely back. She seemed to him 'quite handsome and impressive in her formality'. Her famous hands, he noted, 'were large and expressive'. After a bit of conversation O'Keeffe realized that she hadn't offered Momaday a drink. 'She became quite flustered', he writes. She insisted that he have a Scotch. 'She excused herself and went out of the room.' He goes on,

> Long minutes passed, and she did not return. I grew uneasy, then concerned. There was a din, a rattling of metal objects,

278

which I took to come from the kitchen. I got up, sat down again, wrung my hands; I wondered whether or not I should investigate. Then, to my great relief, she reappeared. But she was empty handed, and there was a consternation in her face. "It's my maid's day off, and I do not know what she did with the key to the liquor pantry," she explained. "Oh, please, don't give it a thought," I blurted. "Really, I'm fine." But Georgia O'Keeffe had got it into her head that I was going to have my drink, and to my deep distress she excused herself again. Another long time elapsed, again the banging of pots and pans, more wringing of my hands. And then, with pronounced dignity and not a hair out of place, she entered the room with my drink on a small silver tray. Later she confided to me with a twinkle in her eye, did this octogenarian, that she had taken the pantry door off at the hinges with a screwdriver.

Jake and I went into a small shop in Abiquiu to buy corn chips. Taxidermy, bleached cow skulls and paint-by-number landscapes decorated the walls. Under the modern-day town is an ancient pueblo. I've read that the Tewa name is 'Phesu'u', which means 'timber point'. No one alive today knows whether the point refers to a prom-ontory of land or to a tree or some other landmark. I've also heard that the name means 'wild choke cherry place'. It was the early Mexican colonists who turned Phesu'u to Abiquiu and the name has stuck.

In my twenties, I had been surrounded by people who worshipped Georgia O'Keeffe. I'd lost count of the rooms in student houses where her unfurling flowers had been Blu-Tacked to walls. I never took to them. In fact I found those pastel colours insipid. But I could see that her work had emanated from the landscape, seamlessly so. Her

paintings were not imposed upon it; they emerged directly from it, were part of it. I saw her paintings differently
now. New Mexico was working on me, too.

I don't know why, but we didn't go into Georgia
O'Keeffe's home and studio museum which is right in
Abiquiu. Maybe it was also closed. It was so hot that day,
and my diary gets skimpy here. My mind was blown by
the rocks, the colours, the sky, the intensity of it all. Jake
and I did, however, head to Santa Fe to see the museum dedicated to O'Keeffe's work. It was a shock after
Abiquiu. Crowded, a brightly lit gift shop and a piazza
lined with stalls selling turquoise earrings, silver belt
buckles and crystals whose hawkers promised me peace
and enlightenment if I handed over some cash.

The Santa Fe described by Simone de Beauvoir is a different place altogether. Artists, poets and bohemians had
taken over Santa Fe's Canyon Road in the early 1900s.
The first artists settled there because they felt the dry air
would cure their tuberculosis and pneumonia. By the
time de Beauvoir got there, Canyon Road was a well-es-
tablished artists' colony. She describes an all-night party
that ended with people falling over drunk, reading their
poetry to anyone who would listen, and dancing as the
sun rose.

Jake and I left Santa Fe and headed to Madrid (pronounced '*Mad*-rid'), a tiny outpost of around 200
people. Most of the little houses lining the main road had
bleached cow skulls nailed over their brightly painted
doors. We drove past dozens of bungalows, their wood-
en railings and their front porches draped with strings
of red chillies. We stopped outside a large building displaying a sign in that old western typeface from 'Wanted'
posters that read, The Mine Shaft Tavern. Inside the old

mine, thick pine beams were hung with coloured lights, a cigarette had been stuck in a bison's taxidermied head, paintings of New Mexican sunsets and cowboys lined the walls. I was in the overlapping middle of a Venn diagram of 'wholesome craftspeople' and 'tattooed bikers'. Jake and I ordered beer and danced to the live band. In fact, everyone danced here. I would have made a spectacle of myself if I hadn't got up and danced. It was that kind of place.

After a few hours, we walked to his pick-up, parked a little ways from the bar. I looked up and gasped. The bowl of black velvety sky was studded with thousands, millions, perhaps billions of enormous stars. I realized that for the duration of this trip, despite moving through some of the most exquisite landscapes in the US, through deserts and mesas, the edges of prairies and along rivers, I had yet to stand outdoors in a place dark enough to see stars with nothing between me and them. This was partly because I was at the mercy of the Greyhound bus and its scheduled stops, which meant that I spent my nights looking out a dimmed bus window, or walking through brightly lit towns, cities, gas stations and parking lots. But there was something else at play here: as a woman travelling on my own, the opportunity to stand alone in a completely dark place simply didn't present itself. Without a car, how can you travel out of the city and into the desert? With a car, how many women feel safe heading into a desert alone at night to see the stars? I couldn't remember the last time I had truly experienced the night and how it takes up all the shadows and details and wipes 'the face of the desert into a simple, uncluttered blackness until there [are] only three things: land, wind, stars,' as Kerouac so perfectly puts it. I had not – until this moment – been able to get close to the transcendence that emerges when one feels oneself being flung through space, when one has been reduced in the words of William Least Heat-Moon 'to mind, to an edge of consciousness'. You become aware that you are standing on a rock being hurled through the universe.

Just beyond my annoyance at the unfairness of being born female (not my fault) and my inability to drive (absolutely my fault), I could just about hold onto the bigger thought that began to fill me: the realization that what I was really looking at as I stared into the sky was the visual embodiment of time. The light I was seeing had travelled from stars that existed before Europeans had set foot on this continent. This was why I was here. If I had just given birth to a child, I would not have been standing here, staring at the emissaries of deep time transmitting their glow from the black bowl of a New Mexican sky. Events had conspired to send me this stranger who had taken me to this place. Here I was on Walt Whitman's 'more than sufficient Earth', where I also did not want the constellations any nearer; where I could feel they were perfect just where they were, as was I. I knew that Karl would also have to see this sky. She would also gaze up and be transported. I would have to get her here so she could see what I was seeing.

Jake dropped me back at my hotel in the middle of that starry, inky night. I flopped into bed and lay there thinking about how I was having one of those days where you feel as if your will has been subsumed by plans that the universe is making behind your back. Days that spin out from travelling, from leaving parts of oneself behind and taking new parts with you. There is a scene in William Least Heat-Moon's *Blue Highways* when he goes to Nameless, Tennessee to find out where the town got its name. He ends up in the home of Virginia and Thurmond

284

Watts, where Thurmond 'cranked up an old Edison pho-
nograph, the kind with the big morning-glory blossom
for a speaker, and put on a wax cylinder' while the author
ate some of Ginnie's buttermilk pie. 'It was one of those
moments that you know will stay with you to the grave,'
he wrote, 'the sweet pie, the gaunt man playing the old
music, the coals in the stove glowing orange, the scent of
kerosene and hot bread.' The two men laugh at the heavi-
ly romantic music. And then Least Heat-Moon adds, 'It is
for this I have come.'

'The plenitude I dream of, which would take me out of
myself,' Simone de Beauvoir wrote, 'will never be more
than a phantom.... The night is merely a setting; if I try to
seize it, to make it the substance of the moment I'm living,
it dissolves in my hands.' These moments are real. They
cannot be digitized or appified. They are lodged in time
and space. They are only given to us outside the sphere
of the machine and if we try and hold onto them, they
dissolve.

Before drifting off to sleep, I thought about the desert,
the sand dunes, the red, ochre and cream-coloured rocks,
the libraries of fossils, the cresting light and blue skies and
the fiery tones of the earth burrowing into the cool shades
of the crumpled mountains. I thought about the 'violet
dark' and the 'unbearably sweet night' that Sal Paradise
moved through on his road trip. And then, I simply didn't
think about anything. I was empty, but utterly whole.

Jake had offered to buy me a farewell breakfast at Java
Joe's in downtown Albuquerque. The same Java Joe's
I tracked down in 2023 where a 26-year-old gave me a
lesson on how to monetize my travels. I found Jake there
the following morning. While he picked up our coffees
from the counter and brought them outside, I overheard

the conversation between two men at the table next to me. One of them was from my hometown of Ottawa and was visiting his friend in Albuquerque, who it turned out was also Canadian. Their conversation shifted from diets, work-out schedules and body mass index to 'flyover country', the parts of America that are rarely explored by people living on the coasts. If there is a phrase that gets my blood boiling, it's 'flyover country'.

'Some guy told me that Iowa is short for "Idiots Out Walking Around",' the Canadian transplant said. There was a snort from Ottawa Guy. 'And Indianapolis is pronounced "India No Place".' More snorts.

Fury at their snobbishness rose in me. Jake handed me a coffee before I got involved, and gave me a copy of one of his favourite books, Terry Tempest Williams' *Refuge*. We ate breakfast burritos and after too many coffee refills, it was time for him to go to work. We stood on Route 66.

'I'd like to see you off, my friend,' he said.

'You don't have to,' I replied.

'I know, but I'd like to.'

'It's the 2.35 a.m. bus,' I told him. 'I'm taking it so I can sleep on the bus. This hotel has blown my budget.'

'I'll be there,' he said.

After my first night in the Econo Lodge in Albuquerque I looked for Bobby, but he'd already gone home after his shift. I wandered along Central Avenue from the front door of the motel and came upon a broken sign that read CROSSROADS MOTEL. I thought it was a funny coincidence, because I happened to be reading Jonathan Franzen's latest novel, *Crossroads*. A guy in a pickup rolled up.

'You looking for Jesse?' he asked.

'Um, no. I just really like this sign.'

'Oh, most people who come here are looking for Jesse. And I tell them, "Jesse has left the building."'

I had no idea what he was talking about. He obviously sensed my ignorance. 'Jesse Pinkman is a character from *Breaking Bad.*'

'Oh, I get it.' I had watched some of the TV show but not enough to know about Jesse Pinkman's stay in this motel. 'I love the sign,' I said. 'The place looks all closed up, though.'

'It's not.'

'Really?' There were no cars in the parking lot. No one coming or going from the motel rooms. Some of the signs were smashed.

'I'm open,' he said.

'To offers?' I thought maybe he was the owner and was selling the place.

'No. I'm open. As in O-P-E-N. I'm not selling.'

'Oh, I see.'

'Despite how it looks on the outside, the rooms are gorgeous.'

'I can imagine.' I paused. 'I'm staying just over there in the Econo Lodge.'

'My parents used to own that. It was called the PanAm back then.'

He reached his hand out of his truck window to shake mine and then sped off.

The night bus to Vegas was leaving at 11 p.m. I decided to walk to the station early as I'd had to check out of my motel and was tired of lugging my backpack around. I was approaching an underpass when I realized it was the very same one I had been too afraid to walk through in search of the Jean Renoir double bill the last time I was in Albuquerque. On this trip, I'd walked through it several times in daylight. The last time, only a matter of hours ago, my path through the tunnel was obscured by a giant piece of tumbleweed – that symbol of the 'Wild West', the ingredient in every Western movie, which in reality is not indigenous to the US at all. Tumbleweed is a Russian thistle originally brought over from Crimea in 1873 and now lodged in our collective imagination.

It was dark as I approached the underpass on my way to the bus station. I felt a bit concerned, but I couldn't see anyone blocking it, so I figured it was probably OK. Just as I'd done my internal risk assessment, a city bus honked and pulled up next to me.

'You going to the station?'

'Yes. The Greyhound.'

'Get in. It's not safe to walk alone here.'

The driver motioned for me to get on. The people on the bus were a sorry lot. Shouting, spitting, one guy coughing up a seemingly endless stream of phlegm, another man in clothes so dirty that the fabric had lost its ability to bend. He sat, legs and arms outstretched, like a scarecrow. He stared at me and smiled, strung out, completely and utterly absent. I felt guilty for registering the smell, unmistakeably a mixture of sweat and human excrement. When I got off the bus, the driver honked at me again. I had turned in the wrong direction and he pointed to where I should be going. I waved and shouted 'thank you' at him.

The first person I saw as I approached the station was a woman with her trousers down by her knees, lying face down. Dozens more lay on the steps of the station. There was little lighting, so I could only really make out their forms, not the details. Some were crumpled up in the foetal position; others hopped from foot to foot like their feet

were on fire. Carrier bags lay scattered. There were single shoes, beer cans, flip flops, empty containers of food, hairbrushes, broken lighters. The words that came to me as I navigated this scenario: 'This is not normal. This is not how it should be.'

I was hoping that once I got into the station, I could sort out my ticket to Vegas. But the station was closed. I didn't know that Greyhound stations now closed between buses to keep the addicts and the homeless out – yet another communal space forbidden to those without money. I still had an hour before my bus. I remembered de Beauvoir's descriptions of bus stations with restaurants, juke boxes, showers, and lockers that she compares to columbariums. I walked to a café where I very slowly nursed a camomile tea. I was still mindful of sticking to my near-dehydration diet so as to avoid having to use a bus bathroom.

I returned to the station five minutes after it opened. There was already a queue at the Greyhound counter. The problem I had was that there were no longer any direct buses from Albuquerque to Las Vegas. On my previous trip, I had changed buses in Flagstaff during the daytime. It was convenient and safe, but this route didn't exist anymore.

I hadn't described Flagstaff in detail in my 2006 journal, but I did note the large parking lots, scrubby spindly trees planted in an effort to provide shade for the parked cars, a McDonald's, a Dairy Queen, a Jack in the Box and one or two nondescript box stores. It was one of those spaces that is ubiquitous in North America for travellers who want their food fast and their gas cheap. It did have an iconic Greyhound sign with mid-century lettering. Apparently, this has been painted over and the station has now been demolished. A quick Google search told me the new station has a Whole Foods and a lululemon nearby among the Pitta Jungle, Crumbl Cookies, Horizon Shooters Gun Shop and the AZ Power & Lawn.

Just to the north of Flagstaff, I remember noticing three snow-topped mountains of the San Francisco range. It was easy to see why these mountains, which are perched on the rim of an eroded, extinct volcano, are sacred to the Navajo, Hopi and Havasupai, among other tribes in the Southwest. The morning sun had crested their peaks, flooding their cool lilac folds with a warm glow.

While I waited in the Flagstaff parking lot for the Vegas bus, a woman approached and clocked my coffee cup from Jack in the Box.

'Is Jack in the Box expensive?' she asked.

'Um, yeah, I guess it is compared to McDonald's,' I told her. When these are your choices, what is your choice, really? I was reminded of another woman on the bus from Indianapolis. She was travelling with her young daughter who was maybe five or six years old. As we got off at a rest stop, she turned and said to me, 'Why do they always have to stop at a McDonald's? I just want to get my kid an apple.'

In my 2006 journal, I jotted down a sign I had seen in the Greyhound bus station in Flagstaff:

ARTICLES PROHIBITED OR SUBJECT TO SPECIAL
CONDITIONS OF ACCEPTANCE ON GREYHOUND, USA:

AMMUNITION
ANIMAL HEADS
ASHES OF CREMATED CORPSES
BULL SEMEN
CORPSES
DANGEROUS ARTICLES
EXPLOSIVES

FIREARMS
FISH, LIVE
MOTION PICTURE FILMS
NEON SIGNS OR BENT TUBING
RADIOACTIVE MATERIAL
REPTILES, LIVE
SNAKES, LIVE
WORMS, LIVE (FISH BAIT)

Before our bus pulled out of the Flagstaff parking lot in 2006, several new passengers had joined us. One woman on the bus whispered to me that all these people had come from an 'insane asylum'. Some of these passengers looked distressed; some were talking to themselves; a woman dressed in head-to-toe magenta was making interesting shapes in the air with her hands. An older man who was the last to board and had only just managed to find a seat spoke what sounded like a stream of nonsense words. He wore a long dark overcoat and smelled strongly of excrement. After he had taken his seat, the driver said, 'Whoever took their shoes off, can they put them back on? We need to breathe!'

A woman called out, 'That's not feet; that's ass. I'm a mother, I know what ass smells like!'

At this point, several passengers got out their deodorant, their hairspray and their cologne and walked up and down the central aisle of the bus spraying their parabens, phthalates, pheromones, polyvinyl alcohol, hydroflurocarbons, carboxymethylcellulose, propylene glycol and synthetic chemicals with a manic determination to 'clear' the air. If I am ever forced to choose between the smell of shit masked with Lynx and aftershave or the smell of shit on its own, I now know what I would choose, but on that bus, I was in the minority.

292

After about half an hour, just as I thought I couldn't stand the fake pine scent, the saccharine vanilla swirl and clawing fake strawberry sweetness of these personal hygiene products any longer, the bus came to a juddering halt. A police cruiser sidled up to it. The driver stood up and grabbed a guy by the arm. He'd been drinking concealed alcohol. As he was hauled off the bus, the man who smelled of excrement also stepped off. He didn't get into the police car, he simply walked out alone into the desert. I wanted to run after him, to ask him what was wrong, to coax him back on. But I just sat there, along with the others in our cloud of poison, and let him leave us behind. I wondered whether he was aware of his smell and had been offended by the aggressive spraying to mask it. I also wondered how long he would last out there in the hot desert in his overcoat without food or water.

Once that drama was over, the young guy sitting next to me wearing a white T-shirt and a pair of khaki shorts reached down to the plastic bag between his feet, got out a hardcover copy of *JFK: The Case for Conspiracy*, and placed it on his lap. He caught me reading the cover and said, 'I just went to Dallas to check out the Xs that mark exactly where JFK was shot.' Then he told me about his work in construction and how he was heading to Vegas to find a job. There was so much more of this kind of conversation back in 2006 before we were all 'connected' via our devices.

'Ever been to Vegas?' Dallas Guy asked.

'Yes, a year ago,' I replied.

He offered me a magazine, also extracted from his plastic bag. It had a fuzzy black and white photo on the front cover.

'Oh, thanks, but I'm going to read my book,' I said and tapped *Refuge* which sat on my lap. It was dark on the bus, but back then the lights often worked.

He opened his magazine and held a page up for me to look at. In the dimness I could just make out a red cross on a grainy, grey road.

'This is where it happened,' he told me. 'I saw the spot with my own eyes.' His finger was planted on the red X, and he shook his head as if he couldn't imagine such horror; he couldn't believe anyone could have been shot in the head like that in a car in Dallas next to his own wife.

I nodded.

'I didn't know the desert could get so cold,' he said, pulling on the hem of his shorts under the JFK book.

'Yes, the desert gets cold at night. It surprises you,' I replied.

'It's a cold that cuts you right in half,' he said.

The bus was quiet. Most people were sleeping. Some just stared out at the darkness.

My diary at this point: 'It is six in the morning and the sky is just lightening. The JFK-obsessed boy next to me is breathing in heavy, low breaths. The bus is still quiet and my eyes are still open.' At Holbrook, the great ball of sun crested above the flat desert and seemed to tumble through the bus windows, filling our little bubble with insane light. It was like magic. Like this was my first sunrise, like I'd been reborn.

I had no idea where I was on the map, but I was far from lost. I was simply where I wanted to be with this great burning star filling my vision. I still thought about Karl, but the other ghosts I had been travelling with – my grief, my losses – seemed to be getting fainter.

Behind me, I could hear some quiet conversation.

'I was a helicopter pilot,' one of the voices said. 'I wanted to retire, but they're making me go out to Iraq again.'

Someone a few seats away overheard this and piped

up, 'I thought Lincoln got rid of slavery!'

People laughed.

Another voice further back spoke up, 'Yeah, they got rid of slavery all right. Now they make you sign on the dotted line, but they don't *call* it slavery.'

More laughter.

Today, if you type 'Albuquerque to Las Vegas' into the Greyhound website's search bar, the most 'direct' route you get is one that leaves Albuquerque at 4.30 a.m. and arrives in Las Vegas at 12.45 a.m. the following day. It takes over 21 hours because it goes via San Bernardino, which is west of Vegas. There are other equally insane routes on offer – one of them taking a whopping 27 hours because it goes via Phoenix and Los Angeles before doubling back to Las Vegas. To give a sense of perspective, driving from Albuquerque to Las Vegas – a trip of 576 miles – takes eight and a half hours by car.

I tried to outsmart the algorithms by booking a ticket from Albuquerque to Flagstaff and then a separate ticket from Flagstaff to Vegas, which would mean nine hours of bus time with a morning to loaf around Flagstaff. I felt very happy with myself for cracking this problem, although it did mean I would be arriving in Flagstaff at 3.15 a.m. This wouldn't be a problem if the station were open. But when I checked the opening hours online, it appeared that the station would be closed and I would have to sit in the dark on a bench outside in the freezing cold until noon, when the next bus would take me to Vegas.

Then I looked into 24-hour diners where I could sit in Flagstaff until the sun came up. There was a 24-hour Denny's. Perfect. But judging from Google Maps, the 20-minute walk at 3.15 a.m. would be isolated and dark, and possibly unsafe. According to the Uber app, there were no drivers in Flagstaff so I tracked down the phone numbers of the three cab companies in town and called them to ask if they would be willing to ferry a middle-aged woman and a backpack from the bus station to the Denny's at 3.15 a.m. Two of them said they liked their sleep, the other one said he was having eye trouble and no longer drove at night. I wondered how bad it would be to sit on a cold bench in the dark outside the Flagstaff bus station from 3.15 a.m. to sunup.

I was willing to risk it, but when I asked the Greyhound worker in Albuquerque, she didn't think it was a great idea. 'It will be really cold,' she said. 'Flagstaff is high up. You'll freeze to death. And you'll probably be all on your own there. I wouldn't recommend it.'

I spoke to my husband Jason back in London. I was getting tired of this trip. Tired of the routes not lining up, the apps not working, the people who seemed sad and driven to addiction, the dark, the filth, the vomit, the shit. He calmed me down and asked a simple question: 'Where does the bus go after Flagstaff?'

'Phoenix.'

'Why don't you stay on and then get a ticket from Phoenix to Vegas?'

Genius!

I returned to the Greyhound woman at the counter and bought a ticket from Flagstaff to Phoenix. Then I needed to buy an extra one from Phoenix to Vegas.

'The bus from Phoenix to Vegas is a FlixBus, not a Greyhound,' she said as she handed it to me. 'But it's got the Greyhound logo on the ticket, so I think you can get your connecting bus from the Greyhound station.' She assured me it would be fine.

I wandered off and found a seat to wait for the bus that would take me the eight and a half hours from Albuquerque to Phoenix. A guy approached and took the seat next to me. Tall, bearded, with a good head of thick grey hair, he wore joggers, boots, a warm coat. He carried two rolled up Navajo-style rugs and a bottle of water.

'I got the cheapest ticket to Pensacola, Florida you can buy,' he said almost triumphantly. 'Three hundred bucks.'

'How long does it take?' I asked.

'Forty hours.'

'That's a long time.'

'I'm going to hitchhike to the Keys to work as a fisherman. I've always wanted to be a fisherman. I love Florida. The heat, the water, the swamps, the birds, the humidity. I have arthritis in my hips and knees. The heat is good for it. I need a good soak.'

He was well spoken, his clothes were clean. I got the sense he was semi-nomadic.

'You know, I haven't eaten anything all day,' he told me.

I gave him what food I had, which wasn't much. Some crackers, trail mix and a box of mini cinnamon swirls. He took them graciously, thanked me and we chatted some more. Eventually he got up and walked off.

When the bus to Pensacola showed up, he wasn't in the queue. I looked around the station to see if I could find him, but he was nowhere to be seen.

The bus from Albuquerque to Phoenix stopped at 1.40 a.m. in Gallup, New Mexico at NK's truck stop and BOMBAY RESTAURANT & BUFFET. When we got off to stretch and get a snack, the driver called out, 'Ten minutes. Don't be late. The next bus west is in ten hours!'

When I boarded the bus again, the driver was standing by the open door. 'Hey! You just going to walk past me like that without saying anything?'

I apologized. 'Sorry, I'm just really sleepy.'

'Where's your ticket?'

'On the bus.'

'Go get it then.' He was being a jerk.

New people were boarding at Gallup, but it's customary for those who've been on the bus to just walk back on without showing a ticket, especially in the middle of the night when it's clear that all their stuff is already on the bus.

As we pulled out, a guy walked to the front of the bus to ask if the driver could turn on the overhead lights so he could find his meds.

'I can't hear you! And no, I can't put the lights on – they reflect off the windshield!'

'How can you answer back if you can't hear me, man?'

'Go sit down!'

Then he did his spiel: 'No alcohol allowed on this bus, no aggression, no violence towards another passenger or me – it's a federal offence. I will pull over, call the police, and you will spend two days in lock-up. It's like Delta or United. You will be charged. Same goes for drinking alcohol. Understand me? Awesome!'

2.30 a.m., Holbrook, Arizona. Incredible signage. The 66 Motel – VACANCY. The K Convenience Store & Gas Station. More people emerged from parked cars, carrying bags. These dark silhouettes came into focus as they entered the bright yellow beams of the bus headlights. In *An American Journey*, Ethel Mannin describes Holbrook as being 'like so many of these highway places throughout America,' she writes, 'a place that is hardly a place. It has no centre, no shape ... it is just a collection of motels and gas-stations and bars and eating-places along a highway, and small, unhappy-looking houses set among thin

trees in the side roads; at one side it is bounded by the railroad, with the desert beyond; at the other side there is just desert.'

At every stop, the driver shouted on the personal address system where we were, how long we had at the stop. The overhead lights went on. It was impossible to sleep. As we cruised through the silent stretches of darkness between stops, my head rested against the window. In the blackness, everything outside took on a ghostly appearance, misshapen, illuminated by lights on the highway, palm trees became monsters, billboards tilted at odd angles, crazy human-made objects lit up from below telling you that unborn lives were sacred, don't drive tired, next exit ALL YOU CAN EAT EVERYTHING.

6.15 a.m.: Out my window on the left-hand side of the bus, the sun was just beginning to crest the horizon. Pinky orange shades, like those of a Creamsicle, melting along the dark outlines of rock formations. Out the other window, saguaro cactuses appeared. I know such trees exist and yet they still take me by surprise, such is their expressiveness: their comical arms outstretched against the dawn light, like giant creatures welcoming us to a new day, a new terrain, a new kind of desert.

6.30 a.m. As we approached Phoenix, we hit a traffic jam. Helicopters appeared overhead, emergency vehicles could be heard wailing nearby. I looked up and saw a glider doing a loop-the-loop above us. Cypress trees, red bushes, palm trees, something that looked like an olive tree, another with feathery leaves – even along this highway there was a huge variety of flora. Mature saguaros lined the tarmac. Many had wooden braces strapped to their bodies to keep them upright. With their braces, they looked like fat green rockets about to take off. And in a sense, they are taking off. Casualties of our overheating world, these cactuses are becoming dehydrated and are dying in large numbers.

When we arrived in Phoenix, I went to the Greyhound counter and stood in the queue. The station was busy. A woman stood nearby with a trolley full of bags. Her phone was plugged into the wall. She was in her early twenties and she was jangly, pacing. She suddenly burst into tears. I had seen this often on this trip. No one comes to the aid of someone in this situation because we know there is very little we can do and it happens so often that we are becoming inured to it. Her tears were most likely a response to a vast, complex and interrelated series of problems. Buying her a meal might have helped. Maybe I should have. But where can you go for such a thing? There are so few bus stations now where you can get a coffee or a donut or a sandwich. Everything is stacked against you unless you have a car, a full tank of gas, an iPhone, and a credit card linked to an array of apps to keep all your devices and vehicles lubricated, with data, oil and money.

When I got to the head of the queue, I asked the woman at the counter where I could get my bus to Vegas. She didn't know of any bus to Vegas. I showed her the ticket I'd bought in Albuquerque, a paper one, which had the Greyhound logo on it.

'Huh. Well, it doesn't go from here. I don't know anything about this bus.'

'But I bought this ticket at the Greyhound station in Albuquerque. The woman there said the bus would be leaving from this station.'

'Well, it's not.'

We both stared at my ticket, trying to decipher it. Under the word 'Station' it simply said, 'Phoenix Glendale (59th

303

Ave/W. Hayward Ave, 85301 Glendale, AZ)'. In other words, I had been given map coordinates as my bus stop.

'Do you know where this is? Is it another station?'

She had no idea. All she knew was that I wouldn't be able to walk there.

I typed in the intersection into Google maps. It was thirteen miles from the Greyhound Station, or a four-and-a-half-hour walk. I had the money for an Uber, but what if I hadn't?

I found a café half-way between the Greyhound station and the map coordinates for the mythical Greyhound bus stop. I ordered a small coffee. The woman in the café said, 'Really? A small one?' I must have looked rough. 'OK, make it a large.' She smiled. I ate a massive breakfast burrito and brushed my teeth in the café bathroom.

I ordered another Uber. When I gave the coordinates to the Uber driver, he was puzzled. 'This is a Greyhound bus stop you're going to?'

'Apparently so.'

'Huh.'

As we chatted, somehow the subject got onto guns. He owned a handgun and an AR-15. He loved his guns. 'I'm a conservative,' he told me, 'which is a dirty word these days.' He paused. 'I used to be a Democrat, but the Democrats today aren't like the JFK Democrats. They're all gone. These ones are extreme. They're messing with kids.'

We got close to the coordinates and drove around trying to find something that might say 'Greyhound Bus Stop' or 'FlixBus Stop'. On a wide, busy six-lane road, we passed a giant Walmart and then I spotted it. A city bus stop with a small plastic sign tacked onto it showing the FlixBus logo. It was maybe the size of an A4 piece of paper. Easy to miss. 'There it is!' I said.

305

'What, *that* bus stop?'
'Yes, I think so.'
'But that's a city bus stop.'
'I know. But I think I can see a sign.'

The Uber driver found a safe place to pull over around the corner. I thanked him and got out. The only other person at this bus stop was a guy with a small tinfoil pipe smoking crack. The sun was beating down, but thankfully there was a cool breeze. It hit me that I might be standing on the wrong side of the road. How did I know that this stop would be the one heading in the direction of Vegas? There was no information on the app. I tried calling FlixBus but their line went dead. A guy in a wheelchair showed up and I asked him if he knew whether the bus to Vegas would be on this side of the road or the other. It was impossible to cross this road with all the traffic. He had just moved to Phoenix from Chicago and didn't know. Another man showed up. He had a shopping trolley filled with some old clothes and looked like he hadn't slept in a while. He heard the word 'Chicago' and piped up, 'I'm from Flint!'

'Oh, I've just come from Detroit,' I said.

'Well, you win!' he replied.

None of them had heard of a bus to Vegas from this stop but they all agreed that this was probably the right side of the road. The A4 FlixBus sign had a QR code on it. I tried to scan it but my phone didn't seem to recognize it. The four of us at the stop chatted for a while and I kept wondering how on earth a bus company could think it was a good idea for people to wait along a six-lane road in Phoenix with no access to a bathroom or a water fountain before boarding a bus for a long journey. Nothing can justify such decision making. I needed to pee and I wanted to refill my water bottle, so I walked to a nearby Taco Bell and used the facilities there. I'm a small, white, middle-class woman. If I had been sleeping in my clothes for days or looked like I'd had too much to drink, I'm not so sure the Taco Bell folks would be so happy to accommodate me. The relocation of bus stops 'curb-side' to the cheaper outer fringes of town, like the one I was standing at in the outskirts of Phoenix, is a move that will further make it impossible for those who rely on public transportation to be able to access it.

The madness of an intercity bus stop by the side of a giant road was all the more visceral and infuriating because, standing there on a hot day, with little shade and no drinking water, could literally kill you. Phoenix is the hottest city in the US. The city's most extreme heatwave to date was in July 2023, when temperatures topped 43 degrees Celsius for thirty-one consecutive days. It is reported that 300 people died from heat-related causes that month and heat deaths have more than quadrupled in Phoenix as global temperatures rise and unregulated urban development turns the city into a sprawling, concrete heat island. The hardest hit are those with no access to housing and no money to seek shelter – even temporarily – from the burning sun. Who would stand there and wait for a bus when they could take to their air-conditioned car?

About a month previously, I'd read the story of Caleb Blair, a Black teenager who had died in Phoenix just hours after being told he couldn't go into a minimart to cool off. 'I can't breathe, I'm hot, I need to sit down. I can't breathe,' he had told the cashier at the Circle K gas station in Phoenix. It was 10 June 2022 and the outside temperature was just above 44 degrees Celsius. Caleb Blair had no choice but to sit outside in the burning sun. The descriptions of the CCTV footage and the transcripts from the 911 calls in his final hours are harrowing.

Blair had been curled up in a ball on the burning asphalt, rolling around and struggling to breathe. He had been suffering with addiction issues for a while and that day he was high on fentanyl and methamphetamine. A Circle K employee had called 911 to say, 'There's a guy outside, he's on something... He's banging his head against my car and he's got blood on the door.' By this point Blair was naked. One caller described him as being in medical distress, 'I can see that his foot is cut, he just puked, it looks like it might be blood. He's been doubled over hitting his head on the ground.' Another said: 'He's obviously on something, beating the ground... it's an African American male, he's got a shoe in his mouth currently, pants around his ankles... he's pulling his own hair.'

Police arrived and handcuffed him. His trousers were still around his ankles and he was dragged into the shade of a mesquite bush. Paramedics arrived and took him to the hospital, where he died. According to the coroner, the cause of death was drug intoxication, with extreme heat and pneumonia as contributing factors. Blair's father, however, believes that his son 'took his last breath naked in handcuffs next to a dumpster'. Deaths like Caleb Blair's lie at the intersection of racial discrimination and the devastating effects of climate change. Bus stops on the side of huge roads with zero shade or water are physical manifestations of this lethal intersection.

The housing crisis in Phoenix means that huge numbers of people are living on the streets. And this number is growing. More than a thousand people have died from extreme heat in Phoenix in the last three years. Rates of

drug abuse – mostly meth and fentanyl – are also high among Phoenix's homeless population. In Maricopa County, where Phoenix is located, Black and Indigenous Americans have the highest rate of heat deaths. Doctors here are treating third degree burns on people who simply touch the tarmac. Paramedics who might kneel to treat a patient on the sidewalk are also getting serious burns.

By the end of July 2023, every single one of the 45 beds in Phoenix's major burn centre was occupied. One third of the patients had fallen to the ground while outdoors. It can take only a fraction of a second to get a 'pretty deep burn', Dr Kevin Foster, director of burn services at the Arizona Burn Center at Valleywise Health, said in an interview. For people who have been on the pavement for ten to twenty minutes, 'the skin is completely destroyed' and the damage often goes down deep, meaning it is a third-degree burn. This affects the elderly, the homeless, the inebriated, the confused. For months every year, Phoenix and all of Maricopa County are under weather warnings because of extreme heat. And it's getting worse.

As I stood in this heat island with no water or shade and no sign of a bus on the horizon, I thought hard about who makes the decisions to send people to a place like this to wait for a bus to Las Vegas. Phoenix and Vegas are major cities in the southwest, so this isn't exactly a minor route. Sending passengers to coordinates on a map in the country's hottest city could prove lethal. There was no provision for unsighted people, for those who are disabled, elderly or a bit fragile. Like so much that I was seeing on this trip, it was nonsensical at best and deliberately cruel at worst. Another reminder that people without cars who cannot easily move from one place to another are a population who do not matter in the US. The connection between the warming globe and the burning of fossil fuels is as clear as a sunny Phoenix afternoon, and yet the forces of capital and the centres of power seem to be doing all they can to keep people in their cars and prevent them from using public transportation to get from A to B.

The crack-smoking guy next to me at the bus stop wandered off. I prayed he wouldn't end up like Caleb Blair. Phoenix in March was tolerable, but as I type this, there are extreme heat warnings. What will become of him, or the guy from Flint, or any of the thousands of others who have been left behind or who are just sitting on a bench waiting for a bus?

The FlixBus did eventually show up. By the time it arrived, two other Vegas-bound passengers had arrived by car, both equally confused about whether a bus would materialize. The driver was perky and friendly. I mentioned that it was confusing to be given coordinates as a bus stop for a long trip and he shrugged.

'Yeah, I guess so.'

A Black woman sat in the seat diagonal to the driver. She was in casual wear; he was in black slacks, a crisp blue shirt and a tie. It seemed like they might know each other. They were chatting away about DEI (diversity, equity and inclusion) and what she called 'HR diktats'.

The woman said, 'I mean, it's crazy, these DEI people get paid so much money just to tell people to respect each other. It's crazy that we legislate this.'

The driver piped up, 'My granddaughter works for an insurance company. She's been working from home and they have a camera on her at all times.'

'I wouldn't like that.'

'I studied engineering and I never thought for a second that engineering would veer off into social engineering. That's what's happening, it's social engineering.'

'Yes, I'm trying to get my son to go into engineering. He's interested in politics, but I told him, "You don't need to *study* politics, you can just turn on the news."'

'I used to work in analytics for casinos in Vegas. I used to study questions like, "How long does someone sit in a chair and is that chair comfortable?" or "How long do people play that specific game?", that kind of thing. My background was electrical engineering, but I moved into software and electronics. It's pretty interesting stuff but then it morphed into the social stuff. We should be dealing with humans, not robots.'

At Wickenburg, we crossed the Hassayampa River.

A passenger behind me: 'Wow. This is the first water I've seen in Arizona'.

Another passenger: 'Yup. Snow melt. They've had flooding. There is still snow in Flagstaff. It's good for poor old Lake Mead, though.'

'Yeah. Is it disappearing 'cuz so many people are moving there?'

'Yeah. And also 'cuz California doesn't capture its rainwater. They took down all the dams to save this fish and that fish. I don't know if we need these fish. Maybe we do. I think they're a little crazy there in California. But maybe they're right.'

'It's gonna take a few more years of rain to fill Lake Mead.'

We headed onto Highway 93 from Highway 60. The earth here was not as red as it was in New Mexico or Texas. In the distance mountains shimmered and in the foreground cactuses bloomed with bright yellow flowers. I spotted some hawks. They soared above the Joshua trees and canyons. What struck me here was the variety

313

of living beings. As we approached Wikieup, shades of green appeared – the result of the Big Sandy River. The last time I did this trip, I didn't know that the Colorado River and the Hoover dam were just ahead and could be seen – albeit only for a second – from the bus. I hadn't looked out the window in time back then, so I made sure to look out for them this time. As we crossed the Colorado River, a thin metallic ribbon like a silver tongue cutting through the rock – the state border between Arizona and Nevada – I caught a quick glimpse of the megalithic Hoover Dam with Lake Mead in the background. Just as they passed from view, it started to rain.

Seeing the Hoover Dam, I felt that terrible stab I always get when I look at these enormous engineering works that are designed to make life better but destroy so much in the process. This dam, built between 1931 and 1936, was created to control the river and impound Lake Mead. 'Control' and 'impound' – these words tell you everything. I tried not to think about all the dead fish, the drowned trees and the stolen land. I focused instead on the rain and the casinos lodged in that landscape like cheap, sparkly trinkets in the desert.

As we got closer to Vegas, traffic appeared along with great glowering skies. The mountains in the distance were dappled with white and violet and black. Shadows from fast-moving clouds skittered over the tract houses and pavements of the Vegas suburbs. I'd forgotten how strangely beautiful the approach to Vegas is. The mountains that encircle the city didn't seem to have much snow on them. We passed a sign: 'SHACKLED BY LUST? JESUS SETS FREE'.

315

On my last trip, on the approach to Vegas, some of the passengers started planning where they would be 'stepping out' – a phrase that sounded incredibly quaint and old-fashioned to me. Two men and a woman, complete strangers, compared notes on the various benefits and drawbacks of injecting versus smoking their first hit of heroin. They had the same conversation about 'crystal'. One of the three had just got out of jail for dealing meth. The woman's son was in prison in Vegas for carrying dope on a city bus. She was going there to bail him out. But first she needed to score. The driver, as we flew through the candy-coloured lights of the city, advised us all to get some rest so we'd have the energy to party.

When we pulled into the old downtown Greyhound station in Las Vegas in the evening, the shadows lengthened and the neon signs lit up the street in succession like a string of dominoes. I checked into the Bridger Inn Hotel on Main Street, just down from the old station. In 2023 it was out of my reach, budget-wise. Back then, this part of Vegas was walkable and close to what was called the Arts District. It's all gone now. Well, perhaps not gone. It's been replaced by upscale cafés, bars, restaurants and shops. The scale felt less human to me than it had in 2006.

On this trip, my bus pulled into the new Las Vegas bus station on Gillespie Street, twelve miles south of the old depot on North Main Street, at 5.15 p.m. sharp. It had been raining. The streets smelled of petrichor and the sky was the colour of lead.

I stood on the street looking at my phone, wondering if I could walk to the Tropicana from the bus station. It would take me an hour. I decided, yet again, to get an Uber. While waiting for it to show up, a young Hispanic guy came over.

'You were on my bus,' he said.

'Oh, yeah.' I didn't recognize him but didn't want to be rude.

'I'm George,' he held out his hand.

I shook it and told him mine.

He was also waiting for an Uber.

'How do you like the US?'

'I love the US. I've lived here on and off over the years. I'm from Canada, so it's kind of home away from home for me.'

He asked me what I thought of it on this visit. I mentioned the alarming levels of poverty, disenfranchisement, addiction and hopelessness I was seeing.

'Most of the poor people here are just lazy,' he said. 'There are jobs; they could work; they just want to complain.'

'But it's real, what I'm seeing. It feels like the problem is deeper than people just being lazy.'

'Don't feel too bad about all the riff raff. Most of them bring it on themselves.'

¶ In 2002, my partner Jason had been offered film work in New York. With his job came an apartment in Battery Park City, a planned residential area on the west side of the southern tip of Manhattan. I moved there too, to be with him. His father had just died and we were talking about marriage and I wanted a kid. His hours were long, and while he was off filming, I spent my days in our apartment working on my PhD, going to the library, seeing friends and reconnecting with family there. It was a calm period for us after some very up and down years. Because Jason was working, we had a bit of money and he thought it would be fun for us to go to Las Vegas. He booked us a room at the Venetian as a surprise and only told me close to the time of departure what he'd done. I freaked out. The room was $250 a night and, because I couldn't go to Vegas 'ironically', I couldn't see this trip as 'fun'. I am frugal. I have never spent that kind of money on anything. I've never *had* that kind of money to spend on things. We compromised that we would still go, but we'd stay in a less flashy and expensive hotel.

We arrived in the evening and went straight to the El Cortez downtown, where we'd booked a cheap room. I was not prepared. The lights, the noise, the ping-ping-pinging, the fake sound of coins coming down a metal chute, the *Ghostbusters* theme tune inexplicably clanging out at regular intervals, the gamblers with their plastic buckets of change feeding the machines, the lack of windows and clocks. An image has stayed with me: a woman in a motorized wheelchair wears a credit card attached to her wrist with what looks like an old telephone cord. The card is stuck in the machine like a baby's pacifier. She is aggressively pumping the arm of the slot machine as money is being sucked from her bank account. There appears to be no end to her losses.

323

After crossing the casino floor and walking up a couple of flights of stairs, we found our room. The leaking air conditioning unit had left a small puddle in the carpet. The window wouldn't open and everything smelled of cigarette smoke. But it was the grim yellow lighting that slightly undid me. Normally, I can do crappy hotels – in fact I quite like them – but because this was Vegas, where you are supposed to have *fun*, I couldn't do it. I left the room, ran down the stairs, walked through the casino, back to where we'd left the car and collapsed in a sobbing heap. The valet looked at me, then at Jason, and asked almost sarcastically, 'Is she OK?'

I sort of loved him for that. The only words I could get out were, 'This shouldn't be here. None of this should be here!'

We contemplated driving to Los Angeles that night, but as it was late and we were tired, we found another room at the slightly less melancholic Sahara Hotel where we spent the night being cold to each other. Me, unable to verbalize why I had reacted the way I had. He, pissed off that his pre-wedding surprise had so spectacularly failed. I felt guilty and he had every reason to be angry. We left the next morning and headed to Los Angeles.

Three years later, Jason got the idea to make a documentary in Vegas and got some backing from Channel 4. In the early 2000s, it was the fastest growing city in the US. Homes were being built at record speed. Every month, thousands of people were showing up looking for work, mainly in construction and hospitality. Between 1970 and 2000, its population went from 270,000 to 1.3 million, and it looked set to continue rising. It was a boom time, a new kind of gold rush, and Jason wanted to see what this kind of explosive urban growth looked like. I can't remember the details – either I volunteered, or he

324

asked me (or maybe it was a bit of both) – in any case, I ended up accompanying him on his shoot.

We arrived in early spring and unlike our previous trip to Vegas, it was chilly when we landed – that night-time desert cold hit us as we stepped onto the tarmac at McCarran Airport (since renamed the Harry Reid International Airport). We booked into the Motel 6 on Tropicana, where we didn't have to walk across a massive casino floor to get to our room; we could drive to our front door, which was a relief. After about a week at the motel, we found an even cheaper room in an Americas Best Inn & Suites on South Maryland Parkway. It no longer exists and I can't find out what has replaced it because I don't remember the cross-street. The apartment block was aiming for bland, corporate clientele, but judging from the shouting and the regular appearances by the police, they weren't hitting their target demographic. In the grounds was a small swimming pool where kids would play in the daytime and where adults would gather to drink in the evenings. The parking lot of the nearby 7-11 was where the prostitutes and rent boys lined up under the streetlights. In the darker corners, people bought drugs.

One evening, Jason and I went to the little kidney bean-shaped pool to cool off. Vegas had hit a spring heatwave, sending temperatures over 40 degrees Celsius. A man and a woman were lying on loungers, drinking beer. Beverly Hills this was not. The pool looked like it hadn't been cleaned in a very long time and the stench of chlorine was overpowering. But we jumped in to cool down. As we sat on the edge of the pool, the male half of the couple approached. He and his girlfriend were really 'open minded', he told us. Jason and I were their type, apparently. He gave us their room and cell phone numbers on

a scrap of paper and told us to stop by. We were flattered but never followed up.

Meanwhile, Jason had placed an ad in the local newspapers asking for people who'd just arrived in Vegas to get in touch. He wanted to make sense of this place through the stories of those who were arriving to start a new life. One of the people who called us was a young woman who had escaped an abusive home and had hitchhiked to Vegas from a small town in California. She'd been picked up on the highway by a much older guy called Robert. She ended up moving in with him. They had a sort of arrangement: she was free to date other men, and although he more-or-less accepted it, he wasn't too happy with the set-up. They invited us over to their house for a drink so Jason could interview them. The young woman had just found a job in a bar off the Strip. They lived in one of those cream-coloured L-shaped bungalows with metal siding, so familiar to me. It was similar to some of the houses where I grew up in Alta Vista or the one Karl had grown up in in Napanee. It was a tract house, a cookie cutter home, straight out of a Robert Adams photograph. The streetlights, the sidewalks, the rows of tidy bungalows facing each other across a newly paved street – they all just ended where the desert began.

This extreme interface between the built-upon and the wild recalled a passage from Robert Venturi, Denise Scott Brown and Stephen Izenour's 1966 book *Learning from Las Vegas*: 'Beyond the town, the only transition between the Strip and the Mojave Desert is a zone of rusting beer cans,' they wrote. Here there were no rusting beer cans. Here there was only air and the lemony-yellow glow of the streetlights in which the wings of tiny moths fluttered.

I did not collapse into a sobbing existential heap on this return trip to Vegas with Jason in 2005, because I was there to be part of his documenting of the city; I was not there to have *fun*. I was an observer, and through this act of mediation, I was able to see Vegas in a different light. We were not living in the post-modern town described in *Learning from Las Vegas*, nor were we engaging with the city ironically, as a joke, as a flimsy cardboard cut-out, a Pop Art construction, the wet dream of populist pleasure makers, or a simulacrum of a city. I could and still can appreciate the 'messy vitality' of the Strip that the authors of *Learning from Las Vegas* exalt in, along with their enjoyment of the unselfconscious creation of a popular aesthetic. I was also aware that this city is a place where people live, work, write poems, worry about their greying hair, their lack of exercise and their kids' college fees. And, yet, I simply couldn't – and still can't – shake my view of Las Vegas as human folly, a mistake, an aberration, and most importantly an environmental catastrophe. I struggle with the post-modern view of the city because it doesn't take into account Vegas as a place where people simply live and work, nor does it address the ecological devastation necessary for it to exist. These opposing forces were at the heart of the Vegas I first laid eyes on, and were possibly what tore me open on that first night.

One reviewer in 1979 discussed how *Learning from Las Vegas* was 'influenced by the "cultural pluralism" that Denise Scott Brown advocated'. He applauded how the authors approached the Las Vegas strip 'non-judgmentally, as the valid expression of a "taste culture" with its own standards and audience' and how they could see virtue in how 'more or less haphazardly, but organically, an order had evolved on the strip', an order that was

'barely perceptible' but seemed to work. The aesthetic of Las Vegas, where replicas are visited instead of the real thing, where trash at the New York, New York casino is collected in garbage trucks disguised as yellow cabs, where signs and signifiers dissolve, fall apart, collide or merge into each other, is an aesthetic that requires some distance, some objectivity, and feels removed from any recognizable human scale. Although my distance from it helped me see the city anew, I could not discard the thought I had had when I first laid eyes on Vegas. *This shouldn't be here. None of this should be here.* There should not be an all-you-can-eat seafood buffet in the middle of a desert. A cheeseburger should not weigh fifteen pounds and underground wells should not be depleted so that fountains outside casinos can jet hundreds of feet into the air all day, every day to piped classical music, while much of their precious water evaporates into thin air. How can we have fun when we are expected to participate in this ecocidal madness?

The spring and summer that Jason and I were living in Vegas coincided with the hundredth anniversary of what some referred to as the 'founding' of the city in 1905. 'Founding' is a strange word, because the place had been the home of Southern Paiutes for hundreds of years. The Spanish, however, named the settlement 'Las Vegas' or 'The Meadows'. Drawn by a spring-fed creek – the only fresh water for miles – Mormons built an adobe fort here. Part of it is still standing and, in 1999, it was turned into a state park. But 1905 has stuck as the year of the city's birth because that was when the railway came to town and when the land auction was finalized, paving the way for Las Vegas to become incorporated in 1911.

Birthday celebrations had been brewing for months,

culminating in the baking of what would be the largest cake in the world. The seven-layer, 130,000-pound vanilla cake measured 102 feet long, 52 feet wide and contained 23 million calories. On the day of the great cake slicing, Jason and I lined up outside Cashman Center, a large building which looked like a cross between a storage facility, convention centre and a high school gym. We were with Matt, one of the people we had been filming with. He was a soft-spoken and thoughtful gambling addict who'd been cast out of the Church of Jesus Christ of Latter-day Saints for falling in love with a non-Mormon. He was currently homeless and often slept in one of the storm sewers or in the Salvation Army shelter when they had a bed.

Thousands of people showed up for cake. Some clutched Tupperware containers, others cardboard boxes, suitcases, even giant plastic garbage bags to lug their chunks back to their kitchens, offices and rented rooms. We shuffled our way inside where a volunteer in a spattered Costco apron handed us each a slice of cake on a paper plate with a plastic utensil stuck into it like a small pitchfork. The three of us found a spot under a tree and watched people leave the Center with as much cake as they could carry. The scene was like a demented children's picnic directed by Tim Burton. The planners of this birthday celebration had wildly overestimated how many Las Vegans would want to queue up in 40-degree heat for free cake. On that evening's news, I watched in horror as dump truck after dump truck brought mountains of leftovers to a local pig farm and shovelled it into pens for the animals to 'pig out' on. If there were ever a film clip needed to illustrate overabundance and society-as-spectacle in the US, this would be it.

Consumption is one of the engines fuelling the Vegas

that many people come to the city to experience. We have the facts about the environmental cost of this consumption. We know about the extraction of resources needed to make the place hum, sing and glow and we know about the garbage and how most of it ends up in landfill, in oceans or incinerated, creating clouds of toxic smoke. The year Jason and I were there, the hotels, casinos and restaurants alone were creating over half a million tons of garbage a year – enough to fill an American football field 10 metres high every day. We know about the waste, but what can we do with this knowledge?

Like all built environments in the American West, you cannot talk about Vegas without mentioning the element on which its existence depends: water. When I think about Nevada, my mind immediately moves towards that hundredth longitudinal meridian first observed and then described by John Wesley Powell in his 1878 'Report on the Lands of the Arid regions of the United States'. This east–west divide runs from the Canadian border in the north to the Gulf of Mexico in the south, through the Dakotas, Nebraska, Kansas, Oklahoma and Texas. Powell had been commissioned by the government to explore the western territories to see if it were viable to continue carving up and handing out 160-acre parcels for farming and homesteading in the West.

After years of travelling, Powell argued that due to its aridity – the West receives on average less than twenty inches of rain per year – it was almost a separate country from the East. A lack of fresh water and rainfall would not sustain high levels of population or intensive agriculture. The government ignored him and, ever since, precious waterways across the West have been dammed, reshaped, exploited and poisoned in the service of progress, development and unsustainable human activity.

The vast Colorado River, the major waterway in the West and Southwest, became the irrigation source for cities and communities springing up in deserts and on arid lands. Its water was so in demand that in 1922 something called the Colorado River Compact was created, which essentially divided the river into two parts. Those to the north – Colorado, New Mexico, Utah and Wyoming – would be allocated 7.5 million acre-feet of river water a year; while California, Arizona and Nevada were allocated another 7.5 million acre-feet plus a million extra. In order for this to happen, the Colorado would need to be dammed. This is where the Hoover Dam comes in, and the creation of Lake Mead. This body of water is called a 'lake' but really it acts as a reservoir and a site for recreation. In *America Day by Day*, de Beauvoir describes it as

> a large sheet of fake blue water that clashes sharply with the pink rocks. This water is as out of place in the desert as a grove of orange trees on a moor, as a fresh stand of birch trees in reddish sand dunes. It's an unreal landscape ... and it has the deceptive colors of Gauguin. Even though it's man-made, it's a real lake we can see with our own eyes.

Las Vegas still gets most of its water from Lake Mead. Lake Powell (note the ironic name), a reservoir 300 miles away in Utah, is supposed to provide the more northern states with water, but it functions as a holding tank for Lake Mead. Water from it flows through the Grand Canyon and eventually finds its way to this 'large sheet of fake blue water'. No one really understand why we've ended up with this set-up. All we do know is that these enormous reservoirs are running out, and at least four million people rely on Lake Mead for their water. There is now a 'bathtub ring' running around the rock walls of the lake, showing how much the water level has dropped in recent years.

There is another lake in Vegas that isn't being drained at such an alarming rate. Lake Las Vegas in Henderson, a well-off southern suburb of Vegas, has its water replenished from Lake Mead. In 2020 it provided 1.2 billion gallons of water to the people of Vegas. Some of this went on golf courses, some for the canals in the Venetian and some went to private residences, like the mansion in Spanish Trails owned by a prince of Brunei, which used 12,327,000 gallons of water in 2020. All this for one single house in the desert.

Back in 2011, after eight years of drought, golf courses started waking up to the problem of keeping their lawns green. In a 2012 article called 'Water Hazard' in *Golf Course Management* magazine, Mark Leslie talks of the water police who can fine you for misusing the precious commodity, and how even watering lawns at the wrong time of day can land you in trouble. He mentions the fact that the evapotranspiration rate in and around Las Vegas is probably the highest in the country and that golf courses in Vegas pay over a million dollars a year for their water. The article describes methods being used by golf courses to help battle the drought, such as making use of the correct nozzles on their irrigation systems to minimize evaporation, running better water audits, and where there are bodies of water, covering them with something called Aquatain, 'a silicone-based product from Australia ... which promises a reduction in surface-water evaporation in ponds'. Basically, using Aquatain is a bit like spraying liquid Saran Wrap onto your pond. According to the company who makes it, it is harmless to people and aquatic life.

The article also mentions xeriscaping – landscaping

with plants that do not need irrigation. Las Vegas golf course managers are 'converting turf to desert landscape' and 'installing heat-tolerant plants such as acacia, mesquite, Texas Rangers, bird of paradise and vitex bushes; grasses like fountain grass; and trees like palo verde, stone pine, Mondale pine, aleppo pine and various ashes', but choices are limited because, as one person interviewed for the article says, 'It's pretty ugly desert. It doesn't even grow cactus out here, it's too cold and dry and rocky.' And then there is the problem of weeds. The author of the article goes on, 'Removing turfgrass exposes very fertile soil, the ideal growth medium for weeds.' Scott Sutton, a superintendent at the municipal Wildhorse Golf Club in Las Vegas and a 'Certified Golf Irrigation Auditor', says that on his limited budget, he 'couldn't afford pre-emergence herbicide, but discovered another solution: a workforce of individuals working off community-service hours for the district court.'

In November 2021, ten years after this industry article was published, a piece appeared in the *Las Vegas Review-Journal* headlined 'New golf courses that come to Las Vegas won't be able to use Colorado River water for irrigation.' The author, Blake Apgar, writes, 'On average, golf courses in Southern Nevada consume 725 acre-feet — about 236 million gallons — every year. One acre-foot is about what two Las Vegas Valley homes use over the course of sixteen months.' Probably the most upsetting fact is that most of the water used to irrigate golf courses is lost to evaporation and cannot be returned to Lake Mead, unlike water used in homes and businesses, which can be returned to the Lake after being treated.

People are becoming aware of the drought, of the lower water levels. The photos of Lake Mead's bathtub rings – messages from the Earth itself that water levels

338

are falling rapidly – have gone viral. However, nowhere in this coverage is there a mention of the sacredness of water, its necessity to the existence of all life forms, and of our place in this story, which should be one that is in service to this precious liquid. Nothing I read about water use, recreation, tourism, or development in the Las Vegas region manages to shift those words I first uttered when I fled the El Cortez and crumpled in a heap. *None of this should be here.*

Despite the pretence 'that much of our waste gets recycled', most of it ends up in landfill. All across Nevada, the stuff we no longer need or know what to do with has been sent into the desert to be incinerated, buried, left to rot, decompose or, in the case of plastics and forever chemicals, left there to sit out the end of time. It isn't just the 'normal' waste – the Styrofoam cups, chicken bones, water bottles and candy wrappers – that are exiled to the desert near Vegas: there is plenty of the more insidious stuff, the stuff which decomposes over hundreds if not thousands of years.

The Mojave Desert has been blown up, blasted and poisoned by the US military since the first aerial atomic bomb was detonated there in 1951 in a place called Frenchman Flat. In the spirit of revisiting my 2006 trip, I decided to take a look on Google maps at the proximity of Frenchman Flat to the Vegas Strip. Google will not give driving directions, but they do tell me that on foot it is 158 miles and would take 52 hours to walk. There are two tourist reviews of Frenchman Flat: 'Not the best hiking spot,' it reads. 'Felt nauseous for some reason and now I'm slowly losing my hair. Would not recommend.' A more recent review from someone called 'farsyde bop' reads, 'Nice hiking spot, felt nauseous but later my muscles

started to grow and I didn't need to wear my glasses anymore. Only annoyance, my skin is getting greenish when I get angry.'

The famous Nevada Test Site (now rebranded as the Nevada National Security Site), in which Frenchman Flat sits, is about an hour's drive from the Vegas Strip and occupies an area slightly larger than Rhode Island. Over the span of forty years, almost a thousand nuclear bombs were detonated here. The last one, in 1991, was an underground atomic blast called the 'Divider'. This land belongs to the Western Shoshone – a fact often overlooked when people talk about the atomic programme in Nevada.

The Treaty of Ruby Valley was signed between the Shoshone people and the American government in 1863. It stipulated that the tribe would continue to own the land, as recounted by Ian Zabarte, the Principal Man of the Western Bands of the Shoshone Nation, 'in exchange for $5,000 a year for twenty years, paid in cattle and other goods'. The US would also be allowed to 'establish military posts on the land' and 'mine for minerals on it'. Zabarte was born in 1964, a year after above-ground testing of nuclear weapons was banned on his ancestral lands. The US continued to test weapons of mass destruction, but did so underground and at the rate of one almost every three weeks. Between 1951 and 1992, nuclear testing on Shoshone lands created 620 kilotonnes of nuclear fallout. As a point of comparison, the bomb dropped on Hiroshima in 1945 created 13 kilotonnes. In a 2020 article Zabarte wrote for *Al Jazeera*, he lists the people he knows with cancer – some of whom are toddlers. 'Every family is affected', he writes. 'I watched my uncle suffer from horrible cancer that ate away at his throat and my grandfather die of an auto-immune disease that is known

341

to be caused by exposure to radiation. They say he had a heart attack, but when your skin falls off, that puts stress on your heart.'

Despite denials from the US Atomic Energy Commission (AEC), incriminating documents were discovered in 1978 in the state archives of Utah, which was downwind from atomic testing in Nevada. These documents revealed that 18,000 sheep were grazing only a few miles to the north and east of the Nevada Test Site in the early 1950s. None of the ranchers or shepherds were alerted to any dangers before bombs were detonated and their concerns since have mostly been dismissed. In 1979, the *New York Times* reported that, after grazing in Nevada, 'the sheep were returned to Utah in the spring of 1953' where 'ranchers noted that many were sick and dying. Ewes had spontaneous abortions and showed burnlike lesions on the face, neck and ears. The majority of lambs were born dead and stunted, and ewes died either during lambing or a few days later, according to the documents.' None of this was enough to convince the AEC that these illnesses and deaths were related to atomic testing. Two autopsies on sheep showed that the concentration of Iodine 131 – a radioactive isotope – in their thyroid glands exceeded 'by a factor of 250 to 1,000 the maximum permissible concentration of radioactive iodine for humans'. Even this was not enough to persuade the AEC to compensate the people of these lands for the increased number of cancers and other illnesses in their animals and loved ones. Court cases for reparations are still ongoing.

To many people, deserts, often represented as blank areas on maps, are great big nothings. Yet to the humans, non-humans and all living things who have acclimatized to these lands over thousands of years, deserts are home, a refuge. 'To say nothing is out there is incorrect,' writes William Least Heat-Moon. 'To say the desert is stingy with everything except space and light, stone and earth is closer to the truth.'

On federal land, adjacent to the Nevada Test Site, sits Yucca Mountain. I say 'federal land' because that is what it is called in Washington. Really, it is Shoshone land. In 1987, Congress decided that this was where America's nuclear waste would be stored, deep underground. Yucca Mountain, like any place designated to house lethal amounts of nuclear waste, was a compromise. There were supposed to be two nuclear repositories in the US – one in the east; one in the west. Politicians in the east complained that their population was too high to make it viable. So, the less populated west won the nuclear waste lottery, partly because of Nevada's low population but also because it has such a small congressional delegation able to oppose such decisions. The question of where to store nuclear waste is always a headache for politicians. Dumping garbage that can kill or maim your constituents is not a vote winner. In 1989, the state of Nevada enacted legislation to make it illegal to store high-level radioactive waste there. For twenty years, the battle over storing nuclear waste in Yucca Mountain has been a political hot potato. In 2002, under President Bush, it was given the go-ahead, only for it to be halted under President Obama. Meanwhile electricity customers in the US continue paying their bills, some of which contribute to a nuclear waste fund which has already collected $22 billion. Like so much to do with the environment, the problem has not gone away; it has simply been pushed aside.

It will be thousands of years before this waste will be safe to handle or even approach. Despite the arguments around where it should be buried – some of it has already been barrelled up and thrown into the Pacific, while some decision-makers believe we should blast it into space – there is a hotly contested issue around the 'DANGER' sign needed at the entrance to any nuclear burial place. The classic nuclear logo might not be recognized by our descendants, who may be walking the Earth or floating around space thousands of years from now. How do you make them understand that something is too dangerous to touch? What languages will they speak? What symbols will they recognize? How much knowledge will they have of things like half-life, nuclear contamination and the ensuing diseases from such dangerous materials? Will humans even be around then?

In 2017, an architectural design company called 'arch out loud', which brands itself a 'platform for exploring the possibilities of architecture and design ... to create innovative solutions for issues facing our world' hosted a competition for a marker to be placed at the entrance of nuclear waste sites. The hope is that we can create symbols, hieroglyphics, plaques, monuments or pieces of land art which will be able to communicate with humans in 10,000 years from now, warning them of the dangers of nuclear waste. The winner, 'Testbed', was a site-specific piece that transformed the area into 'an experimental field of climate engineering that manipulates the geology of the site itself by setting in motion an open-ended assemblage of processes that generate an entangled scientific earthwork of hybrid formations.' The runners up were called 'A crystalline funeral', 'A Storm is Blowing From Paradise' and 'Lodestar'. These earthworks might all be wondrously innovative, but will they deter or even be understood by future generations? And what about the living beings who don't read and write? The plants, the animals, the very soil itself? How will they be protected?

344

Andra, a French company that designs, develops and operates solutions for radioactive waste, states on their website that the

ASN (Nuclear Safety Authority) safety rule of 1 June 1991 provides for 'the conservation of the repository memory, making it extremely unlikely that human intrusion into the repository area is to be found'. For surface storage, ASN prescribes a minimum of 300 years after closure. For deep storage ... ASN considers that a loss of memory cannot be excluded 'reasonably beyond 500 years....'

In other words, they are trying to create a kind of oral and visual tradition, a collective memory, which will warn future humans away from these nuclear sites. Yet, Andra admits that 'No one can predict whether the organizations today responsible for radioactive waste repositories will still exist in several centuries. Measures are then put in place so that the memory of these centers lasts as long as possible, and this despite possible social or political ruptures.' Interestingly, they state that the most efficient means of transmitting the information around nuclear waste burial is to use words on paper:

New information technologies evolve very quickly, some solutions become obsolete in barely ten to twenty years.... This rapid development is a major problem for the transmission of information. As a precaution, paper is preferred as a support. All digital documents are printed on permanent paper, a future proof solution. This paper, first produced in the 1950s, is a special paper created from pure cellulose that can be stored for a long time, unlike ordinary paper which deteriorates over a few decades.... The existence of a storage center must also be anchored in the collective memory. Andra regularly communicates about the storage centers it operates and maintains this knowledge with the surrounding public. The memory of such a site must be shared with its environment, particularly its residents, from generation to generation.

For us to communicate with people of the future, we will need paper manufactured in the 1950s. Surely this is one of the strangest human projects ever embarked upon. Meanwhile, the collective memories of Indigenous people who have stewarded these lands for millennia, who have a rich oral history embedded here, are being wiped away like an inconvenience. It strikes me as yet another example of our culture's schizophrenia that we are inventing a whole new oral and visual tradition – one devoid of creation myths and land connections – in order to warn future generations of the poisons we have lodged deep inside the Earth, which might kill us and every living thing around us. Instead of creation myths, we are writing our own destruction myths while telling ourselves that this is progress.

Gone are the days when the Rat Pack and fellow cocktail drinkers would watch atomic testing from the roof of a casino as a form of entertainment. During the 1950s, Vegas promoted what it called 'Atomic Tourism', with one casino owner declaring that the nuclear blasts were the best thing to happen to Las Vegas. Guests would stay up all night to wait for the spectacular desert sunrise and sip their final highball as nuclear bombs were detonated at dawn. Gone also are the bikini-clad women who jostled for the title of Miss Atomic Bomb. The winner modelled a bathing suit with ruffles up the front emulating the

famous shape of a mushroom cloud. It is still possible to experience a simulacrum of all this in the National Atomic Testing Museum, where for a few dollars you can experience your very own imitation bomb blast or learn how to survive an atomic explosion by going beyond the basic 'duck and cover' position.

Atomic tourism may be a thing of the past, but we are still living in the Atomic Age. The fallout is all around us still. Those who grew up downwind of the bomb blasts – the 'downwinders' as they're called – those who work in nuclear facilities, those whose land was occupied to make way for atomic testing, do not need any of this simulated for them because they are living with the cancers, the deaths and the birth defects. For most people today, the Atomic Age is less of a spectacle or a beauty pageant and more of a slow, poisonous drip, drip, drip.

It took my return to Vegas in 2006 for me to unpick my initial reaction to the place, to put it in the context of a kind of ground truth – the reaction one feels to a place based on observable, or sometimes invisible, information. In my case it manifested physically. Riding in a gondola in the Venetian is quantitively but not qualitatively different from watching atomic blasts from a casino rooftop. They both spring from the human urge to consume and destroy. Sinking a Mojito at the Wynne or playing the slots at the Bellagio is an act of participation in this destruction. Having *fun* in Vegas is a problem for me. *None of it should be here*. And that includes me.

In the months that Jason and I were living in Vegas's Americas Best Value Inn & Suites on South Maryland Parkway in 2002, I got pregnant. On one particularly hot day, we had been filming on the roof of a multi-storey car park under the beating sun when I began to feel

349

light-headed. The temperature had risen to about 45 degrees Celsius and for the past few weeks my morning sickness had been exacerbated by this extreme, unabating heat. I remember burning my fingertips when I touched the door handle of our car. That evening I realized I was somewhere around the ninth week of pregnancy – a danger-point my body remembered from a previous pregnancy. We were driving back to our apartment after a day of filming when I felt the sickness disappear. Just like that, a switch had been flipped. We brought pizzas back to our room and for the first time in two months, I felt hungry. The next day I bled and bled and didn't leave the apartment. I miscarried and felt the life drain from me. The swiftness of it all somehow suited the hot, shiny, angular hardness of the city.

After the months I'd spent with Jason in Vegas, I knew my way around the city. I was able to navigate the Downtown and the Arts District with its small craftsman bungalows – what they called 'cottages' – the second-hand clothing and furniture shops, the graffiti, the mannequins on the sidewalk wearing feather boas and leather jackets, the galleries, bars and auto repair shops. This urban landscape was recognizable, even familiar, to me. It wasn't the Vegas of the Strip, nor was it the Vegas of tract housing. It was something else entirely, more like the student neighbourhood of a college town or Toronto's Queen Street West, circa 1983.

This city is where my novel about Karl comes to a climax. It's where she sees her mother working in a bar at the El Cortez as a waitress. She notices the lipstick, the short skirt, the dyed blonde hair. Karl meets a man in a diner who vaguely knows Jean and she gets her phone

number. They meet for Mexican food and Jean turns out to be as uninterested in Karl as she had been on the day she walked out. I had created a study in selfish mothers. I think I'd created her as a warning to myself. 'You could be Jean,' I often found myself thinking. I, too, was selfish. I, too, found it difficult to imagine myself as a mother. I, too, liked to run away when things got difficult. There were so few women with babies around me who were making art and writing books. And there was also the issue of bringing another consumer onto a planet with limited resources. And yet, the desire still burned inside me for a child.

The Bridger Inn Hotel sits at 301 South Main Street, which in 2006 was lined with motels in various states of decay. It was like a kinetic museum of collapsing mid-century motel architecture and neon signage. I could envision the piles of leases in back rooms not being renewed, the contracts left unsigned and the real estate being sold off to developers. Gentrification was in the ether then.

I wandered into the Hotel Nevada, next door to the Bridger, a white six-storey building with bright blue lettering that matched the vast, cloudless sky. The look was a meeting of Wild West with a 1970s version of 'moderne'. There was a poster on the front door advertising a café in the lobby, but when I went in, I saw that the café was a dark, smoke-filled room, with a drinks machine and people chain-smoking or sleeping off hangovers. I was fascinated by this strange in-between space where it seemed you were free to indulge whatever you wanted while, at the same time, you were at the mercy of this city, or the limits of your luck and survival instincts. This part of Vegas felt on the cusp of being razed to the ground and redeveloped. I could sense it was being primed for something big because everything around me was crumbling. I had seen this kind of thing happen in Toronto, New York and London. You can always tell when the arts district of a city is being taken over by developers. It's a little like that light sleep before an early flight or a job interview, when you keep waking up to check the time, a sort of nebulous consciousness just before something big is about to happen.

¶ The first entry in my journal on my 2006 visit to Vegas was written in the Art Bar on Main Street. This drinking spot would not have looked out of place in Hackney or Brooklyn. The red velvet sofas, the bust of Elvis, the paintings of James Brown and Aretha Franklin reflecting the palette of de Kooning, a few 'drip' paintings. It was dark and the airwaves were channelling Eminem, loudly. I ordered a Corona with a slice of lime as I settled in to write in my journal. The TV was on above the bar. The sound had been muted, but subtitles ran along the bottom of the screen. A brunette with a Barbie-esque figure walked into an office. She sat next to a shiny wooden, presidential desk. She picked up what I thought was a jellyfish. We were not entering the realm of Dadaism, however. The jellyfish turned out to be a silicone breast implant. A man entered the room to join her, but he took the big chair behind the desk. It turned out that he was a plastic surgeon and she was his wife and he had done dozens of surgeries on her and she was thrilled about every single nip, tuck, boob job and fat extraction. They were now choosing a new pair of breasts 'for fun'. No one else had been watching the TV. The other customers were having a good time, chatting and laughing. Karl and her crush Ben would have an argument about this TV show. Ben would be saying 'Why not?' and Karl would be saying, 'But why?' She was not in love with Ben. Her mother was trying to fleece her out of a house. Karl was finding Vegas disorienting.

I drank my beer and wandered down to the El Sombrero, where Jason and I used to eat because it was cheap, lively and served until late. When we were filming in Vegas, First Fridays had only been going for three years – when galleries and businesses opened up late on the first Friday of every month for a bit of a party.

In those days, I heard the area referred to simply as the Arts District; now it had been rechristened 18b after its 18-block length.

Earlier in the day, I'd walked around the brightly painted bungalows off Main Street, wandered into the large Arts Factory with its galleries and studio spaces, and wended my way to the enormous second-hand furniture and clothing store The Funk House. Between 2002 and 2006, the area had seen a small boom, and serious monied art dealers had started moving in. There were locals who wanted to hang onto the grassroots, ground-up, spontaneous running of the Arts District and those who were pushing for a more corporate approach. The divide seemed to be widening. In 2005, a reporter for *Las Vegas Weekly* described a gathering where big-time art dealers with their collections of 'Rauschenbergs, Ruschas and Rosenquists' met with local downtown artists. There was talk of the 'Manhattanization' of Vegas's Arts District and the spectre of gentrification that looked set to price out smaller galleries.

The month that I was staying in the Bridger Inn Hotel choreographing Karl's meeting with her waitress mother and her unhappy affair with Ben, a seminal meeting was going on just down the street in the little wooden cottages across from The Funk House. An artist known as Dray, who was the first to bring his studio to the run-down bungalows, had painted a mural on his cottage called *The Birth of an Arts Scene*. It showed a naked woman holding a flower. Two months after I rolled out of Vegas heading for Los Angeles in 2006, Andre 'Dray' Wilmore painted over all his murals, including *The Birth of an Arts Scene*, after he and fellow tenants were served with eviction notices.

Everything in that area changed for good in 2011 when

Tony Hsieh, CEO of the highly successful online retail business Zappos, purchased the First Friday trademark. Hsieh had a Silicon Valley entrepreneur mentality, as evidenced in an ad he published looking for staff who were: 'Fun-loving ... the heart and soul of our culture.... If you are "fun and a little weird" ... please take a look at our openings.... At the Zappos Family of Companies, over-sized egos are not welcome. Over-sized Eggos, however, are most welcome and appreciated.' Eggos are a kind of packaged waffle you heat up in your toaster.

Hsieh's expanded vision for Downtown Vegas soon became more apparent as he bought up large swathes of it, launching what he called the Downtown Project with $350 million of his own money. This was to create a neighbourhood for his employees and local Las Vegans where they could 'work, live and play'. That same year, in 2011, a twenty-foot-tall showgirl sculpture representing Las Vegas at Burning Man (as part of a partnership between the Burning Man organization and the First Friday organizers) was set alight, the crowd chanting, 'Burn it! Burn it! Burn it!' as her boa and clothes were incinerated. This event was billed as a celebration of 'radical self-expression' rather than what to me sounds like a dystopian scene from the end of the world. The end of the world, meanwhile, was namechecked by the dancers, singers, musicians and showgirls who went on to perform 'The Burning Opera: How to Survive the Apocalypse'. Electronic music blared from a 100,000-watt sound system and the party went through the night. In a *Las Vegas Weekly* article from 2012, Hsieh's First Friday manager explained the significance of the burn as a time when 'everybody really came together and did exactly what they were supposed to do. Total cooperation. And that's what it's all about – working together.'

Some of the long-term businesses and the less well-off population who lived in low-rent motels and apartments, on and around Main Street, were not so happy with the burning of effigies and the radical self-expression. They just wanted to live affordably and stay in business. Things came to a head when the Downtown Project bought the Fremont Family Market and Deli, which catered to the area's low-income residents. Despite having been there for fifteen years and having recently spent $50,000 refurbishing their store to appeal to Zappos employees, their lease was not renewed. They were given four months to leave, and the property was leased to the Downtown Project.

As I walked down Main Street at night in that spring of 2006, it was clear that among those looking for an evening out, a bite to eat, maybe some blackjack or live music, there were others who looked barely able to make ends meet; some were scoring, high, or on the edge of sanity. Many could barely walk. The membrane between me and the outsiders, the weirdos, the drunks, the people struggling, always feels so thin. One small but potentially cataclysmic event could be the difference between being able to sleep in a warm, safe bed and lying on a piece of cardboard on the street.

Tony Hsieh was seen as a visionary, a generous man who dreamed of turning unloved parts of a city into 'collision bowls' and of *Delivering Happiness* – the title of his 2010 book, whose subtitle is *A Path to Profits, Passion and Purpose*. After his controversial development of Vegas, where some locals felt overlooked, Hsieh sold Zappos to Amazon for $1.2 billion but remained its CEO until 2020. At this point, Hsieh had set his sights on purchasing real estate in upmarket Park City, Utah, where he had bought a 16-million-dollar mansion with a private lake. Over the years, his drug use became widely known as did his increasing paranoia and disassociation from reality. The police were often called to his property over complaints of pyrotechnics and loud parties that lasted sometimes for weeks. His behaviour became noticeably more erratic. One newspaper reported in December 2020 that Hsieh 'starved himself of food, dropping weight to under 100 pounds; he tried not to urinate, and he deprived himself of oxygen, turning toward nitrous oxide, which can induce hypoxia... Hsieh's drug addiction was just one component of his increasing rash behavior, which escalated into fascinations with fire.' In 2021, he died of complications from smoke inhalation after a fire broke out in a shed he had locked himself in. He was 46.

In 2023, the Strip still functioned as a magnet for tourists and fun-seekers. After checking in and dropping my bags in my room at the Tropicana, I walked outside to a beautiful spring evening to try and find some supper. The sky was an expanse of rosy pink, but the noise, the crowds, the flashing billboards and the escalators needed to cross the roads that intersect with the Strip were all too much for me that night. What does it do to a space, to a city, to a human being when the streets can no longer be crossed on foot? The scale of it dwarfed and overwhelmed me.

I'd been up for thirty-six hours and just wanted some food before heading to bed. I went back into the Tropicana and took a seat in the first bar I came to, the Trago, where I ordered a ten-dollar Corona. The music was generic, pulsing, a kind of housified Motown being flogged to death. A woman came in and ordered a whisky. She lit up and started playing Keno. The smell of her cigarette was a strangely welcome boost of nostalgia.

I carried on scrolling through the Tropicana website

looking for information on where to eat. I have no sense of direction, especially in windowless spaces, so this was a fruitless exercise. I had zero idea of where to find the Oakville Tuscan Grill, the Red Lotus Asian Kitchen, the Chill'm Bar or even the Starbucks. The noise from the machines, the music, the recirculated air and the artificial lights unmoored me. At this point, I would have settled for a crust of dry bread if it meant being somewhere peaceful. After wandering around the casino, I found Robert Irvine's Public House, billed as a 'classic American pub'. I took a seat at the bar and ordered a beer and a hummus plate. I was tired and had no fight in me. The hummus had a metallic, semi 'off' taste to it but I was too hungry to say anything.

A man took the stool next to mine. Clean-cut. Chinos. A pressed shirt. He was from Spokane, had a wife and a couple of kids. He liked a lot of Trump's policies, although he didn't like Trump, *per se*. He supported Pence because he felt he was 'straight and presidential'. Biden, in his view, 'had no control over the country. There was too much poverty because of the bad economy.'

We were on opposite sides of the political spectrum, but we managed to have a civil conversation. We identified many of the same problems, we simply had different ideas about their solutions. The screen in the restaurant was showing a hockey game between Pittsburgh and Dallas. We got to talking about hockey. We realized that we both liked the Montreal Canadiens. We cheered on Pittsburgh together until my bill arrived.

I took the elevator up to my room with its muted tones, its bamboo furniture keeping to the 'tropical theme' and its general air of easy comfort. I couldn't help but wonder what cities and buildings – in fact the entire built environment – would look like if we applied some of the ethics of ecology to them – some of Aldo Leopold's 'land ethic'. Cities decay, but forests evolve (if we let them), rivers can run dry or burst their banks, deserts can expand and contract; nature is fluid and responsive, and yet cities so often seem to go in one direction: they either fall apart – their skyscrapers scattering on the wind like thistledown – or they become slightly more resilient through gentrification. Even cities that have been gentrified and support greener, more sustainable communities are at risk from climate-change induced disasters like flooding and wildfires.

Perhaps it is our deep knowledge that cities are essentially finite, that they will eventually crumble, that keeps some of us gravitating towards nature for a sign of how to live well on the planet. By 'well', I mean in a constant harmonious state whereby we take what we need to survive and thrive while giving back to the Earth what it needs in return. Aldo Leopold called on humans to recognize that we are members of a 'biotic team' and that we should act in ways that 'preserve the integrity, stability, and beauty of the biotic community'. Surely cities can also be seen as biotic communities. 'We can be ethical only in relation to something we can see, feel, understand, love, or otherwise have faith in,' Leopold wrote. Our ability to reframe the urban as something we can love seems at once out of our reach and yet crucial to the health of human and non-human life on our planet. The sense of beautiful permanence within the fluidity of ecological systems exists in direct contrast to the fact that even the tallest, most expensive skyscraper, even Vegas's MGM Grand or Tony Hsieh's mansion in Park City, will one day fall and will, over time, become dust.

By the time I got to Vegas – both in 2006 and in 2023 – I was hitting that stage in my travels when the end was in sight. In 2006, I hadn't wanted it to stop. I did have a husband to return to and a series of part-time jobs, but there was a sense I could carry on floating indefinitely. I was enjoying it. I was feeling, in the words of the author David Gessner, like a 'polygamist of place', happiest when moving through cities, towns, service stations, highways, sunrises and sunsets with my fellow travellers. The Greyhound bus window was like a movie screen showing a picture I felt I could watch forever. It became addictive.

In 2023, I felt differently. The people around me seemed more desperate than they had in 2006, which made me more aware that my travels on the Greyhound were by choice. I could escape; many couldn't. This added a layer of unease to my journey. A different but equally stark observation was centred around the fact that as an older woman I no longer seemed to have the currency I did in 2006. I got asked for directions, I got asked for money and food, but interactions rarely went much further beyond this. It was difficult to parse how much of this was down to no longer being seen as a sexual being and how much was due to the increased atomization of society, the prevalence of screens, the ubiquity of prescription and non-prescription drugs, and a general social anomie. The paradox of travelling as an older woman was that while I had become more aware of myself and my physical limitations, I was simultaneously less visible to those around me. Much as I was entranced by this recent trip across the continent, it didn't hold me with quite the same tenderness it had seventeen years previously.

In *On the Road*, Sal Paradise had with him a copy of Alain-Fournier's *Le Grand Meaulnes*, but he 'preferred reading the American landscape' as he went along. 'Every bump, rise, and stretch in it mystified my longing,' he wrote. 'In inky night we crossed New Mexico; at gray dawn it was Dalhart, Texas; in the bleak Sunday afternoon we rode through one Oklahoma flat-town after another; at nightfall it was Kansas. The bus roared on.'

Moving helps me think. The nomadic impulse is one I understand. Yet recently I have been thinking more about the place-based environmental approach as espoused by writers I admire, like Wendell Berry, Gary Snyder and Aldo Leopold, who opened my eyes to the wonder of being 'in place' and the knowledge that can arise from closely observing and tending where you are living. Snyder's *Practice of the Wild* is an extraordinary call not only to steward, but to love the Earth you live upon. Berry brings an element of pragmatism through his understanding of sustainable agriculture. Is it possible to create this kind of relationship to one piece of land today, when we are living in such different times, with their own specific social, cultural and economic forces? This place-based environmentalism is in essence sedentary and involves a deep communion with land and a generous, steady approach to nurturing it. The philosophy appeals and entices, but how many of us today can buy or rent a patch of land and give it the time and the care that it needs? As someone who has been peripatetic for much of my life, I dream of such rootedness.

In his 2018 book *The Prophet of Dry Hill*, David Gessner explores this conflict between the desire to stay in one place in order to 'marry' the land, and living in the real world of job instability, high rent, expensive housing and the need to care for dependants. Gessner and his wife had dreamed of making Cape Cod their patch, but it became impossible. His employment there was temporary, they couldn't afford the real estate and if he were to continue in academia and therefore earn a living, they would need to move. While Gessner believed deeply in the value and richness of committing to a place in the way previous generations had, he felt that, 'Maybe it wasn't possible simply to repeat and relive the old verities. The world was more crowded, land more expensive.' When he and his wife left Cape Cod, they felt bereft. 'We had a sneaking suspicion that we were leaving the best place we had ever lived and the best place we would ever live,' he writes. 'We'd be losing something when we left, something subtler than a nice view. We were going to miss the raw stimulation of living so close to the water and the bluff. And we were going to miss a deeper connection that we couldn't yet put into words.' I understood this so well.

In 2014, my husband and I moved from East London to Montana. Living there introduced me to people whose lives were so intertwined with the land that the boundary between them and the soil was almost non-existent. Leaving Montana after two years really did feel like I was turning my back on 'the best place we had ever lived'. Yet economic realities tore us away from the place I still, to this day, yearn for. 'I was giving up not just the place but the idea that I would ever commit to a place,' Gessner writes, echoing my feelings exactly.

The philosophy of living-in-place and connecting closely with the land is appealing, but how feasible is it? Are there other ways of thinking about our relationship to the planet and how best to live on it? I wonder if our desire to be connected to a place has something nostalgic about it, something to do with a past many of us romanticize and one that we can never regain. Those who are not able to put down roots often move around because they have to – they are chasing that job or that cheaper housing or simply trying to better their life. Some of us move around because we are seeking somewhere to lay roots but never quite find the right soil. Even those who do find their place, who tend their patch, risk being uprooted as extreme weather, fewer resources, environmental degradation and less economic stability lead to unplanned but necessary migration.

Buried deep inside my dream of settling in one place lay a very small seed. This consisted of my desire for a child, an anchor to my present, a link to my past, to some kind of future and the cycles of nature. A person can also be a place – a temporal and emotional locus. Yet here I was back in Vegas where, twenty-one years previously, I felt I had seen the most wrong place imaginable. And it was also where I had been pregnant and then felt another little life slip away.

In 2006, at the Bridger Inn Hotel in Vegas, I had a dream. I was rolling around in a white room. My nose began to bleed and I was splattering blood all over the pristine white walls. I wanted it to stop but I couldn't stem the flow. When I woke, my first thought was about death. Then I realised that blood is also life. This dream was about childbirth.

Towards the end of her trip across the US, Ethel Mannin also had a vivid dream. It was, according to her, a dream of her death.

> There was an intense and increasing light, which enveloped me; I was at the heart of it; it intensified all the time, and I knew there was no escape from it, and I said to myself, "So this is it; this is what it is to die." I wasn't afraid, only interested, and sad that it was the end.

Strangely she saw it as a literal dream about her

368

physical death. Since it came at the very end of her trip, I wonder whether it might also have been about the death of her cross-country journey. We are different people when we travel. We are able to leave some of ourselves behind. This is freeing. When these long journeys end, we must take the time to mourn them and to mourn the person who made the journey. She is often not the same person who returns home.

Waking up on the eleventh floor of the Tropicana, I could only make out a blurry sunrise, as the windows were covered with semi-opaque glazing to keep out the harsh sunlight. What view I had was a smear of coloured, abstract shapes. The room was large, clean and comfortable. I'd had a very good sleep. However, the room's efficiency was more than I was used to. The water pressure in the shower hurt my nipples and the steam from it set off the fire alarm. I asked at the front desk if they might have another discounted room. They didn't. Someone who had been in the queue waiting to check in told me that the 66-year-old hotel was being demolished next year to make way for a 1.5-billion-dollar baseball stadium. Vegas loves its reinventions.

The cheapest room on the HotelTonight app was $250 and it was slightly out of town. Taylor Swift was performing in Vegas, so beds were at a premium. I eventually found one at the Downtowner for $139, which was cheap considering it was a Saturday night with one of history's most successful pop stars in town.

I had been to the Downtowner before. When Jason was making his film in Vegas, we went to meet a potential film subject there. He had been an out-of-work actor whose claim to fame had been a brief appearance in *Almost Famous* and a friendship, according to him, with the film's director, Cameron Crowe. I can't remember the details of his story, but he had something he wanted to share with us, so we headed to the Downtowner to meet him. When we got to the motel, he wasn't there. Guys in string vests sat on the stairs outside their rooms smoking, looking like they needed something but didn't know how to get it. The place felt weary, but it definitely had good bones.

Built in 1963, the two-storey, white stucco building was like something dropped in from Palm Springs – all mid-century modern proportions. In 2015, as part of Tony Hsieh's downtown remodelling, it was given a total makeover. There was a slightly sad unused mini-golf course and 1950s-style furniture. My room backed onto North 8th Street, which was a party street on a Saturday night. Not all the parties sounded fun. I also had a set of metal stairs right outside my door which led to the first floor. There was a lot of running up and down those steps, a lot of 'Open the fucking door!' and at one point several hard suitcases ricocheted down them. Around 4 a.m. things got quiet and I managed to get a couple of hours of sleep.

In 2006, I left Las Vegas after two nights and headed to Los Angeles, where I stayed with my friend Alex in Venice Beach. For my last night in Vegas, I had followed Karl around. She and I went to the Sports Bar in the California Hotel, which was a five-minute walk down Main Street from the Bridger Inn. Despite the name, the California is a Hawaiian-themed hotel. We ordered a Corona with a slice of lime. The guy next to us, a real joker, asked the pretty blonde bartender when the dancing girls would be coming on. She did a fake laugh and shrugged it off. Just as Karl and I were getting a bit fed up of this guy's nervous energy – you could feel him trying to come up with baited lines to reel the bartender in with – his phone rang. You're not allowed phones in casinos, so he ducked down behind his bar stool to take the call. It was obviously his wife asking what he was doing because, after a short pause, he whispered, 'I'm just here lusting after my wife.'

Karl and I headed back to our hotel where the next morning I prepared to say goodbye to her and to Vegas. I could leave her here to fend for herself now as I had found the ending to her story. After I had written the scene of Karl arguing with Ben about the plastic surgeon, the denouement of the novel emerged: Karl ended up playing pool in a downtown bar with an older woman called Eileen who was having a farewell party with friends as she was in the process of moving to St. Louis. Karl got blind drunk and ended up going home with Eileen who took care of her. They spent several days and nights together and then Eileen drove off to St. Louis, while Karl got on a Greyhound to head back to Napanee where she would be starting from scratch: no home, no job, no family and the emotional upset of meeting her selfish, aloof mother. In the Tulsa Greyhound station, Eileen calls Karl. After this phone conversation Karl realises she is in love. She changes course and heads to St. Louis. It was important for me that despite everything, Karl would find safety. The novel had found its resolution.

This is where my April 2006 journal ends. I have no notes about the final part of my trip. I recorded none of my six-hour bus journey to Los Angeles, neither on paper nor in my memory. It is like a desert on a map: empty. But just like a real desert, it is full of life, conversations, dreams – it is just that I can't recall them. I do remember my friend Alex picking me up at Union Station in Los Angeles (the one with lockers like columbariums) and hugging me when I stepped onto the concourse. How good it was to lay eyes on her. I remember her little craftsman bungalow in Venice Beach surrounded by bougainvillea, roses and dwarf palm trees. I remember having a shower when I arrived and the soft towel she gave me. We walked along the beach and talked about babies, or our lack of them. She was also at a point in her life when she wanted to become a mother and was struggling with it. We watched an unseasonal downpour for several days as the streets flooded. It was cold and grey. I had never experienced Los Angeles like this. She asked about my novel and I told her the ending. We drank tea. We slept. Then I had to leave. My trip was over. So was Karl's.

In 1947, Simone de Beauvoir felt immense sadness at leaving the United States. She wasn't just leaving the US, she was leaving her lover Nelson Algren. Although she doesn't talk about their love affair in *America Day by Day*, this separation must have added to her sense of melancholy at returning to Paris. She wrote:

> Yes, I believe that this is what moves me so strongly at the moment of my departure: America is one of the pivotal points of the world, where the future of man is being played out. To "like" America, to "dislike" it – these words have no meaning. It is a battlefield, and you can only become passionate about the battle it is waging with itself, in which the stakes are beyond measure.

It is indeed a pivotal point of the world. But it isn't only battles that are being played out. There are strangers sleeping in buses next to each other, feeling nothing but warmth for the people around them. There are sunsets and sunrises and little clouds of sand and soil being whipped up in winds somewhere in the deserts of New

Mexico or Arizona or Texas. There are people laughing and there are human connections being made outside the digital world, in the world of the senses. It is these things that matter. The stars exist just where they should, all around the 'more than sufficient Earth' that Walt Whitman conjured. When life conspires to bring you to a patch of land under a trail of stars in our more than perfect sky, look up. Look up and keep looking up until you can't any longer.

In 2023, I also spent two nights in Vegas before heading to Los Angeles. History was repeating itself. My friend Alex had left Venice Beach and was now living in Santa Monica. This journey was the last lap of my trip. The bus was leaving Las Vegas at a respectable 11.30 a.m., so I took advantage of the beautiful spring morning and the bowl of blue sky to walk around Downtown and take photos. Fremont Street was just outside my front door at the Downtowner. I wandered along it, between Maryland and 14th Street, a block lined with falling-down mid-century motels just waiting to be demolished and developed. All those 1950s signs, the rooms full of stories and dreams and losses. The optimism of that mid-century architecture, when the word 'atomic' meant good, big, expansive, fun, full of life.

Quite a few people had bedded down on the street outside my motel, but it was so quiet that I could hear birds singing. I found a café called PublicUs, yet another establishment that wouldn't accept cash. On top of this drive towards cashlessness there was an increasingly annoying 'tipping' theme I'd been noticing. I am a good tipper. I know what it's like to rely on tips because I put myself through three years of university and four years of art school by waitressing in Toronto. But a strange new system has crept in. After tapping your card on an electronic reader, you are now asked how much tip you would like to add. Even when you buy a bottle of orange juice at a deli counter or a muffin in a bakery or a plant in a flower shop, a tipping function is added, where the option is to give an extra 18, 20, 25 or even 30 per cent. Often the 'service' in question consists of a member of staff removing an item from a refrigerator or handing you a product from a shelf. When I asked the servers if they actually received this added tip, many didn't know.

Turning the tip function off and simply paying for your item's advertised price requires some fiddling with the machine – and in my case, putting on my reading glasses. There is also a sense of embarrassment over the fact you might be ungrateful for the server's polite and cheerful delivery of a cup of coffee. This new form of extraction from a customer is what's known as 'tip creep', and my instincts around its iniquitousness were right. When the worker in the flower shop or the deli turns the Apple Pay machine around for you to tap with your debit or credit card, and a prompt for a tip pops up, that worker can be classified as a 'tipped worker'. In 43 states in the US, a tipped worker can be paid as little as $2.13 an hour. Well-known chains have normalized this. It's a good way for companies to pay their workers less while appearing to care for them. In fact, it's quite the opposite.

The bus from Vegas to Los Angeles was full, but I won the Greyhound lottery and got a seat to myself. As people filed on, the driver stood at the door of the bus checking tickets. A young woman with matted hair stood talking to him. She wore black leggings, a white T-shirt, flipflops and white socks, which were grey with dirt. Her ankles were noticeably swollen. She looked seriously unwell.

She was pleading with the driver to let her on. She had no ticket and he wasn't having it.

As passengers filed on, the woman sitting in the front seat – the spot that calls to the chatty eccentrics – said to a young and very made-up woman as she walked past, 'Look at your eyelashes! Some people can't get them on straight. Yours are just perfect!'

'Thank you so much,' came the reply as the young woman headed to the back of the bus.

The driver took his seat and we pulled out of the station.

Chatty Woman asked the driver if Greyhound were related to FlixBus.

'They own us!' he replied, not sounding too happy about it.

She asked him to tell her where we would be stopping and he obliged.

'We'll be at Barstow for a 30-minute food break in two and a half hours. We'll be getting into San Bernardino at 3.45 and L.A. at 5 p.m.'

'Thank you for letting me sit here,' she said to the driver. 'Last time I was on the bus, I had a seizure. A girl kept kicking me. She thought I was a drug addict.'

I was already feeling nostalgic. I was going to miss this strange soundscape of overheard conversation, these snatches of insight into people's histories you are privy to on a Greyhound.

We were sailing through the Mojave Desert. I've done this route several times and yet each time, I am lulled into a sort of desert trance. I look out waiting for anything new that might show up along the far-off horizon rippling with distant mountains. Just beyond the Nevada–California state line, we came upon a vast solar farm of 350,000 giant computer-controlled mirrors, each one roughly the size of a large garage door. The site looked like something a set designer would make if tasked with creating a futuristic place of worship or a mad king's desert palace. In the background, the Clark Mountain range showed off its pink and violet palette.

This facility, the Ivanpah Solar Electric Generating System, was built on 5 square miles of public land. When it opened in February 2014, it was the world's largest thermal power station and had been given the green light by California's then-governor Arnold Schwarzenegger, who broke ground for the project in 2010. Since its opening, there has been controversy over the facility. In its first year of operation the Associated Press reported that it was producing 'about half its expected annual output'. The state of California's energy commission laid the blame inexplicably on 'clouds, jet contrails and weather'. Weather?

The Wall Street Journal wrote in 2015 that 15 months after starting up, the plant was producing just 40 per cent of what was expected. For those who supported and invested in this plant, namely the Federal Government who put $1.6 billion in loan guarantees into it, along with NRG Energy, Google Inc. and BrightSource Energy, these were mere teething problems. For critics of the solar farm these issues were emblematic of a kind of greenwashing, of trying to satisfy unsustainable levels of consumption with equally unsustainable and underproductive energy generation.

By 2017, the facility finally met its contractual obligations for energy output: enough to power 140,000 homes, however this seems a paltry number considering both the enormity and the environmental impact of the array. The technology developed for Ivanpah is different from the average photovoltaic panels you see on rooftops.

The plant runs instead on something called a solar-thermal system. In this system, the mirrors reflect sunlight to boilers which sit on 140-metre-high towers – slightly taller than the Great Pyramid of Giza. The boilers produce steam, which is converted into mechanical energy in a turbine, which in turn powers a generator to produce electricity. It was originally thought that steam from these boilers would be needed for only an hour a day, during startup of the facility each morning. But it turned out that in order to function, the boilers needed four and a half hours of gas powering. State energy regulators granted this increase, which meant that the natural gas usage to power the plant went up by 60 per cent. There is also the challenge of keeping the mirrors dust-free in a desert which is made up of dust and sand and wind.

The commission which granted the use of extra natural gas for the running of the site stated that, 'Because the plant requires sunlight to heat water and turn it to steam, anything that reduces the sunlight will affect steam conditions, which could damage equipment and potentially cause unsafe conditions.' It seems strange that such a Heath Robinsonesque set-up could be justified for the powering of a mere 140,000 homes.

And then there are the birds. You can't talk about the Ivanpah Solar Plant without mentioning the estimated 6,000 birds who die every year because of this facility. Louis Sahagún in the *Los Angeles Times* wrote, 'A macabre fireworks show unfolds each day along I-15 west of Las Vegas, as birds fly into concentrated beams of sunlight and are instantly incinerated, leaving wisps of white smoke against the blue desert sky.' The unsuspecting birds are chasing the insects they need for survival – which in a desert environment is already precarious. 'Workers at the Ivanpah Solar Plant have a name for the

377

spectacle: "Streamers".' These streamers 'spiral constantly through the superheated air surrounding Ivanpah's towers'. NRG Energy Inc claim they are doing everything they can to mitigate the horrific and painful death of these desert birds.

'If there's a silver bullet out there, maybe we'll find it,' said David Knox, a spokesman for NRG Energy Inc. According to Knox, NRG Energy has tried a whole host of techniques for preventing the thousands of bird deaths each year, such as replacing floodlights with LED bulbs to attract fewer insects and therefore fewer birds. They've also attached 'anti-perching spikes to the towers', along with 'devices that broadcast digital recordings of loud, high-pitched shrieking noises'. So much for noise pollution in this pristine desert. My favourite 'solution' is the fitting of machines onto the towers that emit a 'non-lethal avian respiratory irritant derived from grape juice concentrate'. But Knox himself says, 'We know these deterrents are effective in general commercial use. Are they effective in a solar energy plant? We're trying to figure that out.' Migratory birds rely on the Mojave Desert as a travel corridor. The presence of this facility is causing what Garry George, the energy director for Audubon California, calls a 'bird sink'. Ivanpah 'continues to operate', he says, 'as though there's an endless supply of birds to burn'.

Birds are one casualty of the plant. Desert tortoises, bats and chaparral birds (AKA road runners) are also victims of this technology. The knock-on effect of such an enormous construction on this precious and fragile land is unimaginable. And yet we want to heat our homes and drive our cars. Those living in cities like Vegas or Phoenix rely on air conditioning to survive the heat. We have to charge our iPads, iPhones and laptops in order to

378

do our jobs and keep in touch with each other. And therein lies the crux of it all. Our entire society is built upon consumption and growth, and this isn't going to stop any time soon.

If the Ivanpah Solar Plant is shaped like the semi-circle of an ancient Greek auditorium radiating out into the desert, then the stage area is occupied by the Primm Valley Golf Club. As our bus glided past it, I took in the lush emerald-green grass covering the fake little hillocks. The visual juxtaposition of a giant solar array with lawns manicured for putting a ball around in a desert seemed to encapsulate our relationship to the Earth – a mad, extractive one.

Still on the I-15, the bus was quiet. I was enjoying the empty seat next to me as I watched the desert roll by. We passed a sign saying 'MP Materials Mountain Pass Mine'. According to their website, the 'Mountain Pass Rare Earth Mine and processing Facility is the only scaled site of its kind in the Western Hemisphere' and its facility is 'equipped with state-of-the-art environmental systems, including a dry tailings facility that recovers and recycles more than one billion liters [sic] of water per year'. They mine nine different rare earth minerals for use in all manner of manufacturing, from night vision goggles, cars and military and medical devices to lenses, LED lighting and mobile electronic devices.

The mine site was originally discovered in 1949 when prospectors stumbled upon a radioactive vein in the ground. With the advent of the Atomic Age, the prospectors were hoping to discover uranium. It wasn't uranium, but rather bastnaesite, along with a treasure trove of other rare earth metals. The Molybdenum Corporation

of America (which later changed its name to Molycorp) bought most of the mining claims and began digging in 1952. Europium, used in colour televisions, was mined here, along with other metals, for thirty years. By the 1980s, the 50-acre open pit mine met most of the world's needs and all of the country's needs for rare earth metals.

To help with production and meet growing demands, Molycorp built an underground wastewater pipeline between the mine and the Ivanpah Dry Lake. They gave their word to California state regulators that the pipeline would only be used to transport uncontaminated salty water. Because of their promise, they were permitted to dump this water into the dry lakebed, where it would evaporate (unless of course the lakebed filled with water as it has in the past). However, in 1996, Molycorp accidentally ruptured the pipeline during a routine cleaning. This caused a massive spill which in turn triggered an investigation. According to some reports, there have been sixty spills of this supposed uncontaminated wastewater. Upon inspection, it turned out that the 'salty water' Molycorp had been piping for fifteen years contained high levels of heavy metals and radioactive matter. The spills deposited over a million gallons of poisonous wastewater into the ancient lakebed. A civil lawsuit was brought against Molycorp for violating California state drinking water laws. The company was ordered to pay $3.6 million to clean up their mess and they were also slapped with an additional $410,000 for not reporting hazardous radioactive spillage containing lead and uranium. The company suspended operation in 1998, but there was still the problem of what to do with the millions of kilos of toxic radioactive sludge that had accumulated in the Ivanpah Dry Lake.

Eventually a site in Utah was found for the dumping

of this waste, a place called the White Mesa Mill. This uranium mill had been built on White Mesa in the late 1970s – a stunningly beautiful patch of Utah desert, home to hundreds of members of the Ute Mountain Ute tribe. The facility was originally designed to break up rocks containing natural uranium ore dug up at mines – such as the Mountain Pass mine – across the Southwest, and to process them, thus creating a concentrated uranium powder known as 'yellowcake'. This was to be shipped elsewhere in the US and abroad to be further refined and made into fuel for nuclear reactors. In the 1980s, the uranium market slumped and the White Mesa mill faced closure unless it could find an alternative revenue stream. This is where the garbage comes in. The mill now makes millions of dollars from storing waste that is too dangerous or radioactive to put into normal incinerators or storage facilities. Currently its massive waste pits hold almost 320 million pounds of toxic soup. In order to build these storage ponds, important archaeological sites and burial places dating back to the Basketmaker and Ancient Puebloan societies were bulldozed. A quick peek at Google maps shows rectangular azure lakes with rounded corners, like giant airplane windows, shimmering blue against the ochre ground of the desert.

In 2017, a group of private equity investors, under the name MP Materials, bought the mine in order to revive the rare earth metals industry. These investors made the mine public in 2020 and have ramped up production since. The relationship between the White Mesa Mill and MP Materials has continued. Through a complicated series of deals and with Utah regulators' authorization, toxic waste continues to be sent to White Mesa, which it should be noted is about a mile from Bears Ears National Monument. This historic and sacred piece of land became newsworthy when President Barack Obama proclaimed it a National Monument in December 2016. The site is named after the two main buttes which jut up from the desert floor like two bears' ears. Every one of the tribes – the Hopi, Zuni, Ute and Navajo – who have all lived here for millennia call the monument 'Bears Ears', such is its place in their history. There are over 100,000 sites of archaeological importance within the monument and the buttes themselves are considered sacred. Exactly one year after Obama's proclamation, President Donald Trump reduced the size of the Monument by 85 per cent in what appeared to be an act of spite towards his predecessor. President Joe Biden subsequently restored the territory to the tribes. It's been a contentious issue in Washington for years, yet the people whose land it is have had very little say over its stewardship. It remains to be seen what future administrations might do with this land.

As if this ecological violence in the form of the White Mesa Mill weren't enough, the Ute Mountain Ute people are also suffering. They have relied on deer and rabbits for food, the nearby springs for fresh water and the willow for their baskets throughout their long history. They have described seeing massive trucks heading to the mill with radioactive sludge spilling onto the road their children travel along to get to school. Traces of nitrate and chloroform have been detected in their groundwater and the mill also emits lethal pollutants into the air, such as radon, sulphur dioxide and nitrogen oxide, yet the Nuclear Regulatory Commission gave the mill its blessing.

Since the 1990s, the White Mesa Mill was processing radioactive materials from federal atomic testing (including remnants from the Manhattan Project) along with waste from other industries. According to the Grand Canyon Trust, a non-profit body monitoring environmental issues in the American Southwest, 'The mill charged less than facilities built specifically to dispose of low-level radioactive waste, pocketing millions. Before long, radioactive waste was pouring in from all over North America.' It's the garbage can of Superfund sites – meaning polluted sites identified by the EPA as ones that require long-term decontamination. In the mid-2000s, the mill accepted $6 million from the Japan Atomic Energy Agency to take radioactive material deemed a threat to the health of their citizens. The state of Utah didn't feel they needed a license amendment for this, which seems not only imprudent but insane.

Manuel Heart, the Ute Mountain Tribal Chairman, put it simply: 'They are bringing in uranium wastes the mill is not equipped to handle safely,' and yet the storage facility adheres to its business model and takes money for whatever comes its way. The Environmental Protection Agency also noted that 'no risk assessments on the combination or resultant effects of mixing these different types of wastes with uranium/thorium byproduct/tailings material and impacts on ground water' had been done.

The tailing ponds sit atop the Navajo Aquifer, the main source of drinking water for southeastern Utah. One crack in the rock and this pristine geologic water will be not only undrinkable, but lethal. If the lining of the pits should leak from an untested combination of chemicals capable of eating away at the plastic, the area's springs and the San Juan River could also be infected. Because these waste ponds at the mill were not designed to hold a radioactive soup, the three oldest waste ponds are lined only with a single layer of plastic.

When you dig down into any location where extraction is being done for profit, you find a global web of intricate financial transactions and the pocketing of large sums of money at the expense of ecological and human health. The White Mesa Mill isn't the only place where money is exchanged so that toxic and atomic waste can be stored 'out of the way' – this phrase being shorthand for 'in a place where those affected have no voice'. On it goes, just another environmental catastrophe waiting to happen.

There are thousands of such sites all over the US and across the world. I dread the day when I see the headline 'Navajo Aquifer breached by Toxic Tailings from White Mesa Mill'. Thelma Whiskers, a Tribal Elder from the Ute Mountain Ute White Mesa Community has this to say: 'I've been fighting the White Mesa mill for years, years, years. Why can't they listen to us people here that live on this Ute reservation? My people are sick! And they won't listen!'

The bus roared on through the desert past MP Materials. Everyone was very quiet. We still had about five hours until we would be in Los Angeles. I was reminded of James Rorty who, in 1922, had been commissioned to write an advertising pamphlet for the state of California, about the very lands I was moving through. In his words, he made 'a hack job' of it:

> Certainly, what needed to be said about California in 1922 was not what I had written in that booklet.... I reflected that if I ... had said and done those necessary, intransigent things in 1922, perhaps I would not have now found myself entering a valley still reeking with the stench of violence, the misery of starved and terrorized workers.

Rorty's writing is incredibly prescient. He saw the depletion of resources, the exploitation of labour through globalization, the corruption of those in power. It's striking how his words resonated with what I was seeing from the seat of the Greyhound:

> There is the possibility that, after the clear demonstration that capitalism cannot plan, cannot release the forces of production, cannot finance consumption, there will come a fundamental change in our social psychology.... [T]he dream-making apparatus, while still substantially intact, is being progressively deflated during the present period of capitalist decline.

Rorty castigated the 'grabbing and exploitation of mineral and oil resources, of water and its yield of power and irrigation', as well as the 'legal banditry, of successive waves of peon labor'.

The desert filled the windows on both sides of the Greyhound. Joshua trees and creosote stood in solidarity. I tried to focus on that and not dwell on the golf course sucking up fresh water, the solar mirrors incinerating birds, the waste from a mine sending radioactive material into giant swimming pools threatening the drinking water of Native Americans, the prescient words of a writer we should have paid more attention to. It was all there, all of it, curled up and huddled in the final lap of this trip like a sick dog.

When we got to the San Gabriel Mountains, just outside Los Angeles, I recognized Mount Baldy. My diary says, 'Snow-covered mountains. Angry dark clouds approaching the peaks. Sad to be ending my trip. Ending it like I did last time with a few nights with Alex. We didn't have kids then.'

¶ During the Covid pandemic, as I started immersing myself in the literature of the road and sifting through diaries from my 2006 Greyhound bus trip, I noticed a remarkable coincidence with its timing. I realized that it was on 3 April 2006 that I had arrived in Napanee to start my solo Greyhound journey across the United States with Karl. In 2007, exactly one year later – to the day – I lay on a bed in the Royal London Hospital and gave birth to my daughter.

In a strange form of serendipity, the pregnancy happened as soon as I had given up any hope of becoming a parent. I remember where I was when I realized I was pregnant. My husband Jason and I had gone to see the mentalist Marc Salem perform in London. When Jason brought me a beer, the smell of it turned my stomach. I looked at him and said, 'I think I might be pregnant.' I could tell he didn't believe me. This one stayed, and the following April, my daughter was born. The Greyhound trip had worked a kind of magic on me. It had reminded me that not having a child would be OK, that moving across a continent with strangers and writing a novel were themselves important creative acts. I had realized I could find fulfilment in doing things that did not involve giving birth and raising a child. I had surrendered to my loss and it had rewarded me with gain.

I also realized during the period shortly after my sister died that books about grief never mention the solace of moving through space as one person among many, as one living, breathing human in a group of living, breathing humans. About how other people's stories can swallow and consume your own stories, turning a heavy, leaden weight into a ghostly, almost translucent thing. That movement can perform a kind of alchemy, that you can trust in strangers; that without trust, there is nothing.

Giving birth in the era of climate catastrophe is an act full of contradictions. Where had my desire for a child come from? Some of it was an unquenchable human need to actively express hope. I wanted to believe that I was capable of creating something outside of myself, something that came from me but wasn't actually mine. Giving birth on a planet already suffering from the results of our over-consumption was the ultimate expression that I was not ready to give up on humans.

The author John Tallmadge confesses his irrational decision to have a child in his 2005 book *The Cincinnati Arch: Learning from Nature in the City*. His experience chimed with mine profoundly: 'We knew many couples who had chosen not to have children for reasons they were very willing to share,' he writes. The first, of course, is 'the environmental crisis ... Why create one more mouth to gnaw at the stricken earth?', he asks. I had interrogated myself about this incessantly for years, but I couldn't shake the fact that so many decisions stem from irrationality. Falling in love doesn't *make sense*. Sitting in a room on one's own writing books is a bizarre compulsion. So many wonderful human activities are not driven by efficiency or empirical decisions. My desire to bring a living being into existence was a way of manifesting my faith in the irrational, in the things humans can make with their hands and bodies. Having a child was another way to cement my link to the infinitely complex web of life. I am an animal and I wanted to truly experience my animalness, my wildness, my desire for something that simply could not be tamed or explained. It was a selfish desire, but one I could not ignore.

John Tallmadge's environmental friends 'just smiled and shook their heads' when he told them about his and his wife's decision to have a child. I remember those difficult conversations with people who simply could not understand why someone who cared so profoundly about the planet and its dwindling resources could also contemplate creating another 'consumer'. Having a child for me was a way of saying *there is a possible future*, of accepting wonder and believing in regeneration. I took the accusations of selfishness and accepted them. My critics weren't all wrong.

A very close friend recently reminded me of an email I had written to him just after giving birth. There is a phrase in it where I talk about the 'dark cosmic cave of womanhood' I'd had to enter to find the strength to push my daughter out of my body. We still laugh about it, and I feel embarrassed, but it is accurate. I simply did not have the vocabulary at the time to describe what it felt like to make a whole human being inside my body – every fingernail and hair and eyelash and limb – and then the feral instinct to push this being out of myself. It was both surreal and very, very real. Like having sex or being at a deathbed, giving birth is both ancient and timeless. Our near-total severance from the Earth and its cycles, from ritual, from our bodies and our essential animalistic desires meant that I simply couldn't discuss with any intelligence what I had felt and thought as my daughter worked her way through me and took her first breath.

John Tallmadge is wonderfully unafraid to express his feelings around the birth of his daughter. He compares her birth with 'the essence of wildness at the very heart of the organism'. I had never read an account that rang as true to me as Tallmadge's, even though his prose, at times, veers into purple. He mentions how, on the night they conceived, he 'sensed an energy flowing through' him and his wife that he had never felt before. 'It was not sex,' he writes, 'but something far more powerful, affirming yet oddly impersonal, like a current of molten light.... I knew for certain that we had conceived. We had opened ourselves and received something holy and alive, borne into us on some sort of hot current originating God knows where.' I can't join him here, as I have no idea when I conceived my daughter, and I can't say there was anything holy about it. But, he goes on, '[i]t was only much later that I realized how the choice to become parents, the choice itself, had broken the addictive hold of our life and so made us, in a tiny little way, part of what was emerging to hold the human world.'

Cars and roads and extraction and blasted landscapes are all part of the contemporary American psyche, the myth, the dream, the nightmare, air-conditioned or centrally heated. Having a child is inextricably linked to this. Bringing yet another being onto our planet can easily be interpreted as the creation of another greedy human destined to guzzle more of our Earth's finite resources. But then again, if life is like a story, then having a child could be seen as the climax leading to a denouement and the acceptance that one's own death is not far off. This narrative of one's life as a generator for yet more life was a narrative I had internalized so profoundly that I couldn't picture my future without a child. This is not to say that having a child is necessary to making sense of one's narrative trajectory – it absolutely isn't – but it was central for me. This communal narrative, however, is in the process of being rewritten and reshaped, as more and more of us question our desire to have a child and as more and more of us choose not to.

The act of creating a human inside one's body does connect one to the 'cosmic' – for want of a better word. Through the act of creating life, our animal selves become aligned with other living beings on Earth. If life on our planet has emerged from stellar explosions, and if every element on Earth is partially made of stardust, then so are we.

For a child, everything unfolds with a deeply radical innocence. Knowledge of this fragile innocence and sincerity often leads me to feel dread as I doomscroll through the news of floods and wildfires and famines and eroding topsoil and the acidification of the oceans, the bleaching of coral reefs, the extinction of species, the extraction of cobalt from the earth by seven-year-olds, the dumping of forever chemicals and the sheer magnitude of micro-plastics in just about everything including our own bodies – in other words, the total wrenching apart of the web of life. My love and hope for the Earth and my love and hope for my daughter are connected. How can they not be? The unseen, a happy accident, an act of faith – or something I have yet to name and understand – led me to having a child. I have accepted it all.

By journeying across the US, I was indulging the part of myself that is happiest when moving. By having a child, I embraced the basic need to stay and connect with place and the people who live in it with me. Where I have settled in London, I am not able to live as close to the Earth as I would like, although I plant what seeds I can, make dark, rich compost, and get my fingers dirty whenever possible. But it's not enough. It might never be enough. I sometimes wonder whether this increasing desire to be close to the Earth – we hear this phrase a lot – is something that also comes with age. I wonder whether this desire to literally dig into the Earth until the membrane between us and the soil is non-existent is also an acceptance of death. This getting closer to the Earth – our final point, our destination – is ultimately fulfilled when one's body returns to it. When you stop moving, you have to accept being in one place. I may never like it, but I can learn to accept it, and to accept that despite being in one place for now, I am still moving ever closer to the Earth, as there is no stopping time. It is time that shuttles us all forward on the one journey we all share, the circle of life and death.

Playlist from my Greyhound Bus Trips

Blues Gals
1. Billie Holiday: Strange Fruit
2. Bessie Smith: Careless Love
3. Dinah Shore: Blues in the Night
4. Billie Holiday: These Foolish Things
5. Lee Morse & her Bluegrass Boys: Moanin' Low
6. Bessie Smith: Cake Walkin' Babies
7. Ma Rainey: Daddy Goodbye Blues
8. Billie Holiday: A Fine Romance
9. Mildred Bailey: Smoke Dreams
10. Geechie Wiley: Last Kind Word Blues
11. Bessie Smith: On Revival Day
12. Greta Keller: Blue Moon
13. Billie Holiday: The Man I Love
14. Bessie Smith: Nobody Knows When You're Down and Out
15. Mattie May Thomas: Dangerous Blues
16. Billie Holiday: Am I Blue?
17. Odetta: 900 Miles
18. Bessie Smith: Lock and Key
19. Billie Holiday: St. Louis Blues
20. Mahalia Jackson: God's Gonna Separate the Wheat from the Tares
21. Bessie Smith: Long Old Road

Blues Guys
1. Duke Ellington: Mood Indigo
2. Walter Huston: September Song
3. Bo Didley: Bo Didley
4. Jelly Roll Morton: The Original
5. Leadbelly: Where Did You Sleep Last Night?
6. Edmond Hall Celeste Quartet: Profoundly Blue
7. Howlin' Wolf: Smokestack Lightning
8. Memphis Jug Band: Oh, Ambulance Man
9. Bascom Lunsford: Mole in the Ground
10. Kansas City Kitty & Georgia Tom: How Can You Have the Blues?
11. Ella Fitzgerald & The Inkspots: I'm Making Believe
12. Jelly Roll Morton: The Crave
13. Blind Lemon Jefferson: See That My Grave is Kept Clean
14. Benny Goodman: Blue
15. Howlin' Wolf: How Many More Years
16. Jelly Roll Morton: King Porter Stomp
17. Bo Didley: Roadrunner
18. Tampa Red: Denver Blues
19. Jelly Roll Morton: King Porter Stomp

20. Howlin' Wolf: I Asked for Water
21. Mezz Mezzrow: Blues in Disguise

Songs by Girls
1. Dusty Springfield: The Look of Love
2. Roberta Flack: Killing Me Softly
3. Maria McKee: If Love is a Red Dress
4. Patti Smith: Free Money
5. Janis Joplin & Moondog: All is Loneliness
6. k.d. lang: Tears of Love's Recall
7. Gladys Knight & The Pips: Every Beat of my Heart
8. Jeanette: Porque te vas?
9. Dusty Springfield: Put a Little Love in your Heart
10. Nico: Elegy to Lenny Bruce
11. Gladys Knight & The Pips: Tracks of my Tears
12. Roberta Flack: Angelitos Negros
13. Brenda Lee: Funny How Time Slips Away
14. Dusty: Son of a Preacher Man
15. k.d. lang: Still Thrives This Love
16. Roberta Flack: The First Time Ever I Saw Your Face
17. Patti Smith: Elegie
18. Dusty Springfield: You Don't Have to Say You Love Me
19. Nina Simone: Ne me quitte pas

Songs by Boys
1. Leonard Cohen: The Stranger Song
2. Elliott Smith: Everybody Cares, Everybody Understands
3. The Kinks: All of the Day and All of the Night
4. Eric Burdon and The Animals: House of the Rising Sun
5. Glen Campbell: Galveston
6. Smokey Robinson: Tears of a Clown
7. The Kinks: You Really Got Me
8. The Stone Roses: I Wanna Be Adored
9. Terence Trent D'Arby and Booker T. & the M.G.s: A Change is Gonna Come
10. All Green: How Can You Mend a Broken Heart?
11. Jim White: Still Waters
12. Tim Hardin: Tribute to Hank Williams
13. Smokey Robinson: Tracks of my Tears
14. Papa M.: Over Jordan
15. The Stone Roses: Waterfall
16. Nick Drake: River Man
17. Smokey Robinson: You Really Got a Hold on Me
18. Procol Harum: A Whiter Shade of Pale

A Bunch of Great Songs
1. The Kinks: Waterloo Sunset
2. Jefferson Airplane: Somebody to Love
3. The Band: Whispering Pines
4. The Smiths: Hand in Glove
5. k.d. lang: Constant Craving
6. Gladys Knight & The Pips: I Heard it Through the Grapevine
7. Nick Cave & P.J. Harvey: Knoxville Girl
8. Tim Hardin: Hang Onto a Dream
9. Jimmy Cliff: Many Rivers to Cross
10. K.C. White: No, No, No
11. The Smiths: How Soon is Now?
12. Dusty Springfield: Wishin' and Hopin'
13. Terry Callier: I'm a Drifter
14. Patti Smith: Break it up
15. The Smiths: Last Night I Dreamt That Somebody Loved Me
16. Nick Cave and Kylie Minogue: Wild Rose
17. Bob Dylan: Blind Willie McTell
18. Gene Pitney: 24 Hours from Tulsa

P.J. Harvey, *Dry* (plus...)
1. Oh My lover
2. O Stella
3. Dress
4. Victory
5. Happy and Bleeding
6. Sheela-Na-Gig
7. Hair
8. Joe
9. Plants and Rags
10. Fountain
11. Water
12. Angelene
13. A Perfect Day Elise
14. The River
15. Missed
16. Ecstasy
17. There Will Never Be a Better Time

Neil Young (Mixed)
1. Only Love Can Break Your Heart
2. Revolution Blues
3. On the Beach
4. Motion Pictures
5. Ambulance Blues

6. Tell Me Why
7. After the Gold Rush
8. Southern Man
9. Oh, Lonesome Man
10. Don't Let it Bring You Down
11. Birds
12. When You Dance I Can Really Love
13. I Believe in You
14. Cripple Creek Ferry
15. Harvest Moon
16. Natural Beauty

Nick Cave (Mixed)
1. And No More Shall We Part
2. As I Sat Idly by her Side
3. Oh, My Lord
4. Fifteen Feet of Pure White Snow
5. Sweetheart Come
6. God is in the House
7. We Came Along This Road
8. Darker with the Day
9. Carry Me
10. O, Children
11. Babe, You Turn me On
12. Spell
13. The Ship Song

Bob Dylan, *Blood on the Tracks*
1. Tangled up in Blue
2. Simple Twist of Fate
3. You're a Big Girl Now
4. Idiot Wind
5. You're Gonna Make Me Lonesome When You Go
6. Meet Me in the Morning
7. Lily, Rosemary and the Jack of Hearts
8. If You See Her, Say Hello
9. Shelter from the Storm
10. Buckets of Rain

Will Oldham (Mixed)
1. O Let It Be
2. Master and Everyone
3. Wolf Among Wolves
4. Even If Love
5. We All, Us Three, Will Ride

Bibliography

Books

Marc Augé, *Non-Places: Introduction to an Anthropology of Supermodernity*, trans. John Howe (London: Verso, 1995).

Laurence Buell, *The Future of Environmental Criticism* (London: Wiley-Blackwell, 2005).

Michel Butor, *Mobile*, trans. Richard Howard (Funks Grove, IL: Dalkey Archive Press, 2004 [1962]).

Harlan Paul Douglass, *The Suburban Trend* (New York: The Century Co., 1925).

Greta Gaard, *The Nature of Home: Taking Root in a Place* (Tucson, AZ: University of Arizona Press, 2007).

David Gessner, *The Prophet of Dry Hill* (Boston, MA: Beacon Press, 2005).

David Harvey, *The Condition of Postmodernity* (Oxford: Blackwell, 1989).

Ursula Heise, *Sense of Place, Sense of Planet* (New York: Oxford University Press USA, 2008).

Bela Hubbard, *Memorials of a Half-Century* (New York: G.P. Puttnam's, 1887).

Carlton Jackson, *Hounds of the Road: A History of the Greyhound Bus Company* (Bowling Green, OH: Bowling Green State University Popular Press, 2001 [1984]).

John B. Jackson, *Discovering the Vernacular Landscape* (New Haven: Yale University Press, 1984).

Jack Kerouac, *On the Road* (London: Penguin, 1991 [1957]).

Irma Kurtz, *The Great American Bus Ride* (London: Fourth Estate, 1993).

Belden C. Lane, *Landscapes of the Sacred: Geography and Narrative in American Spirituality* (Baltimore, MD: JHU Press, 1988).

D. H. Lawrence, *Phoenix: The Posthumous Papers of D. H. Lawrence*, Sussex: Delphi Classics, 2017 [1936]).

William Least Heat-Moon, *Blue Highways* (London: Picador, 1984).

Aldo Leopold, *A Sand County Almanac*, (London: Penguin Classics, 2020 [1949]).

C. S. Lewis, *A Grief Observed* (London: Faber & Faber, 1961).

Ethel Mannin, *An American Journey* (London: Hutchinson & Co., 1967).

Leo Marx, *The Machine in the Garden: Technology and the Pastoral Ideal in America* (Oxford: Oxford University Press, 1964).

Henry Miller, *The Air-Conditioned Nightmare* (New York: New Directions, 1970).

N. Scott Momaday, *House Made of Dawn* (London: Weidenfeld & Nicolson, 2020 [1969]).

David E. Nye, *Conflicted American Landscapes* (Cambridge, MA: The MIT Press, 2021).

James Rorty, *Where Life is Better: An Unsentimental American Journey* (New York: John Day Publishers, 1936).

Lauret Edith Savoy, *Trace: Memory, History, Race, and the American Landscape* (Berkeley, CA: Counterpoint Press, 2015).

John Steinbeck, *Travels with Charley*, London: Penguin, 2000 [1962]).

Gregory D. Squires, *Urban Sprawl: Causes, Consequences, and Policy Responses* (Washington, D.C.: Urban Institute Press, 2002),

John Tallmadge, *The Cincinnati Arch: Learning from Nature in the City* (Athens, GA: University of Georgia Press, 2004).

Alexis de Tocqueville, *Democracy in America*, trans. Gerald Bevan (London: Penguin, 2003 [1835–1840]).

Yi-Fu Tuan, *Topophilia: A Study of Environmental Perception, Attitudes, and Values* (New Jersey: Prentice-Hall, 1974).

Robert Venturi, Denise Scott Brown and Stephen Izenour, *Learning From Las Vegas* (Cambridge, MA: The MIT Press, 1977).

Walt Whitman, *An American Primer*, ed. Horace Traubel (San Francisco:

City Lights, 1970 [1904]).

The Zetkin Collective and Andreas Malm, *White Skin, Black Fuel: On the Dangers of Fossil Fascism* (London: Verso, 2021).

Essays, Articles and Poems

Blake Apgar, 'New Golf Courses Can't Use Colorado River Water, Las Vegas Board Says', *Las Vegas Review-Journal* (2 November 2021).

Hazel E. Barnes, 'Simone De Beauvoir's Journal and Letters: A Poisoned Gift?' *Simone De Beauvoir Studies* (8, 13–29, 1991).

William Beaver, 'The Demise of Yucca Mountain', *Independent Review*, (14:4, 535–47, 2010).

Eckardt C. Beck, 'The Love Canal Tragedy', *EPA Journal* (January 1979).

Michael R. Blood, 'Huge Solar Plant Lags in Early Production', *Associated Press* (17 November 2014).

Laurence Buell, 'An Exchange on Thoreau', *New York Review of Books* (2 December 1999).

Jen Christensen, 'It's So Hot in Arizona, Doctors are Treating a Spike of Patients who were Burned by Falling on the Ground', *CNN* (24 July 2023).

David Cieslewicz, 'The Environmental Impacts of Sprawl', in Gregory D. Squires (ed.), *Urban Sprawl* (*op. cit.*).

Francis Davidson, 'Open-sourcing Sonder's Culture', https://www.linkedin.com/pulse/open-sourcing-sonders-culture-francis-davidson/?trackingId=8SemtEPoTNeFmM8M5lkDqg%3D%3D (29 March 2023).

R. L. Duffus, 'A Revealing American Journey: Mr Rorty Reports on The Temper of The Country Today', *New York Times* (19 January 1936).

EPA (United States Environmental Protection Agency), River Rouge Remedial Action Plan Annual Report. More information can be found at www.epa.gov/great-lakes-aocs/rouge-river-aoc

–––.'EPA Announces $4.2 Million for Habitat Restoration Work at River Rouge River Area of Concern', https://www.epa.gov/newsreleases/

epa-announces-42-million-habitat-restoration-work-rouge-river-area-concern (28 July 2020).

Philip J. Finkelpearl, '*Learning from Las Vegas* by Robert Venturi, Denise Scott Brown, Steven Izenour', *Journal of the Society of Architectural Historians* (38:2, 203–05, 1979).

Ford Motor Company press release, 2000. More can be found on the greenroofs.com website and at https://www.greenroofs.com/projects/ford-motor-companys-river-rouge-truck-plant/

Paul Gilroy, 'Driving While Black', in Daniel Miller (ed.), *Car Cultures* (Oxford: Berg, 2001).

William Goldberg, 'The Birth of an Arts Scene', *UNLV Theses, Dissertations, Professional Papers, and Capstones*, (May 2016).

J. P. Harrington, 'Old Indian Geographical Names around Santa Fe, New Mexico', *American Anthropologist* (22:4, 241–59, 1920).

Paul Harris, 'Monsanto Sued Small Farmers to Protect Seed Patents – Report', Guardian (12 February 2013).

Gabu Heindl, 'Bin City, Las Vegas', *Journal of Architectural Education* (59:2, 5–12, 1984).

Anastasia Hufham, 'Utah has the last conventional uranium mill in the country. What does it do?', originally published in the *Salt Lake Tribune* (7 October 2024). Republished in the MIT Climate Portal, climate.mit.edu

Elizabeth Kolbert, 'The Lost Canyon Under Lake Powell', *New Yorker* (16 August 2021).

Stephen Leahy, 'Exxon Valdez Changed the Oil Industry Forever – But New Threats Emerge', *National Geographic* (22 March 2019).

Mark Leslie, 'Water Hazard', *Golf Course Management* (January 2012). Retrieved at https://www.usga.org/content/usga/home-page/custom-search.html#q=mark%20leslie&type=news&startIndex=1

Stephen Lester, 'Here's the Real Reason the EPA Doesn't Want to Test for Toxins in East Palestine', *Guardian* (2 March 2023).

Ingrid Lunden, 'Germany's FlixMobility acquires Greyhound Lines, the Iconic US Bus Company, in $78M Deal', *Techcrunch* (21 October 2021).

Leo Marx, 'The Idea of Nature in America', *Daedalus* (137:2, 8–21, 2008).

--. 'The Struggle Over Thoreau', *New York Review of Books* (24 June 1999).

--. 'The American Ideology of Space', in *Denatured Visions: Landscape and Culture in the Twentieth Century* (New York: Museum of Modern Art, 1991).

Corey Mintz, 'Outrage at Starbucks' Tipping Prompt Shows People Don't Get How the Tipping Con Works', *NBC News* (9 December 2022).

N. Scott Momaday, 'Discovering the Land of Light', *New York Times* (17 March 1985).

Roderick Nash, *Wilderness and the American Mind* (London: Yale University Press, 2014 [1967]).

Geoff Nicholson, *The Suburbanist: A Personal Account and Ambivalent Celebration of Life in the Suburbs with Field Notes* (Whitstable: Harbour Books, 2021).

Louis Sahagún, 'This Mojave Desert Solar Plant Kills 6,000 Birds a Year. Here's Why That Won't Change Any Time Soon', *Los Angeles Times* (2 September 2016).

Michael Sainato, 'Leaked Audio Reveals US Rail Workers Were Told to Skip Inspections as Ohio Crash Prompts Scrutiny to Industry', *Guardian* (3 March 2023).

Darcy Spears, 'Draining Las Vegas: Here is Who is Using the Most Water in the Valley- Top Commercial Residential Water Users Listed', *KNTV* (27 September 2021).

Cassandra Sweet, 'High-Tech Solar Projects Fail to Deliver', *Wall Street Journal* (12 June 2015).

Marianne Taylor, 'The Woman Who Listens: Interview with Long-time Cosmopolitan Agony Aunt Irma Kurtz, *The Herald* (28 February 2016).

Walt Whitman, 'Song of the Open Road', in *Leaves of Grass*, first published in 1855 and available at whitmanarchive.org.

Ian Zabarte, Principal Man of the Western Bands of the Shoshone Nation of Indians, 'A Message from the Most Bombed Nation on Earth', *Al Jazeera* (29 August 2020).

Illustrations

Page 9, 005
Self-portrait, Fox Motor Inn, Napanee, Ontario, 2006.

Page 14, 002
Petro-Canada station, Highway 41, Napanee, Ontario, 2023.
or
003, Royal Napanee Inn sign, Highway 41, Napanee, Ontario, 2023.

Page 15, 006
Exterior of Fox Moto Inn, Napanee, Ontario, 2006.

Page 16, 007
The Napanee River, Napanee, Ontario, 2023.

010, Interior of TheSuperior Restaurant, Dundas Street West, Napanee,
Ontario, 2006.

Page 17, 015
Napanee, Ontario, 2023.

Page 18, 014
Napanee Baptist Church, Napanee, Ontario, 2023.

012, Len's Bakery, Dundas Street East, Napanee, Ontario, 2006.

Page 19, 016
Napanee train station, Napanee, Ontario, 2006.

017, Looking through a boarded up window, Napanee train station, Napanee,
Ontario, 2023.

Page 20, 018
Napanee water tower, East Street, Napanee, Ontario, 2006.

Page 21, 019
View from a taxi to the Tunnel Bus depot, Windsor, Ontario, 2023.

Page 23, 020
'Condos For Sale', Detroit, Michigan, 2006.

021, Building renovation on East Cranfield Street, Detroit, Michigan, 2006.

Page 32, 026
My room at the Milner Hotel, Detroit, Michigan, 2006.

027, The old Milner Hotel, now the Ashley Apartments, Detroit, Michigan, 2023.
or
023, LaGreen's Arcade, Downtown Detroit, Michigan, 2006.
or
028, The old Westin Hotel, Detroit, Michigan, 2006.
or
029, The new Westin Hotel, Detroit, Michigan, 2023.

Page 33, 023.A
View from the bus on East Jefferson Avenue, Detroit, Michigan, 2023.

Page 34, 022
Downtown construction area, Detroit, Michigan, 2006.

Page 36, 030
View from the Ford Factory Plant, Dearborn, Michigan, 2023.

Page 41, 031
The Lafaytette Greens garden space, part of the Greening of Detroit, Downtown Detroit, 2023.

032, Meldrum Street, Detroit, Michigan, 2023.

Page 43, 033
Alleyway near the Capuchin Soup Kitchen, Detroit, Michigan, 2023.

Page 44, 035
Hantz Farms building, 2140 McClellan Avenue, Detroit, Michigan, 2023.

Page 46, 036
2245 McClellan Avenue, Detroit, Michigan, 2023.

037,Exterior of Cheap Charlie's, 1461 Gratiot Avenue, Detroit, Michigan, 2023.

Page 48, 038
Cauliflower seedlings in one of the Keep Growing Detroit hoophouses, Detroit, Michigan, 2023.

Page 51, 041
Empty phone booths, Tulsa Greyhound bus station, Tulsa, Oklahoma, 2023.

Page 52, 042
'Welcome to Toledo' sign at the Greyhound bus stop, Toledo, Ohio, 2006.
or
044, 'Christ is the answer', United States Plastic Corp, as seen on the I-75 from the Greyhound bus, Lima, Ohio, 2023.

Page 56, 045
Empty warehouse, Lima, Ohio, 2023.

046, Hofeller, Hiatt & Clark, menswear specialists since 1898, Lima, Ohio, 2023.

Page 58, 047
Sparrows in the Columbus, Ohio Greyhound station, 2023.

Page 71, 049
Greyhound bus stop at the Economy Inn (now a Motel 6) on I-70, Terre Haute, Indiana, 2006.

Page 73, 050
Greyhound bus terminal, St. Louis, Missouri, 2006.

051, Greyhound bus station, St. Louis, Missouri, 2023.

Page 76, 052
View of the Mississippi River, St. Louis, Missouri, 2006.

Page77, 053
View from outside my room at the Americas Best Value Inn and Suites, St. Louis, Missouri, 2023.

054, St. Louis, Missouri, 2006.

Page 78, 055
'Pre Pay Inside', St. Louis, Missouri, 2023.

Page 81, 056
Watching *Giant* in my room at the Americas Best Value Inn and Suites, St. Louis, Missouri, 2023.

Page 88, 057
View from a Greyhound bus on Route 66, looking down Gabriel Boulevard, Duenweg, Missouri, 2023.

Page 92, 058

View from a Greyhound bus, outside Joplin, Missouri, 2023.

Page 97, 060
Waffle House as seen from a Greyhound bus on I-81 at Neubrecht Road, Lima, Ohio, 2023.

Page 102, 061
Econo Lodge (now an Americas Best Value Inn and Suites) lobby breakfast area, St. Louis, Missouri, 2006

062, Lobby area of the Americas Best Value Inn and Suites (once an Econo Lodge), St. Louis, Missouri, 2023.

Page 103, 063
View from a Greyhound bus, Bluffton, Ohio, 2023.

Page 106, 064
Broken down Greyhound bus, near Springfield, Missouri, 2006.

Page 108, 065
Rose Company Pawn Shop (now permanently closed), Tulsa, Oklahoma, 2006.

Page 110, 067
Fire in the distance as seen from a Greyhound bus on the I-44 near Vinita, Oklahoma, 2023.

Page 115, 069
The Petroleum Club, Tulsa, Oklahoma, 2023.

Page 116, 068
Tulsa as viewed from my hotel the morning after watching *Trudell*, Tulsa, Oklahoma, 2006.

Page 119, 070
Broken down Phoenix-bound Greyhound bus, 2006.

Page 123, 073
Desert as seen from a Greyhound bus on the I-40 en route to Amarillo, Texas, 2023.

Page 125, 072
The Cross of Our Lord Jesus Christ Ministries as seen from a Greyhound bus, Groom, Texas, 2023.

Page 125, 074
Downtown Amarillo, Texas, 2023.

Page 126, 075
San Jacinto District, Amarillo, Texas, 2006.

Page 128, 076
The boarded-up diner in the Amarillo Greyhound terminal (now closed), Amarillo, Texas, 2023.

078, Exterior of the Amarillo Bus Center, Amarillo, Texas, 2006.

Page 129, 080 or 080.A
Downtown Amarillo, Texas, 2023.

Page 132, 081
My room at the Civic Center Inn (now closed), Amarillo, Texas, 2006.

Page 136, 082
A cattle feedlot as seen from a Greyhound bus, Texas panhandle, 2023.

083, Windmill in the desert as seen from a Greyhound bus on the I-40 in New Mexico, just over the border with Texas, 2023.

Page 137, 084
The Tucumcari rest stop, New Mexico, 2023.

Page 141, 085
Cloud as seen from a Greyhound bus somewhere near Tucumcari, New Mexico, 2006.
And 086
The Econo Lodge on Central Avenue, Albuquerque, New Mexico, 2023.

Page 142, 089
The Hotel Blue, Albuquerque, New Mexico, 2023.

Page 143, 090
The Wash Tub laundromat, Albuquerque, New Mexico, 2023.

Page 144, 091
Mercado Carniceria Los Nogales, Albuquerque, New Mexico, 2006.
And/Or 092
Motel Hiway House, 'Sleep is our business', Albuquerque, New Mexico, 2006.

2005.

Page 185, 129
Las Vegas Motel (now closed), Fremont Street, Las Vegas, Nevada, 2023.

Page 190, 130
'Wildest Dreams' sign, Fremont Hotel (now closed), Fremont Street, Las Vegas, Nevada, 2023.
and/or 130.A, The fenced Gables Motel (now closed), Fremont Street, Las Vegas, Nevada, 2023.

Page 200, 131 or 132
The Ivanpah Solar Electric Generating System in the Mojave Desert as seen from a Greyhound bus, California, 2023.
and/or 133, Primm Valley Golf Club as seen from a Greyhound bus, Nipton, California, 2023.

Page 209, 135
The Pacific Ocean, Santa Monica, California, 2023.

Page 211, 136
The Greyhound bus station, Santa Fe, New Mexico, 2006.

Acknowledgements

I would first like to thank Jacques Testard, Tamara Sampey-Jawad, Joely Day, Clare Bogen, Charlotte Jackson and the whole Fitzcarraldo Editions team who have been on the *Greyhound* bus journey with me for some time and have kept the faith enough not to jump off. A big thank you, as well, to Mensah Demary, Dan Smetanka, Dan Lopez and everyone at Soft Skull for joining the ride. And thank you to Seren Adams at Lexington Literary for believing in me.

Sam Kelly at MIT Press, thank you for alerting me to the writing of David E. Nye and the incredible research in *Conflicted American Landscapes*.

I am massively grateful to Hamish Robinson and the staff and trustees of the Hawthornden International Retreat for Writers at Hawthornden Castle in Scotland. My month of silence and the incredible support from the other writers (you know who you are) were instrumental in getting these words onto paper.

I owe a debt of gratitude to Shelley Warren and Joy Stacey at the Arts Foundation and to the judges who awarded me the 2021 Environmental Writing Fellowship. Without the Arts Foundation's financial support this book could simply not have been written.

Financial assistance was also generously provided by the Society of Authors and the Royal Literary Fund, to whom I am hugely grateful.

The bursary from the Eccles Centre & Hay Festival Writer's Award in partnership with the British Library has been a massive boost, as was the support from the Nature Chronicles Prize for Nature Writing.

The people I met on the road and the people who gave me names and addresses, those who brought joy, shared meals and friendship on an often lonely journey, 'Thank you': Jon Jost, Danila Rumold, Mike Score of Hantz Farms, Ashley Atkinson at Keep Growing Detroit, Amanda Fortini, Alex Tinley and all the people along the way whose conversations, advice, snacks and opinions have made me and this book richer.

The first public outing of an extract from his book was in the form of an essay in *Dark Mountain 20: Abyss*. Thank you Nick Hunt, Charlotte DuCann and the editors at *Dark Mountain* for providing a platform, and for always having intelligent things to say about writing and its place in the world.

Chloe Aridjis, Lorna Scott Fox and Dinah Wood (whose gift of an old-fashioned *Lonely Planet* guidebook was a godsend) – I am so grateful for your friendship and your constant cheering me on. Thanks to my brother Philip Pocock, who likes to remind me of the power of words and who has always believed in his little sister. Melanie Manchot, Terence Gower and Chloe Ruthven – I am so grateful to you for reading very early drafts of *Greyhound* and telling it to me straight.

And, finally, massive thanks and all my love to Eve and Jason, my co-travellers, my confidantes, my partners in crime, who are always with me no matter where I go. Jason Massot's film *Road to Las Vegas*, mentioned in these pages, premiered at the Edinburgh Film Festival in 2010, had a two-week run at the ICA in London and was aired on Channel 4.

My novel about Karl, the androgynous teenager, is still called *Tulsa*. Maybe Karl needed to appear here first or maybe this will be her only appearance on the page. Who knows.

The authorized representative in the EEA is
eucomply OÜ, Pärnu mnt 139b-14,
11317 Tallinn, Estonia.
hello@eucompliancepartner.com
+337 576 90241

Fitzcarraldo Editions
8-12 Creekside
London, SE8 3DX
Great Britain

ISBN 978-1-80427-138-4

Design by Ray O'Meara
Typeset in Fitzcarraldo
This ARC printed by Aquatint

fitzcarraldoeditions.com

Fitzcarraldo Editions